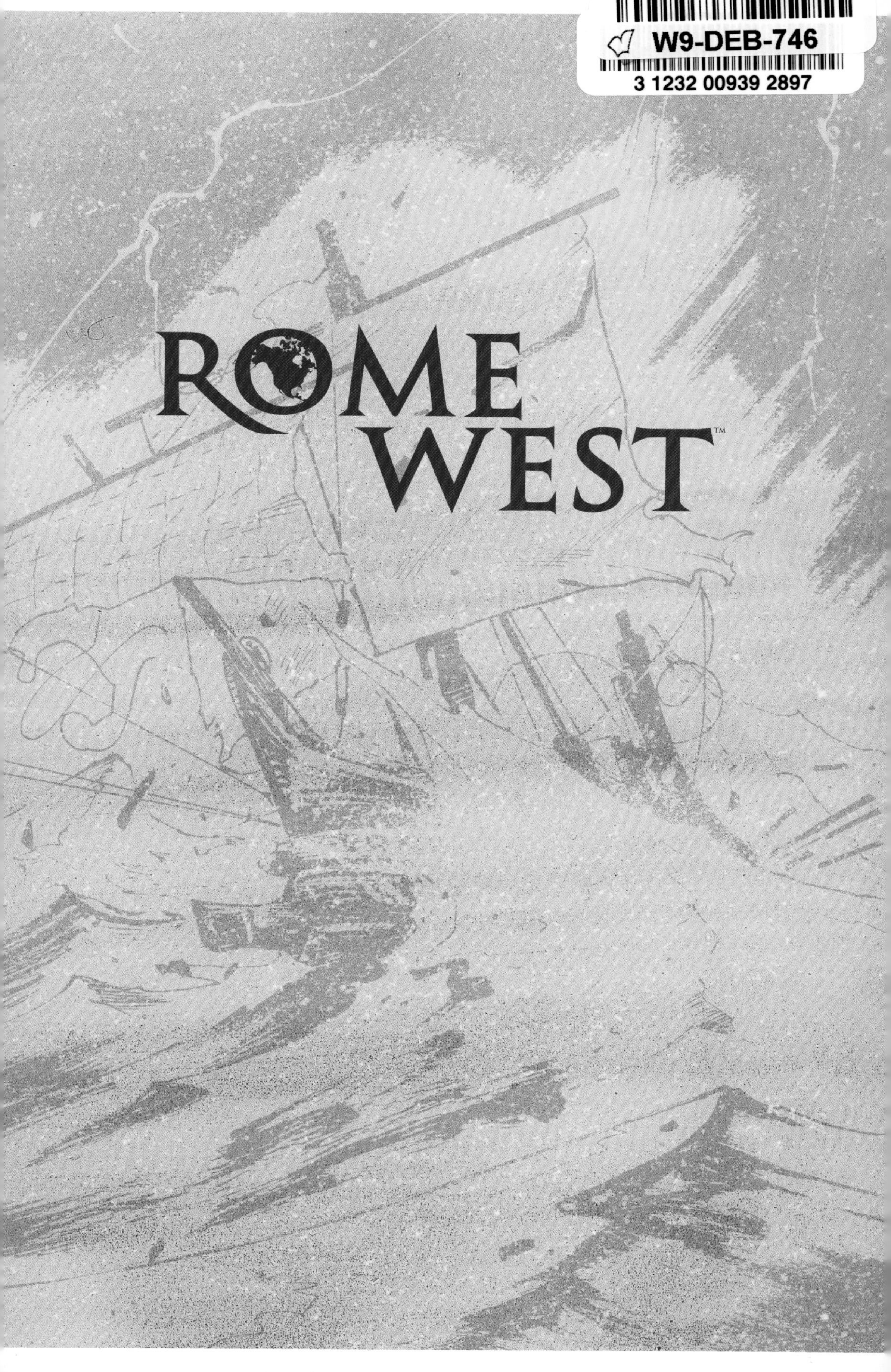

ROME WEST™

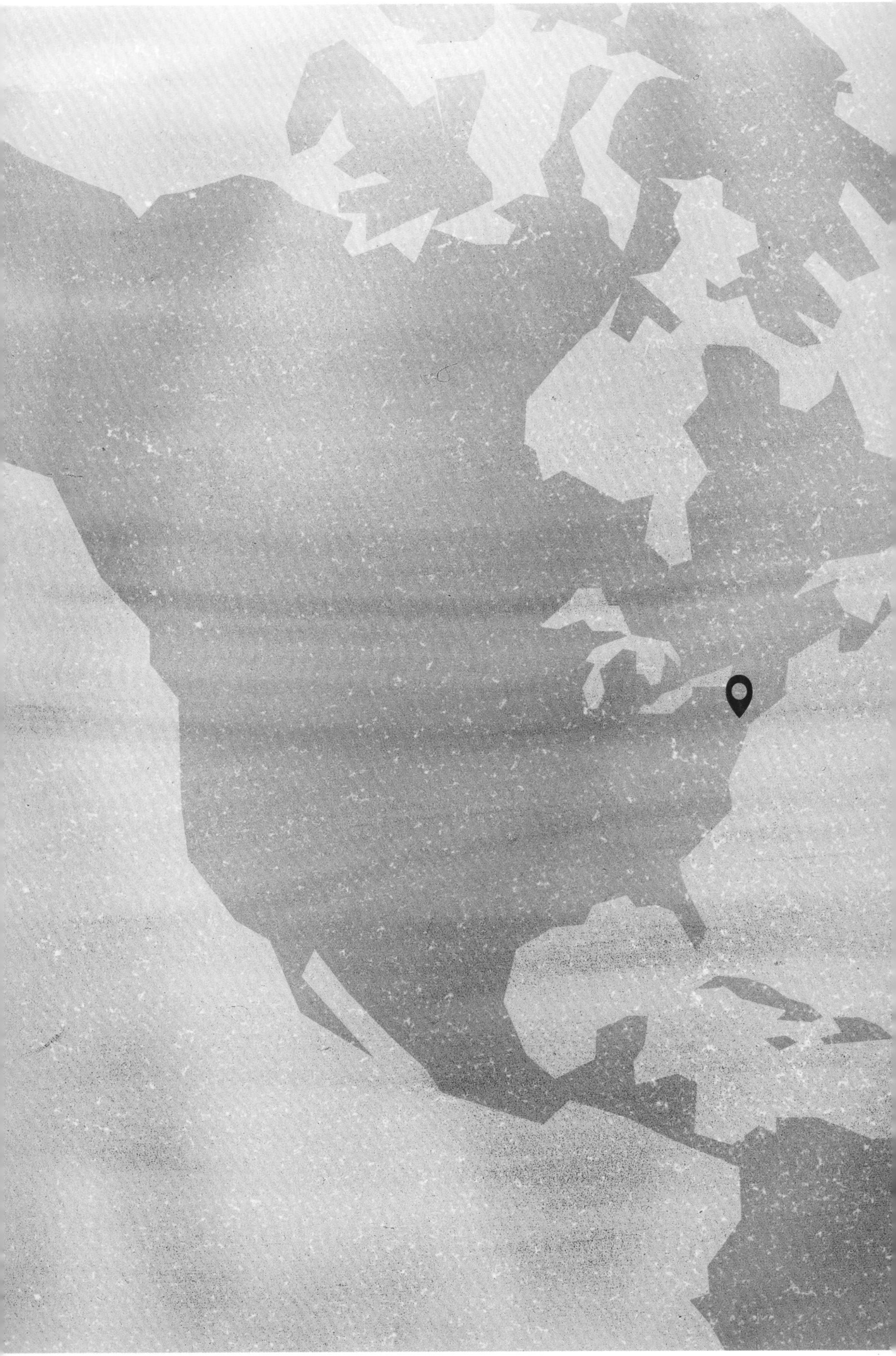

ROME WEST

SCRIPT
**JUSTIN GIAMPAOLI
& BRIAN WOOD**

ART
ANDREA MUTTI

COLORS
LEE LOUGHRIDGE

LETTERING
JOHN AND RYANE HILL

COVER ART
MATTHEW TAYLOR

DARK HORSE BOOKS

PRESIDENT AND PUBLISHER
MIKE RICHARDSON

COLLECTION EDITOR
SPENCER CUSHING

COLLECTION ASSISTANT EDITORS
KEVIN BURKHALTER
JENNY BLENK

COLLECTION DESIGNER
ANITA MAGAÑA

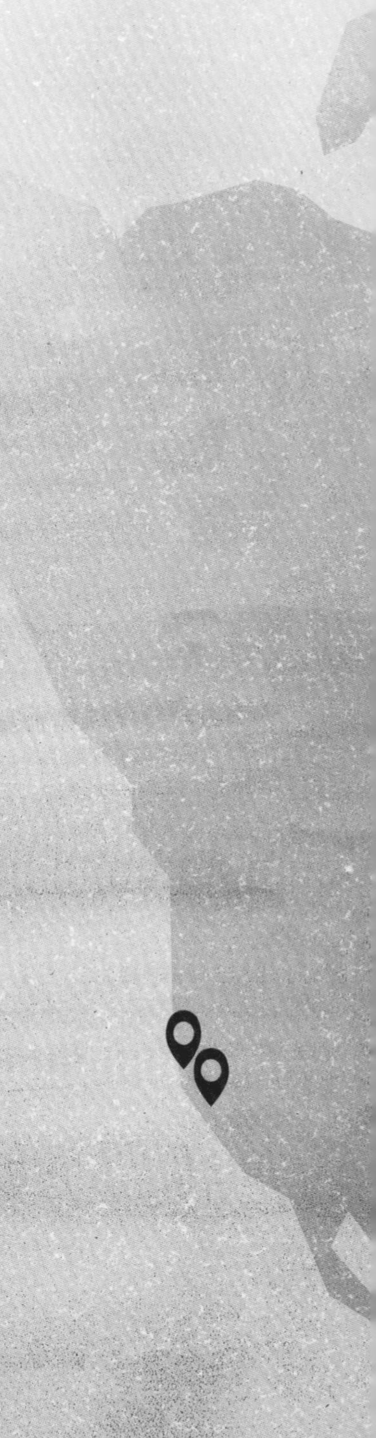

DIGITAL ART TECHNICIAN
CHRISTIANNE GILLENARDO-GOUDREAU

This volume collects the digital comic series *Rome West* #1–#12,
originally edited by Jim Gibbons and published by Stela.

Published by Dark Horse Books
A division of Dark Horse Comics, Inc.
10956 SE Main Street | Milwaukie, OR 97222
DarkHorse.com

To find a comics shop in your area, visit comicshoplocator.com

First edition: July 2018
ISBN 978-1-50670-499-9

1 3 5 7 9 10 8 6 4 2
Printed in China

Neil Hankerson, Executive Vice President · Tom Weddle, Chief
Financial Officer · Randy Stradley, Vice President of Publishing · Nick
McWhorter, Chief Business Development Officer · Matt Parkinson,
Vice President of Marketing · Dale LaFountain, Vice President of
Information Technology · Cara Niece, Vice President of Production
and Scheduling · Mark Bernardi, Vice President of Book Trade and
Digital Sales · Ken Lizzi, General Counsel · Dave Marshall, Editor in
Chief · Davey Estrada, Editorial Director · Chris Warner, Senior Books
Editor · Cary Grazzini, Director of Specialty Projects · Lia Ribacchi,
Art Director · Vanessa Todd-Holmes, Director of Print Purchasing ·
Matt Dryer, Director of Digital Art and Prepress · Michael Gombos,
Director of International Publishing and Licensing · Kati Yadro,
Director of Custom Programs

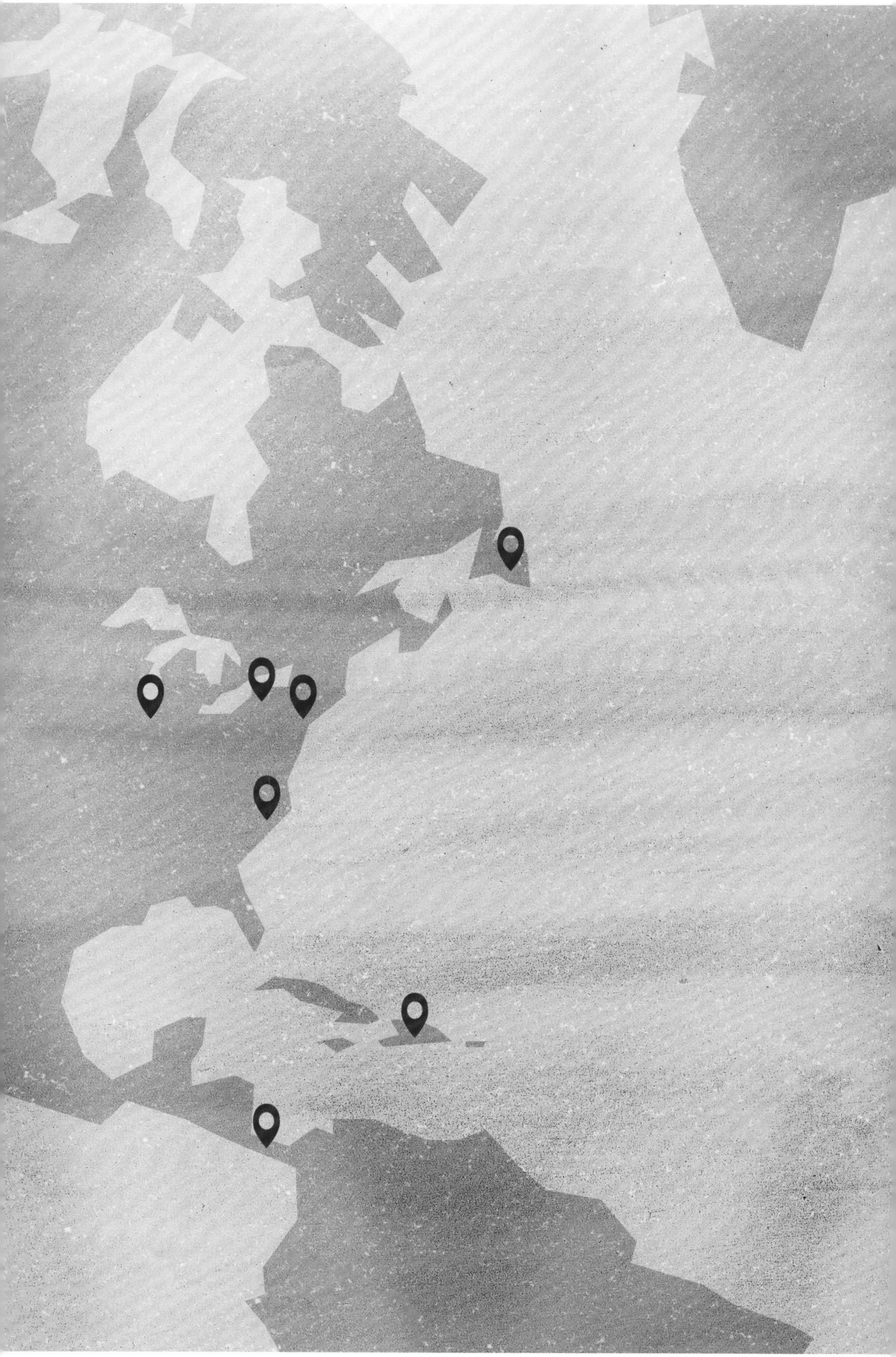

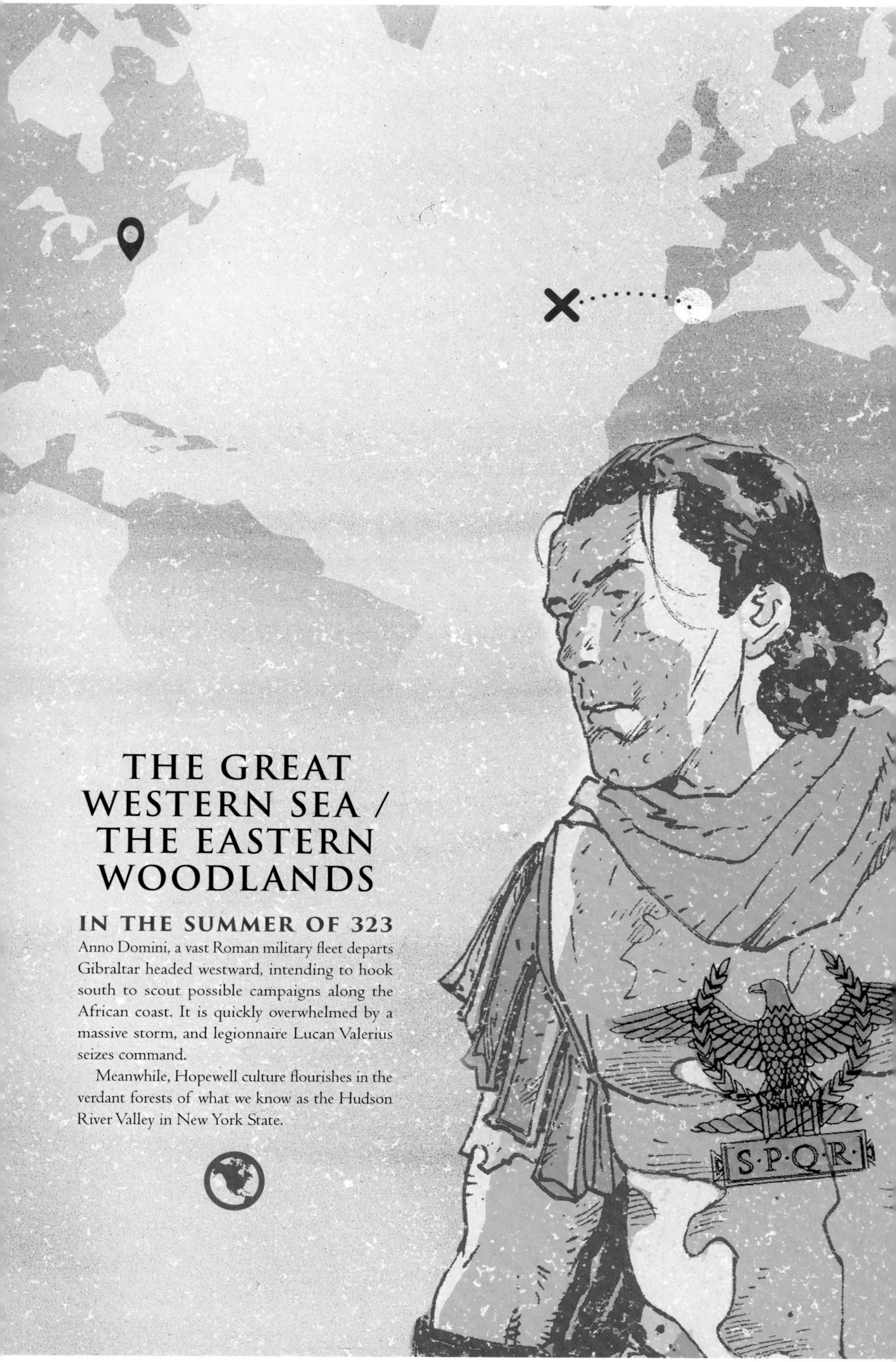
S·P·Q·R

THE GREAT WESTERN SEA / THE EASTERN WOODLANDS

IN THE SUMMER OF 323

Anno Domini, a vast Roman military fleet departs Gibraltar headed westward, intending to hook south to scout possible campaigns along the African coast. It is quickly overwhelmed by a massive storm, and legionnaire Lucan Valerius seizes command.

Meanwhile, Hopewell culture flourishes in the verdant forests of what we know as the Hudson River Valley in New York State.

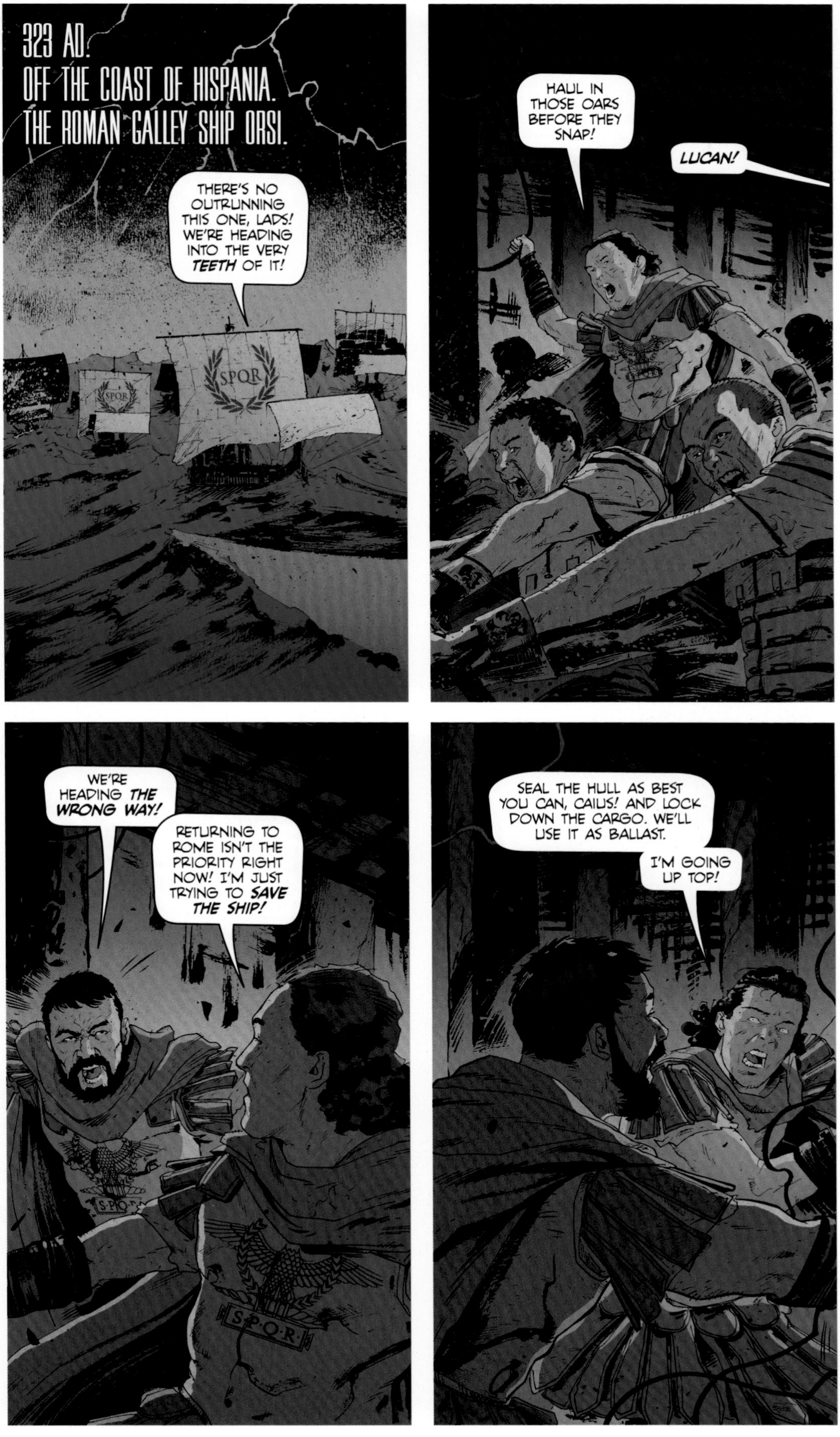
323 AD.
OFF THE COAST OF HISPANIA.
THE ROMAN GALLEY SHIP ORSI.
THERE'S NO OUTRUNNING THIS ONE, LADS! WE'RE HEADING INTO THE VERY TEETH OF IT!
SPQR
SPQR
HAUL IN THOSE OARS BEFORE THEY SNAP!
LUCAN!
WE'RE HEADING THE WRONG WAY!
RETURNING TO ROME ISN'T THE PRIORITY RIGHT NOW! I'M JUST TRYING TO SAVE THE SHIP!
S·P·Q·R
SEAL THE HULL AS BEST YOU CAN, CAIUS! AND LOCK DOWN THE CARGO. WE'LL USE IT AS BALLAST.
I'M GOING UP TOP!

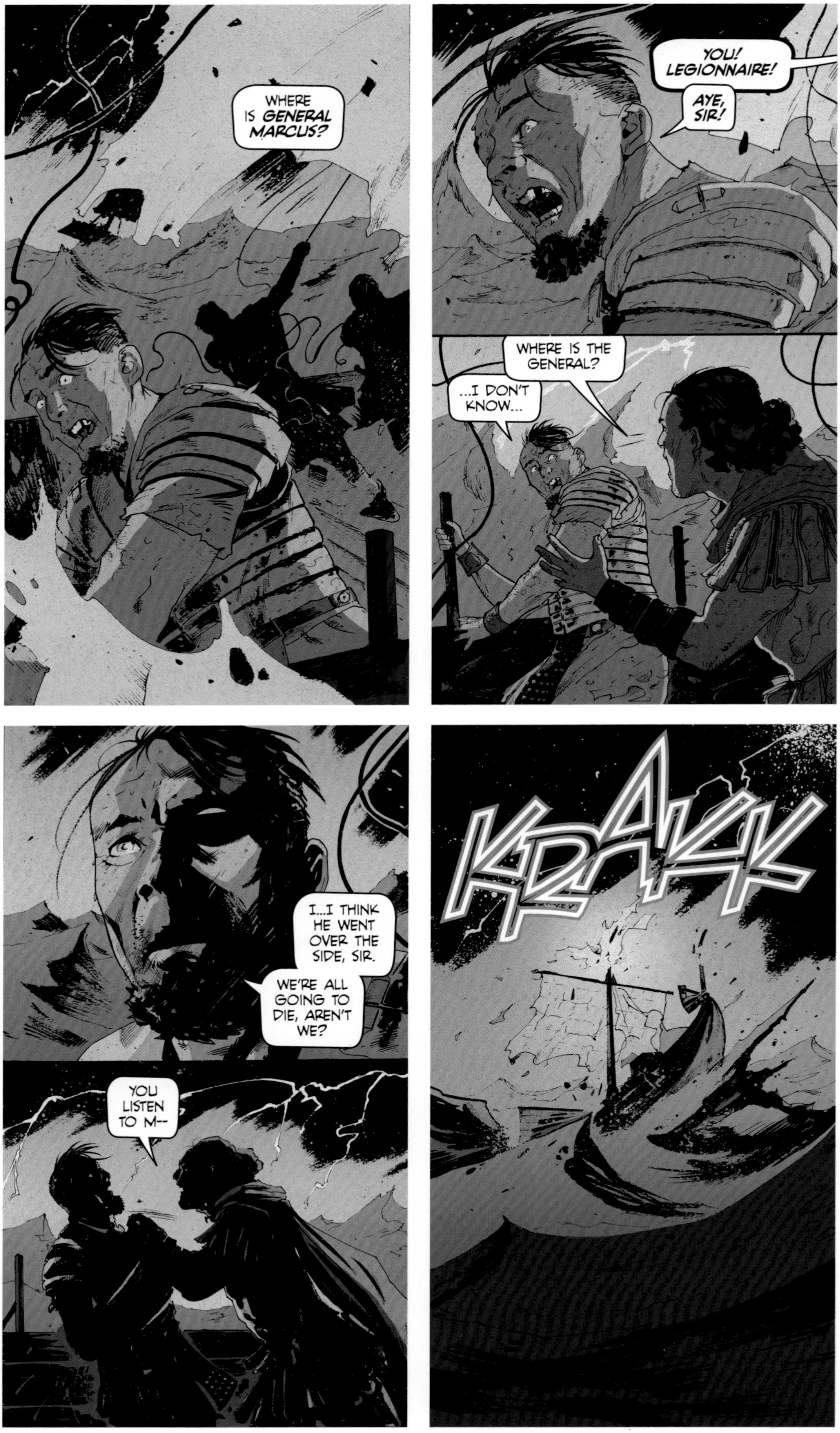
WHERE IS GENERAL MARCUS?
YOU! LEGIONNAIRE!
AYE, SIR!
WHERE IS THE GENERAL?
...I DON'T KNOW...
I...I THINK HE WENT OVER THE SIDE, SIR.
WE'RE ALL GOING TO DIE, AREN'T WE?
YOU LISTEN TO M--
KRAKK

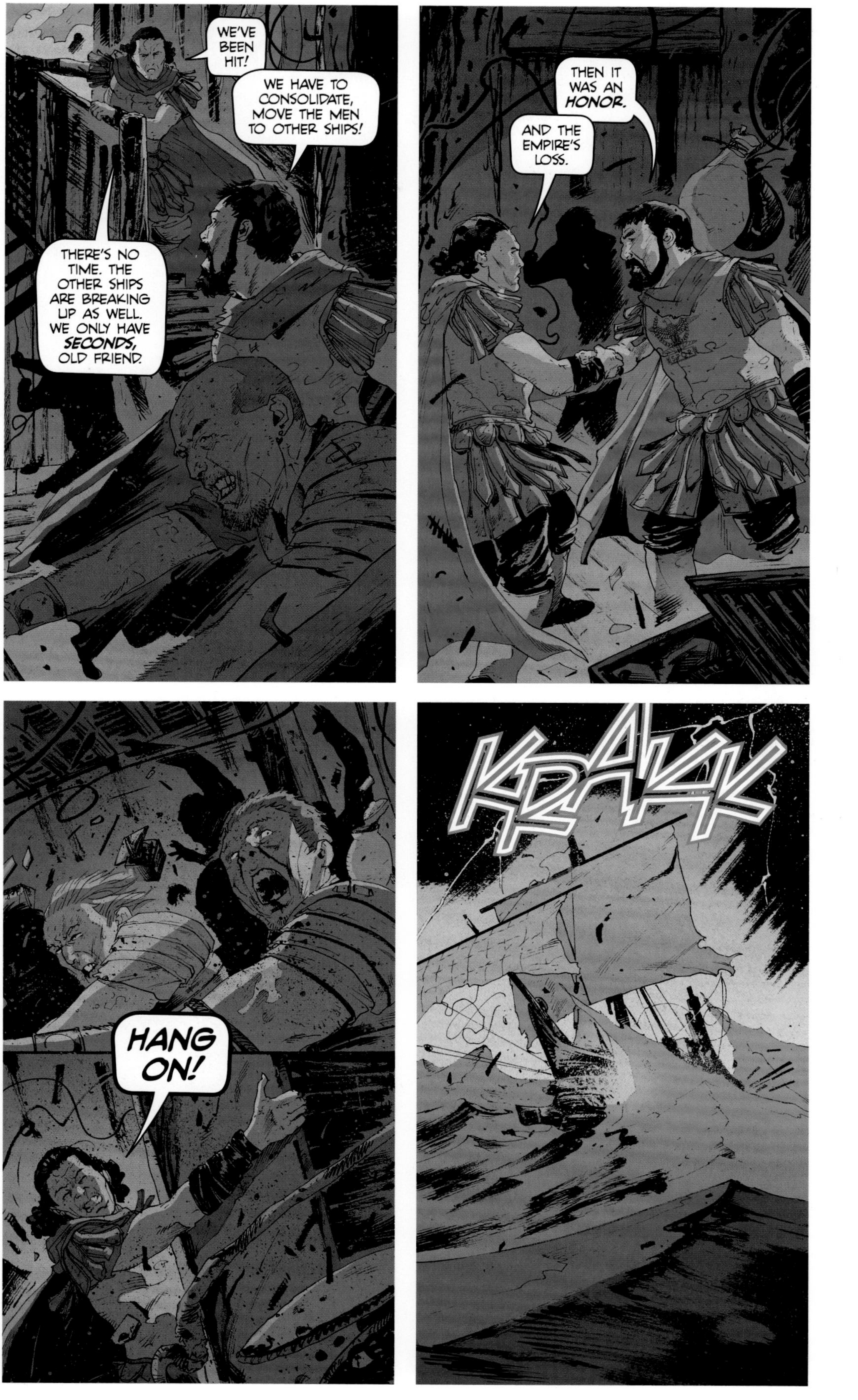
WE'VE BEEN HIT!
WE HAVE TO CONSOLIDATE, MOVE THE MEN TO OTHER SHIPS!
THERE'S NO TIME. THE OTHER SHIPS ARE BREAKING UP AS WELL. WE ONLY HAVE *SECONDS,* OLD FRIEND.
THEN IT WAS AN *HONOR.*
AND THE EMPIRE'S LOSS.
HANG ON!
KRAKK

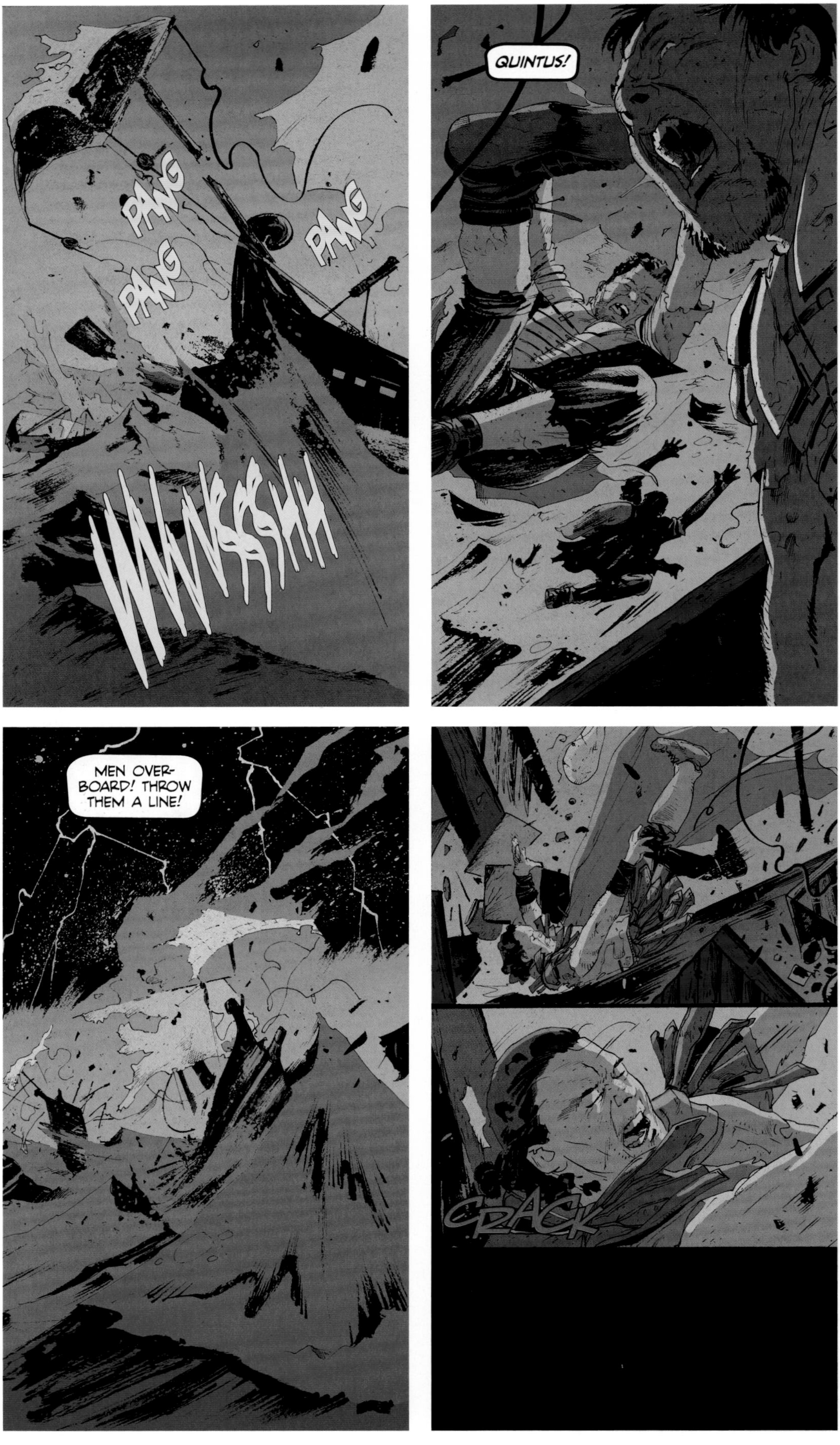
PANG
PANG
PANG
WWVSSHH
QUINTUS!
MEN OVER-
BOARD! THROW
THEM A LINE!
CRACK

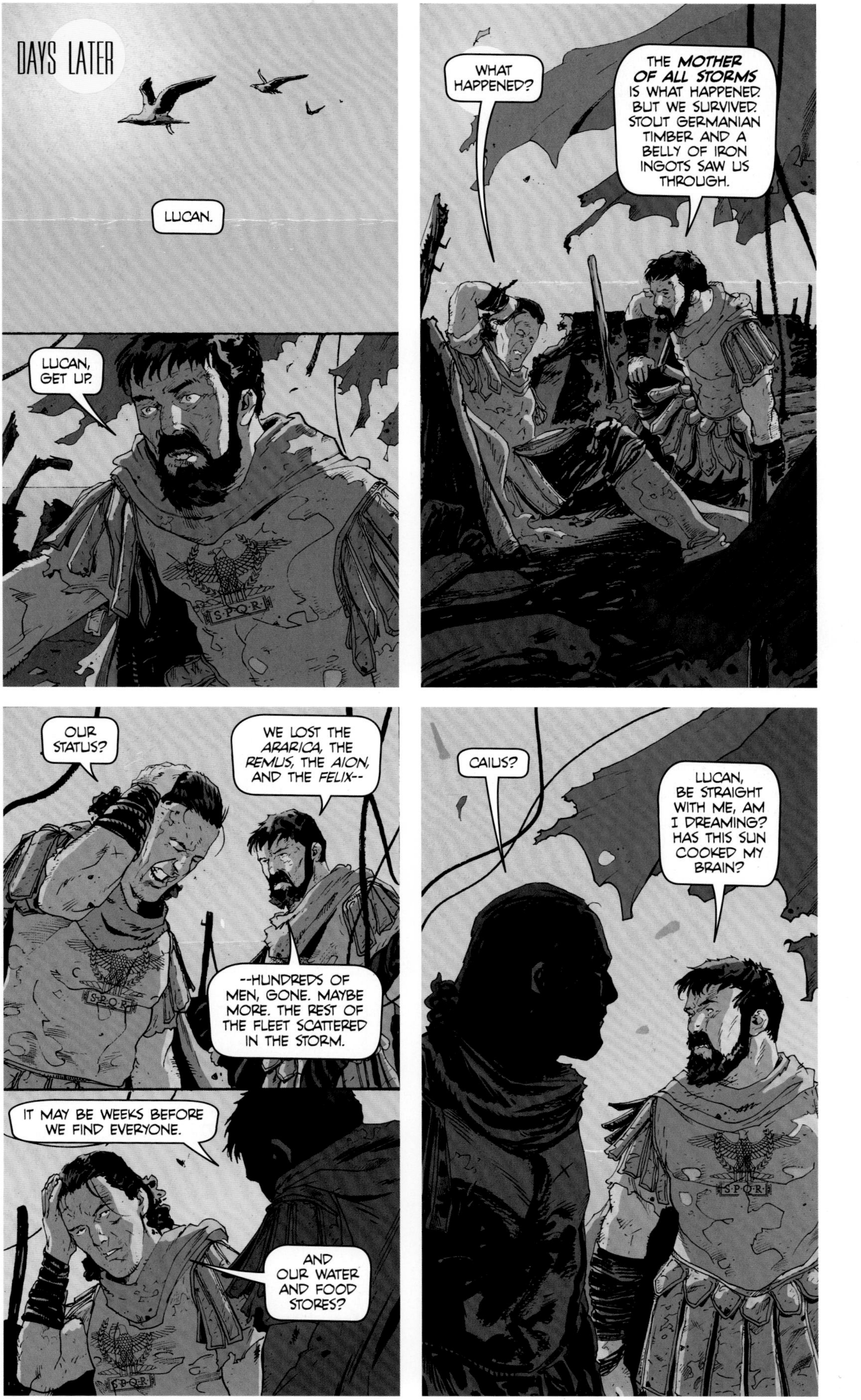
DAYS LATER
LUCAN.
LUCAN, GET UP.
WHAT HAPPENED?
THE MOTHER OF ALL STORMS IS WHAT HAPPENED. BUT WE SURVIVED. STOUT GERMANIAN TIMBER AND A BELLY OF IRON INGOTS SAW US THROUGH.
OUR STATUS?
WE LOST THE ARARICA, THE REMUS, THE AION, AND THE FELIX--
--HUNDREDS OF MEN, GONE. MAYBE MORE. THE REST OF THE FLEET SCATTERED IN THE STORM.
IT MAY BE WEEKS BEFORE WE FIND EVERYONE.
AND OUR WATER AND FOOD STORES?
CAIUS?
LUCAN, BE STRAIGHT WITH ME, AM I DREAMING? HAS THIS SUN COOKED MY BRAIN?

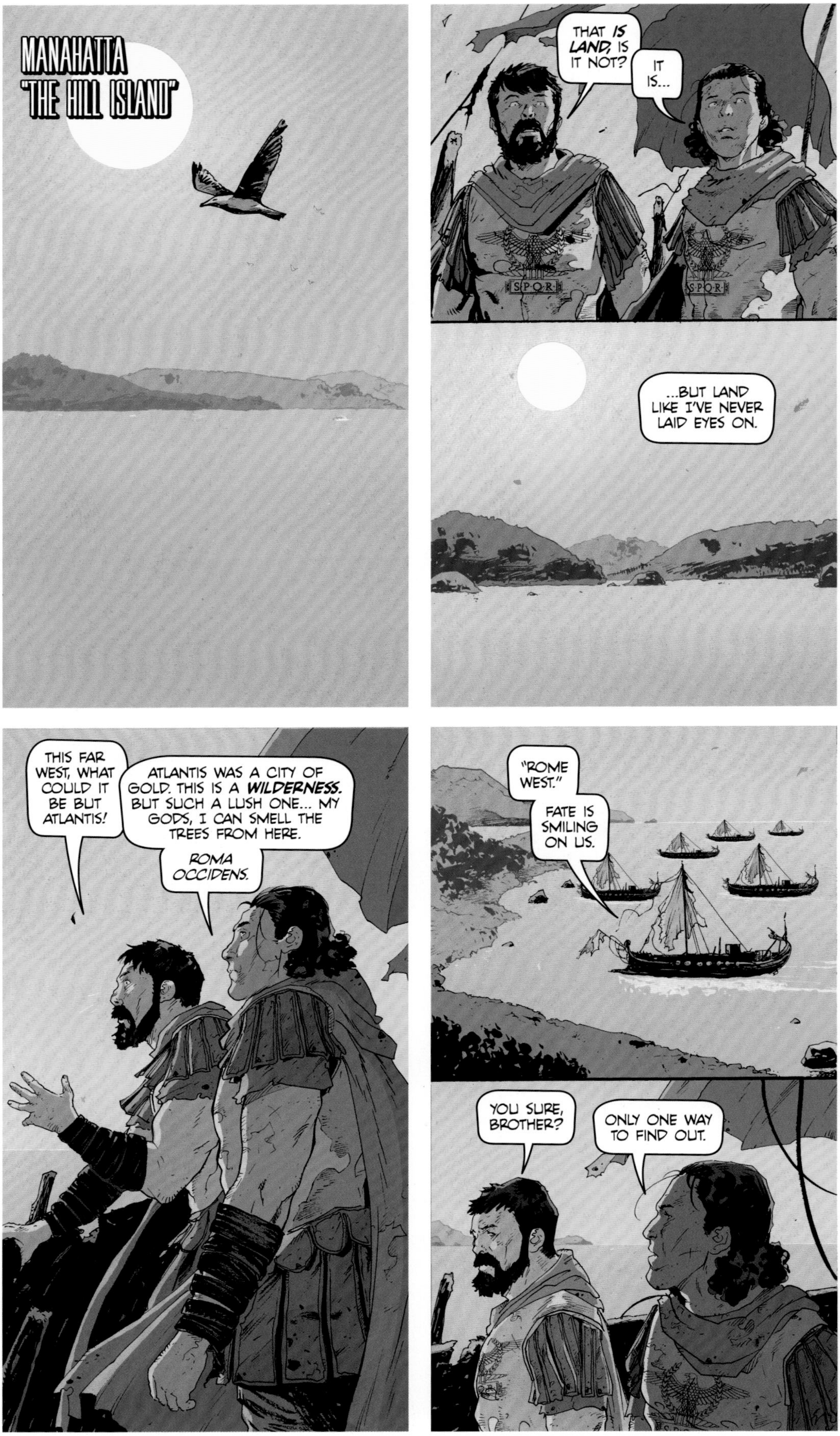
MANAHATTA
"THE HILL ISLAND"
THAT *IS* *LAND,* IS IT NOT?
IT IS...
...BUT LAND LIKE I'VE NEVER LAID EYES ON.
THIS FAR WEST, WHAT COULD IT BE BUT ATLANTIS!
ATLANTIS WAS A CITY OF GOLD. THIS IS A *WILDERNESS.* BUT SUCH A LUSH ONE... MY GODS, I CAN SMELL THE TREES FROM HERE.
ROMA OCCIDENS.
"ROME WEST."
FATE IS SMILING ON US.
YOU SURE, BROTHER?
ONLY ONE WAY TO FIND OUT.

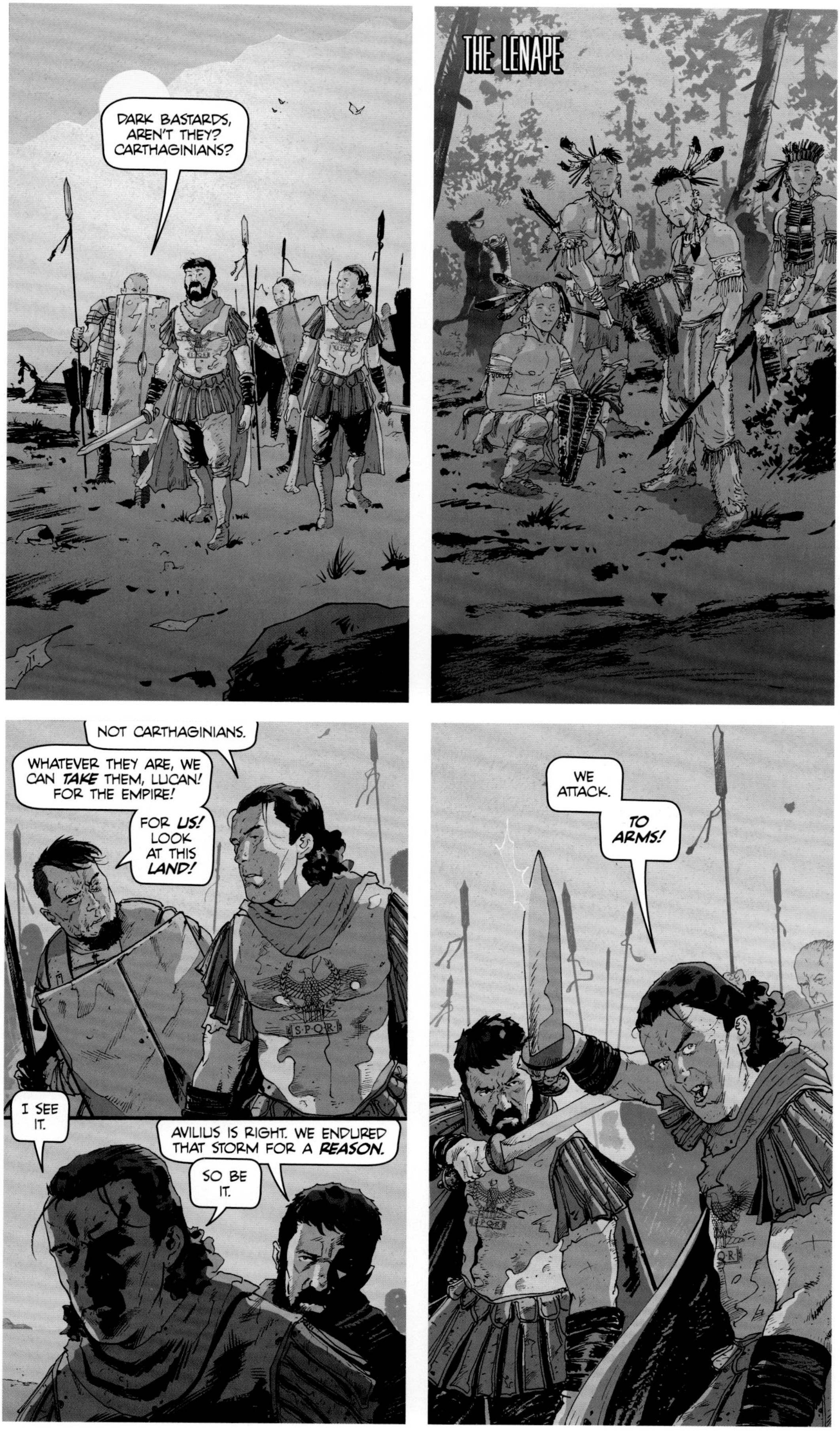
DARK BASTARDS, AREN'T THEY? CARTHAGINIANS?
THE LENAPE
NOT CARTHAGINIANS.
WHATEVER THEY ARE, WE CAN *TAKE* THEM, LUCAN! FOR THE EMPIRE!
FOR *US!* LOOK AT THIS *LAND!*
I SEE IT.
AVILIUS IS RIGHT. WE ENDURED THAT STORM FOR A *REASON.*
SO BE IT.
WE ATTACK.
TO ARMS!

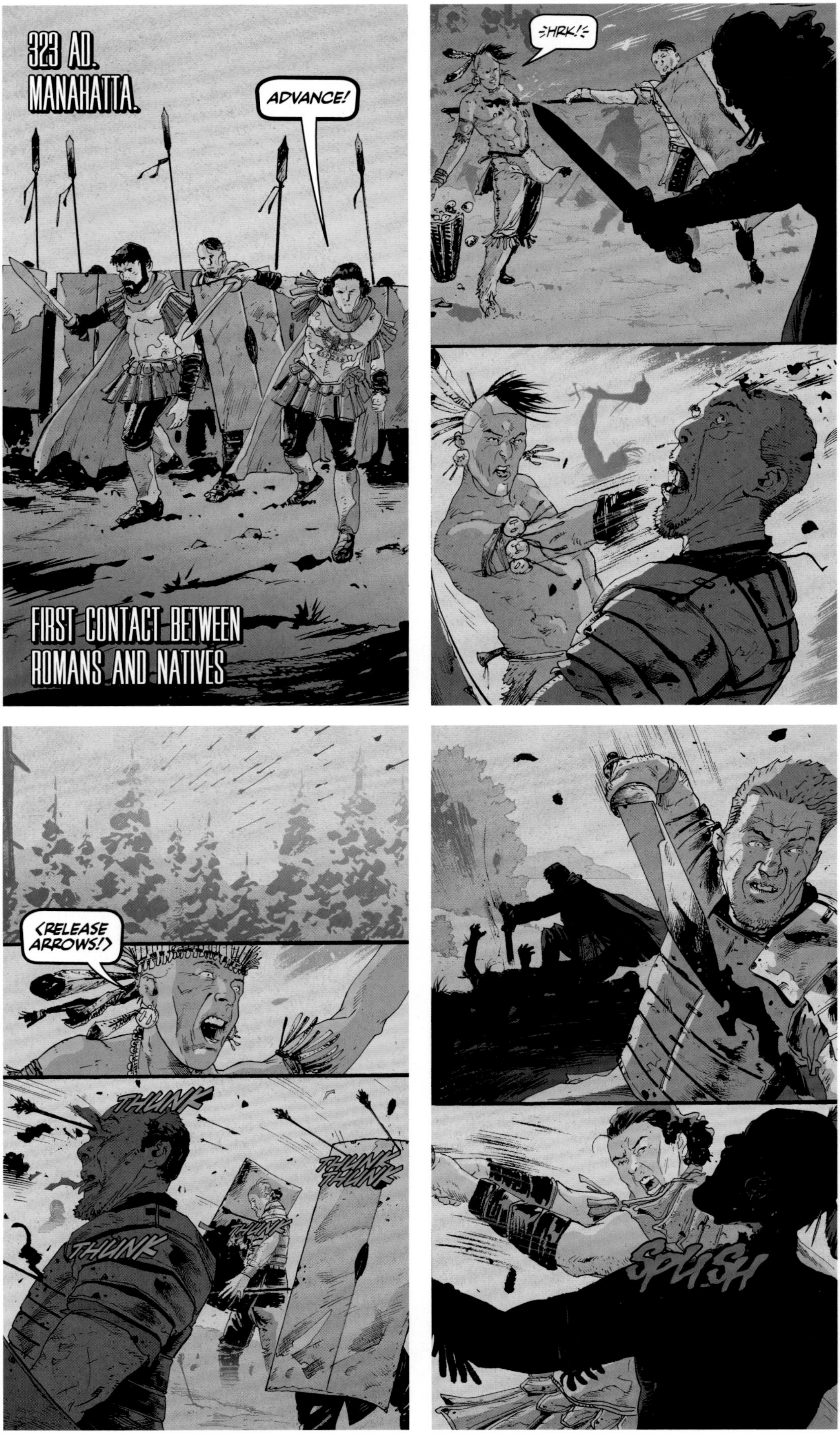
323 AD.
MANAHATTA.
ADVANCE!
FIRST CONTACT BETWEEN ROMANS AND NATIVES
HRK!
<RELEASE ARROWS!>
THUNK
THUNK THUNK
THUNK
THUNK
SPLISH

LEGIONNAIRES, *HOLD!*

<WAIT! WAIT! WE DON'T WISH TO HARM YOU!>

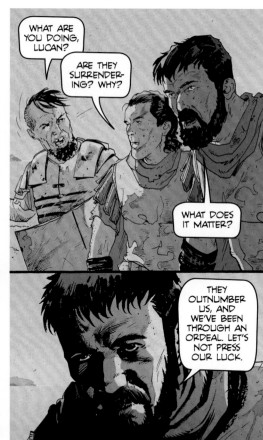

WHAT ARE YOU DOING, LUCAN?

ARE THEY SURRENDER-ING? WHY?

WHAT DOES IT MATTER?

THEY OUTNUMBER US, AND WE'VE BEEN THROUGH AN ORDEAL. LET'S NOT PRESS OUR LUCK.

<WE DESIRE *NO BLOOD* BE SPILT. WE DESIRE TALK.>

<I AM *MURACO,* OF THE EASTERN WOODLANDS.>

WE SHOULD *KILL THEM,* LUCAN!

WAIT.

CAIUS IS *RIGHT.* IF WE FIGHT, WE WILL DIE. IF WE TALK, WE WILL LIVE. AND *LEARN.*

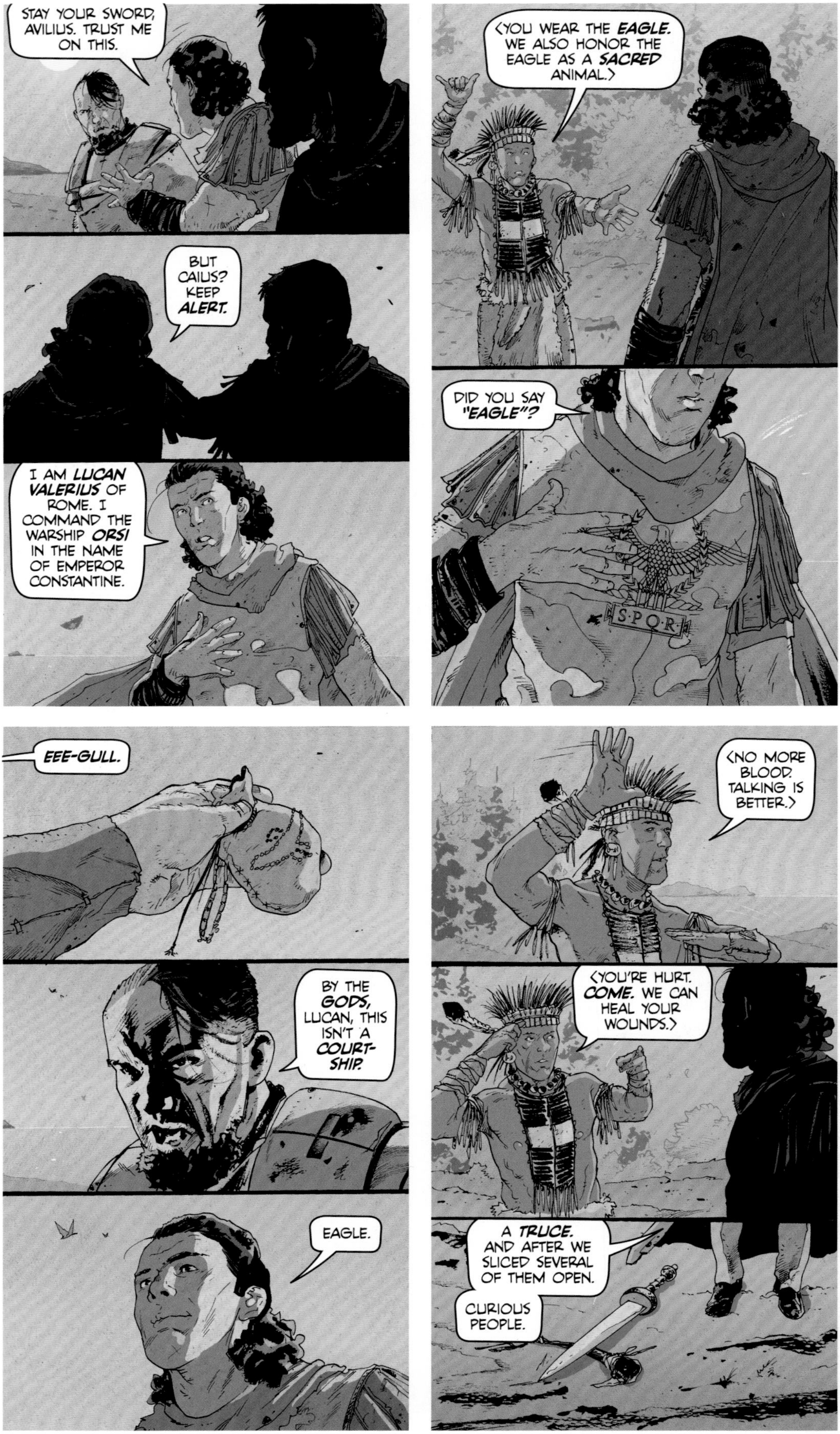
STAY YOUR SWORD, AVILIUS. TRUST ME ON THIS.
BUT CAIUS? KEEP ALERT.
I AM LUCAN VALERIUS OF ROME. I COMMAND THE WARSHIP ORSI IN THE NAME OF EMPEROR CONSTANTINE.
<YOU WEAR THE EAGLE. WE ALSO HONOR THE EAGLE AS A SACRED ANIMAL.>
DID YOU SAY "EAGLE"?
S·P·Q·R
EEE-GULL.
BY THE GODS, LUCAN, THIS ISN'T A COURTSHIP.
EAGLE.
<NO MORE BLOOD. TALKING IS BETTER.>
<YOU'RE HURT. COME. WE CAN HEAL YOUR WOUNDS.>
A TRUCE. AND AFTER WE SLICED SEVERAL OF THEM OPEN.
CURIOUS PEOPLE.

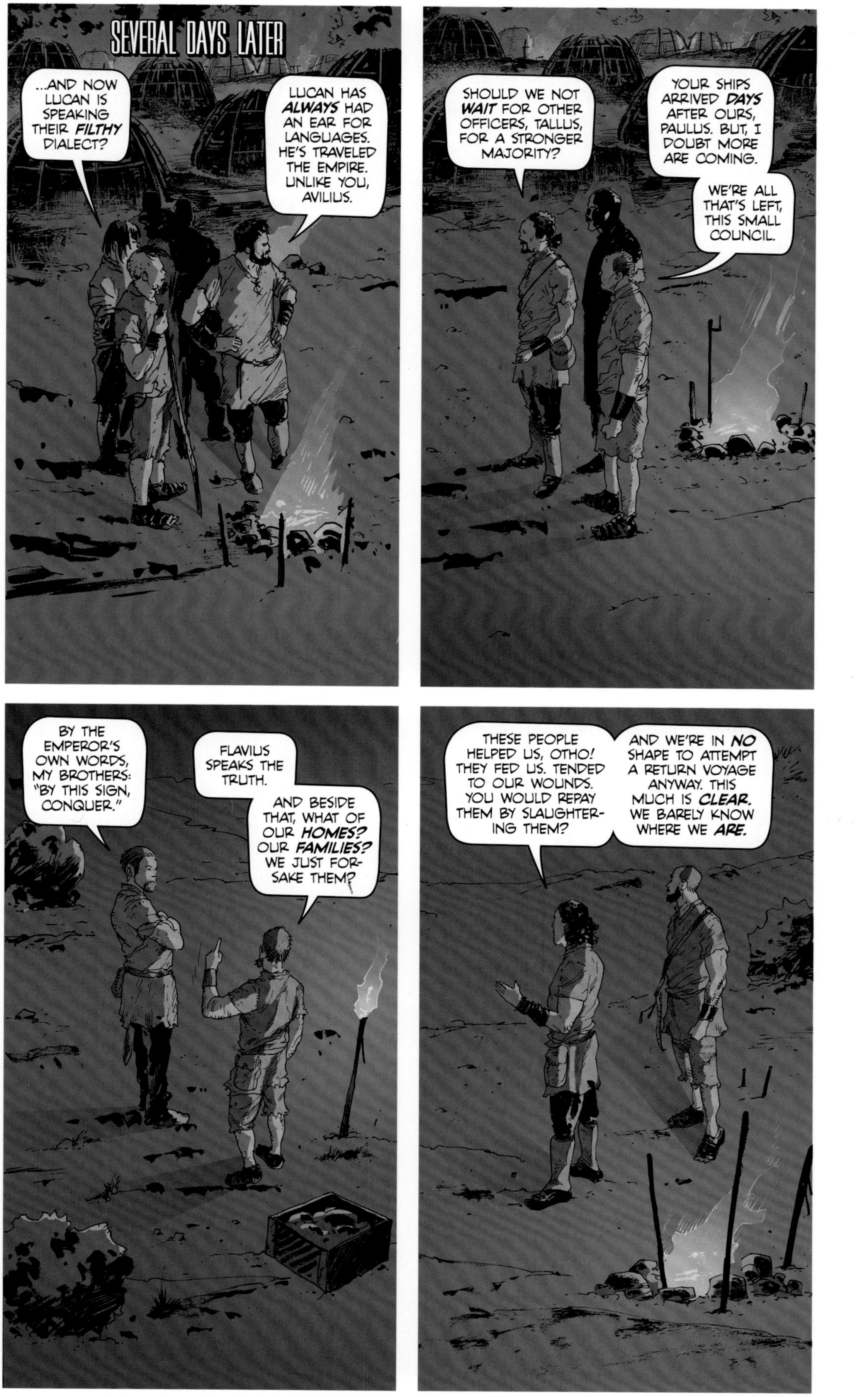
SEVERAL DAYS LATER
...AND NOW LUCAN IS SPEAKING THEIR FILTHY DIALECT?
LUCAN HAS ALWAYS HAD AN EAR FOR LANGUAGES. HE'S TRAVELED THE EMPIRE. UNLIKE YOU, AVILIUS.
SHOULD WE NOT WAIT FOR OTHER OFFICERS, TALLUS, FOR A STRONGER MAJORITY?
YOUR SHIPS ARRIVED DAYS AFTER OURS, PAULUS. BUT, I DOUBT MORE ARE COMING.
WE'RE ALL THAT'S LEFT, THIS SMALL COUNCIL.
BY THE EMPEROR'S OWN WORDS, MY BROTHERS: "BY THIS SIGN, CONQUER."
FLAVIUS SPEAKS THE TRUTH.
AND BESIDE THAT, WHAT OF OUR HOMES? OUR FAMILIES? WE JUST FOR-SAKE THEM?
THESE PEOPLE HELPED US, OTHO! THEY FED US. TENDED TO OUR WOUNDS. YOU WOULD REPAY THEM BY SLAUGHTER-ING THEM?
AND WE'RE IN NO SHAPE TO ATTEMPT A RETURN VOYAGE ANYWAY. THIS MUCH IS CLEAR. WE BARELY KNOW WHERE WE ARE.

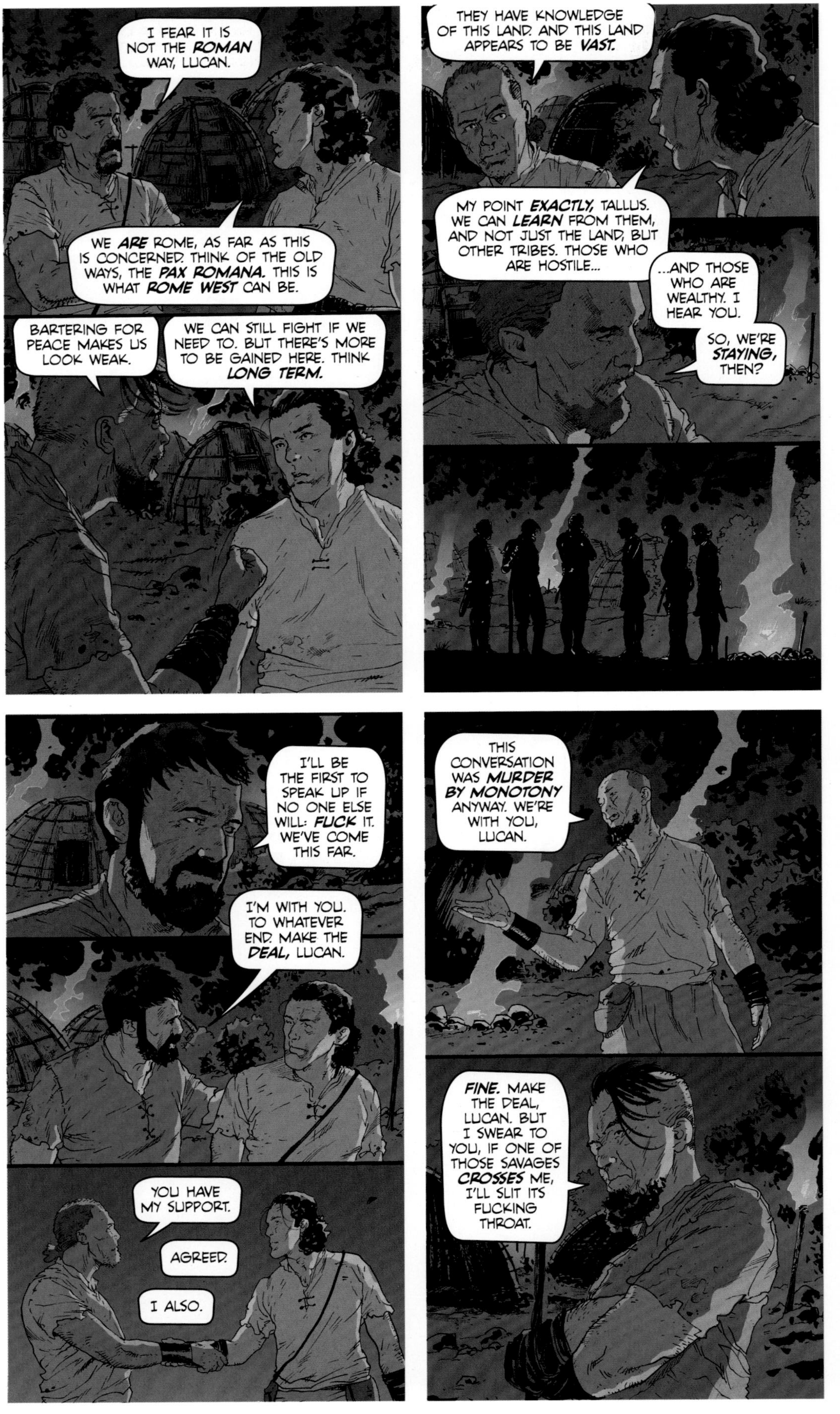
I FEAR IT IS NOT THE ROMAN WAY, LUCAN.
WE ARE ROME, AS FAR AS THIS IS CONCERNED. THINK OF THE OLD WAYS, THE PAX ROMANA. THIS IS WHAT ROME WEST CAN BE.
BARTERING FOR PEACE MAKES US LOOK WEAK.
WE CAN STILL FIGHT IF WE NEED TO. BUT THERE'S MORE TO BE GAINED HERE. THINK LONG TERM.
THEY HAVE KNOWLEDGE OF THIS LAND. AND THIS LAND APPEARS TO BE VAST.
MY POINT EXACTLY, TALLUS. WE CAN LEARN FROM THEM, AND NOT JUST THE LAND, BUT OTHER TRIBES. THOSE WHO ARE HOSTILE...
...AND THOSE WHO ARE WEALTHY. I HEAR YOU.
SO, WE'RE STAYING, THEN?
I'LL BE THE FIRST TO SPEAK UP IF NO ONE ELSE WILL: FUCK IT. WE'VE COME THIS FAR.
I'M WITH YOU. TO WHATEVER END. MAKE THE DEAL, LUCAN.
YOU HAVE MY SUPPORT.
AGREED.
I ALSO.
THIS CONVERSATION WAS MURDER BY MONOTONY ANYWAY. WE'RE WITH YOU, LUCAN.
FINE. MAKE THE DEAL, LUCAN. BUT I SWEAR TO YOU, IF ONE OF THOSE SAVAGES CROSSES ME, I'LL SLIT ITS FUCKING THROAT.

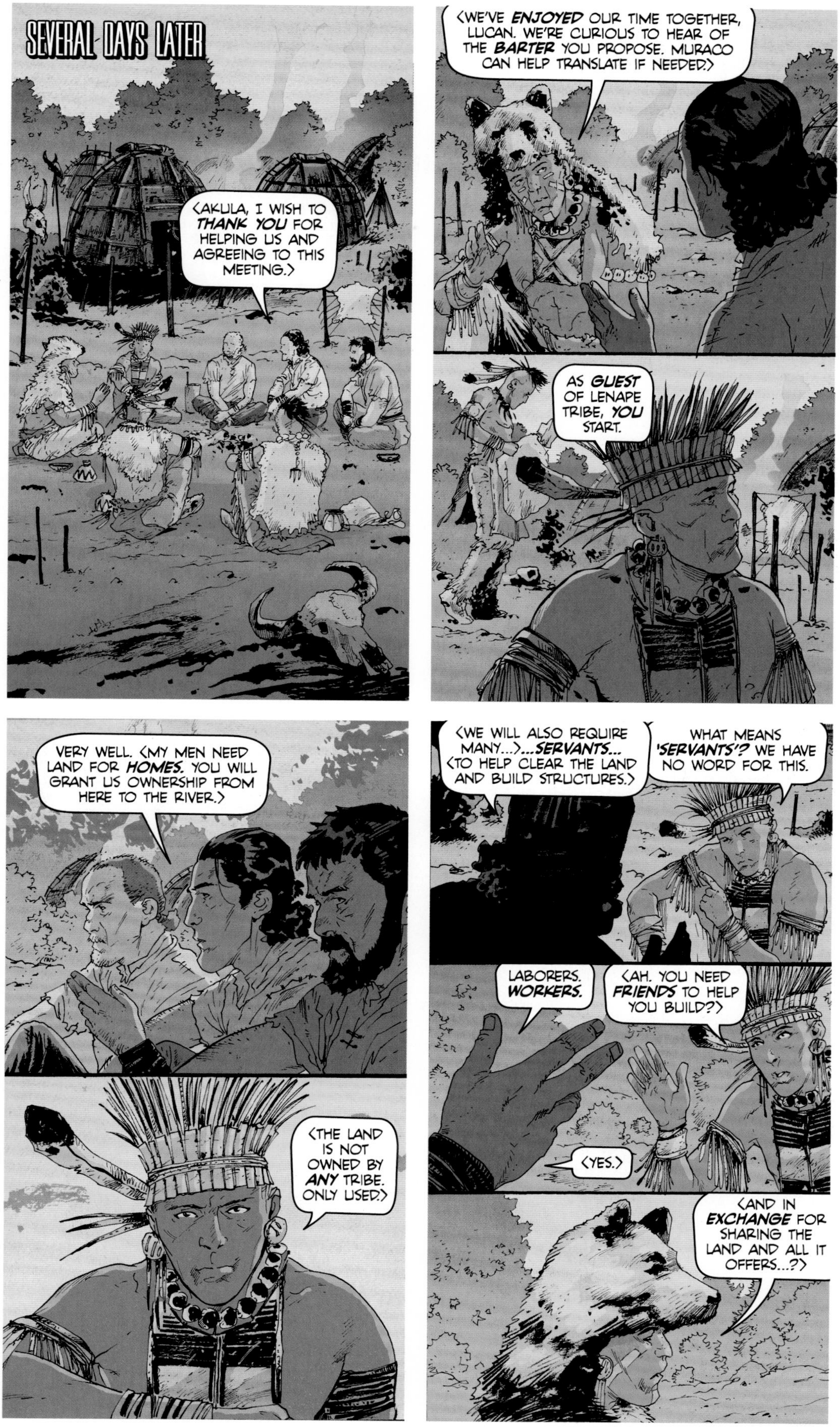
SEVERAL DAYS LATER
<AKULA, I WISH TO THANK YOU FOR HELPING US AND AGREEING TO THIS MEETING.>
<WE'VE ENJOYED OUR TIME TOGETHER, LUCAN. WE'RE CURIOUS TO HEAR OF THE BARTER YOU PROPOSE. MURACO CAN HELP TRANSLATE IF NEEDED.>
AS GUEST OF LENAPE TRIBE, YOU START.
VERY WELL. <MY MEN NEED LAND FOR HOMES. YOU WILL GRANT US OWNERSHIP FROM HERE TO THE RIVER.>
<THE LAND IS NOT OWNED BY ANY TRIBE. ONLY USED.>
<WE WILL ALSO REQUIRE MANY...>...SERVANTS... <TO HELP CLEAR THE LAND AND BUILD STRUCTURES.>
WHAT MEANS 'SERVANTS'? WE HAVE NO WORD FOR THIS.
LABORERS. WORKERS.
<AH. YOU NEED FRIENDS TO HELP YOU BUILD?>
<YES.>
<AND IN EXCHANGE FOR SHARING THE LAND AND ALL IT OFFERS...?>

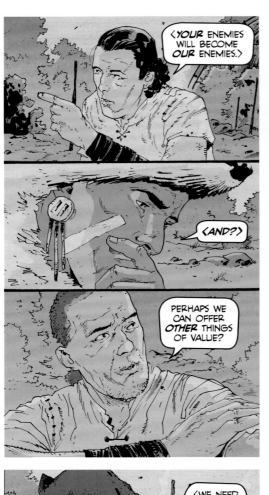

⟨*YOUR* ENEMIES WILL BECOME *OUR* ENEMIES.⟩

⟨AND?⟩

PERHAPS WE CAN OFFER *OTHER* THINGS OF VALUE?

⟨WE CAN TEACH YOU HOW TO BUILD WITH STONE. STRONGER THAN YOUR STICK HUTS.⟩

⟨WE CAN ALSO BUILD STONE...⟩... *AQUEDUCTS*... ⟨A WAY TO MOVE *BIG* WATER.⟩

⟨THIS IS *INTERESTING.* I WOULD LIKE US TO LEARN, BUT STONE IS NOT SO EASY TO PACK UP AND FOLLOW THE HUNT, IS IT?⟩

⟨WE NEED SOMETHING *MORE* TO MAKE THE BARTER FAIR.⟩

⟨*METAL.* WE CAN TEACH YOU HOW TO FORGE STEEL WEAPONS. BETTER SPEARS. ARROW HEADS. *SWORDS.* FOR HUNTING.⟩

⟨YOUR BARTER IS *ACCEPTED,* LUCAN. OUR TRIBES WILL LIVE *TOGETHER* AND LEARN THE WAYS OF THE OTHER.⟩

⟨THEIR WEAPONS! WELL DONE, AKULA.⟩

⟨FINALLY, A TRADE WORTH MAKING.⟩

⟨WE WILL BENEFIT FROM THIS. WE WILL PROSPER. WE WILL DOMINATE.⟩

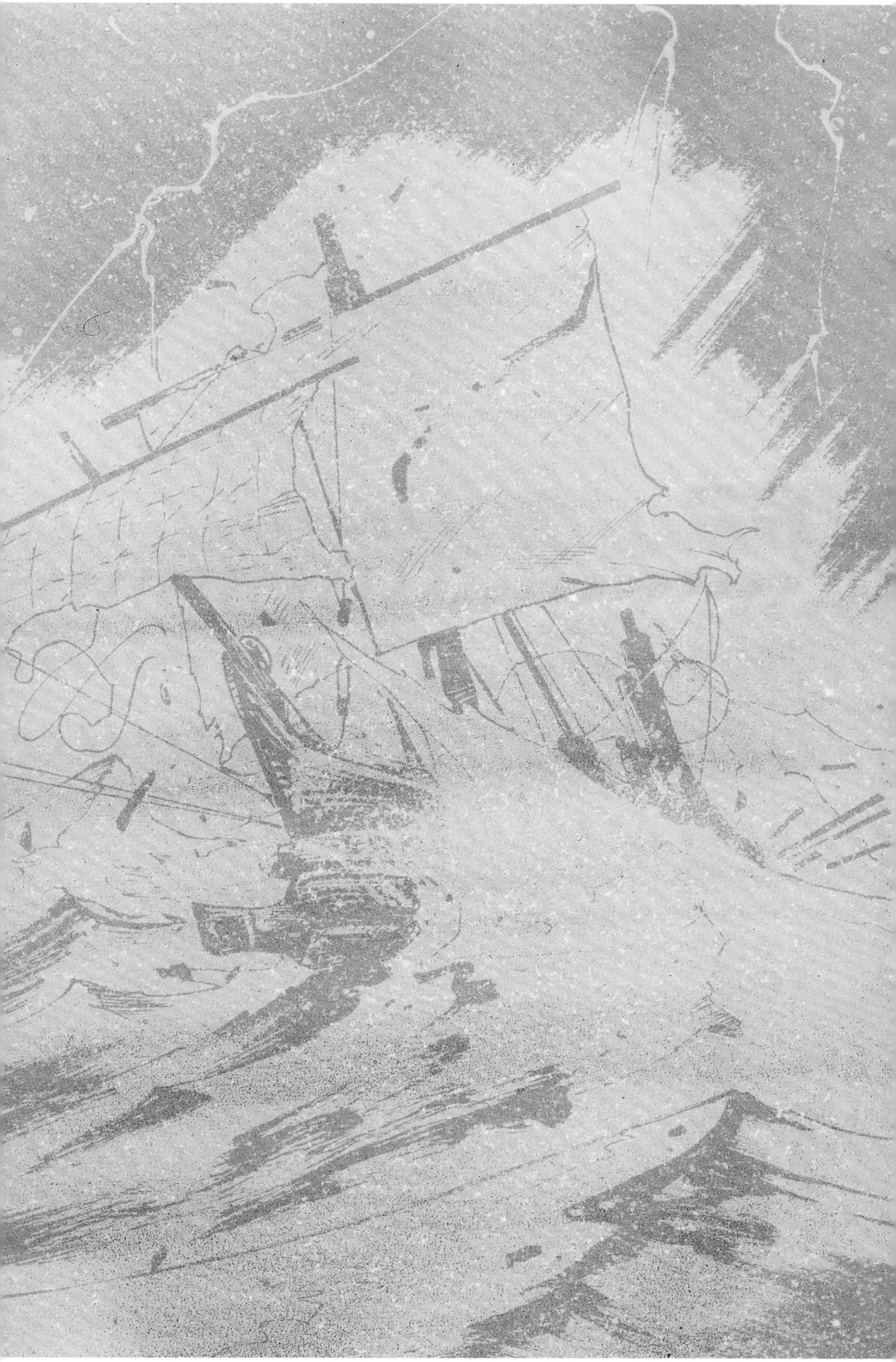

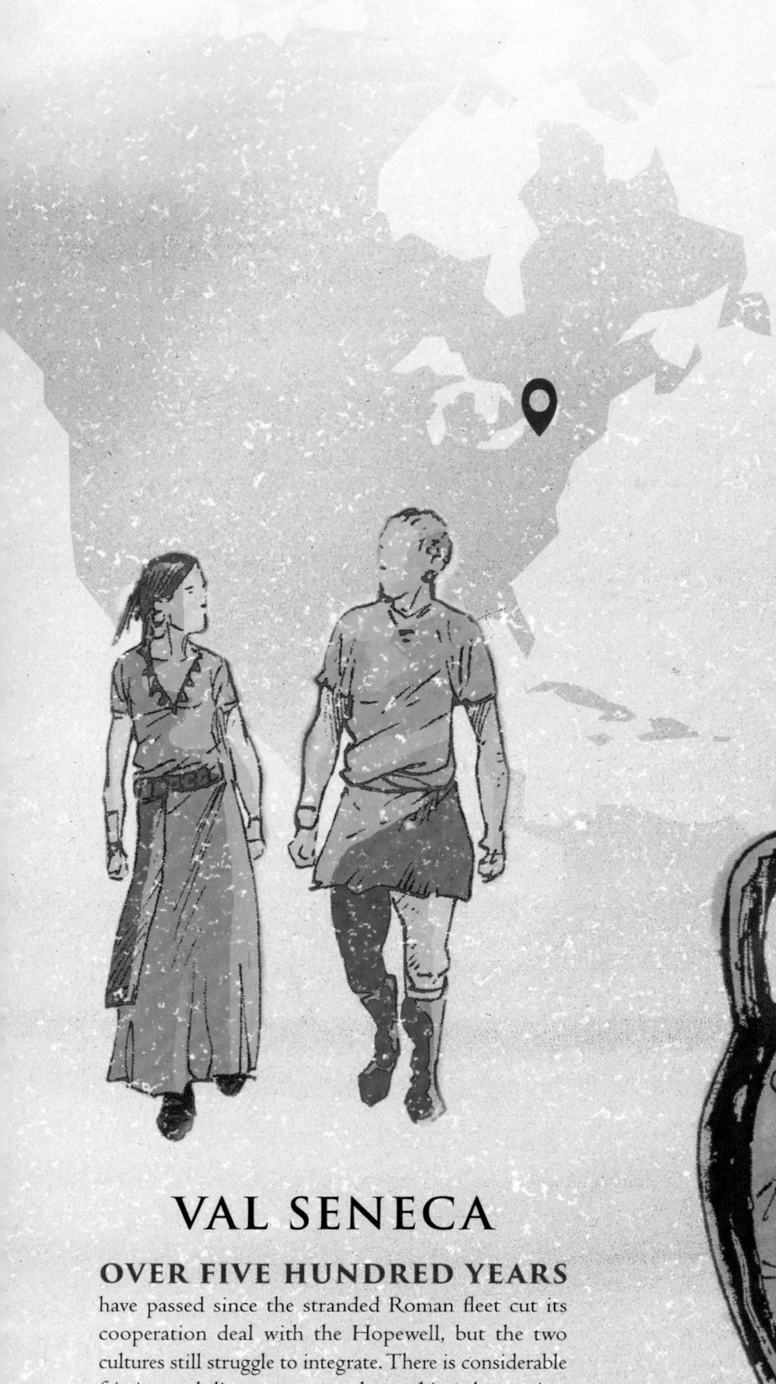

VAL SENECA

OVER FIVE HUNDRED YEARS have passed since the stranded Roman fleet cut its cooperation deal with the Hopewell, but the two cultures still struggle to integrate. There is considerable friction and dissent amongst the working-class natives and the Roman politicos, but Janus Valerius, a member of the ruling family, seeks to force social progress by any means necessary.

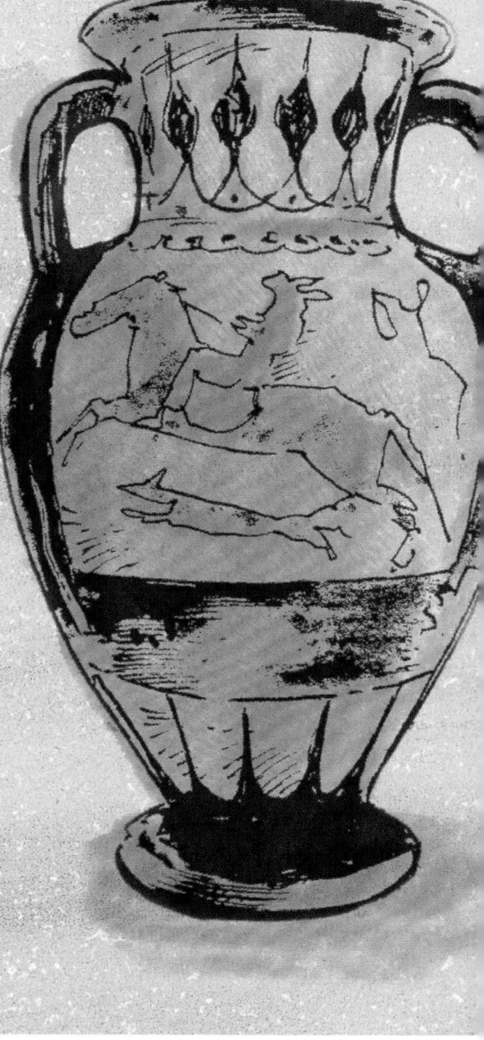

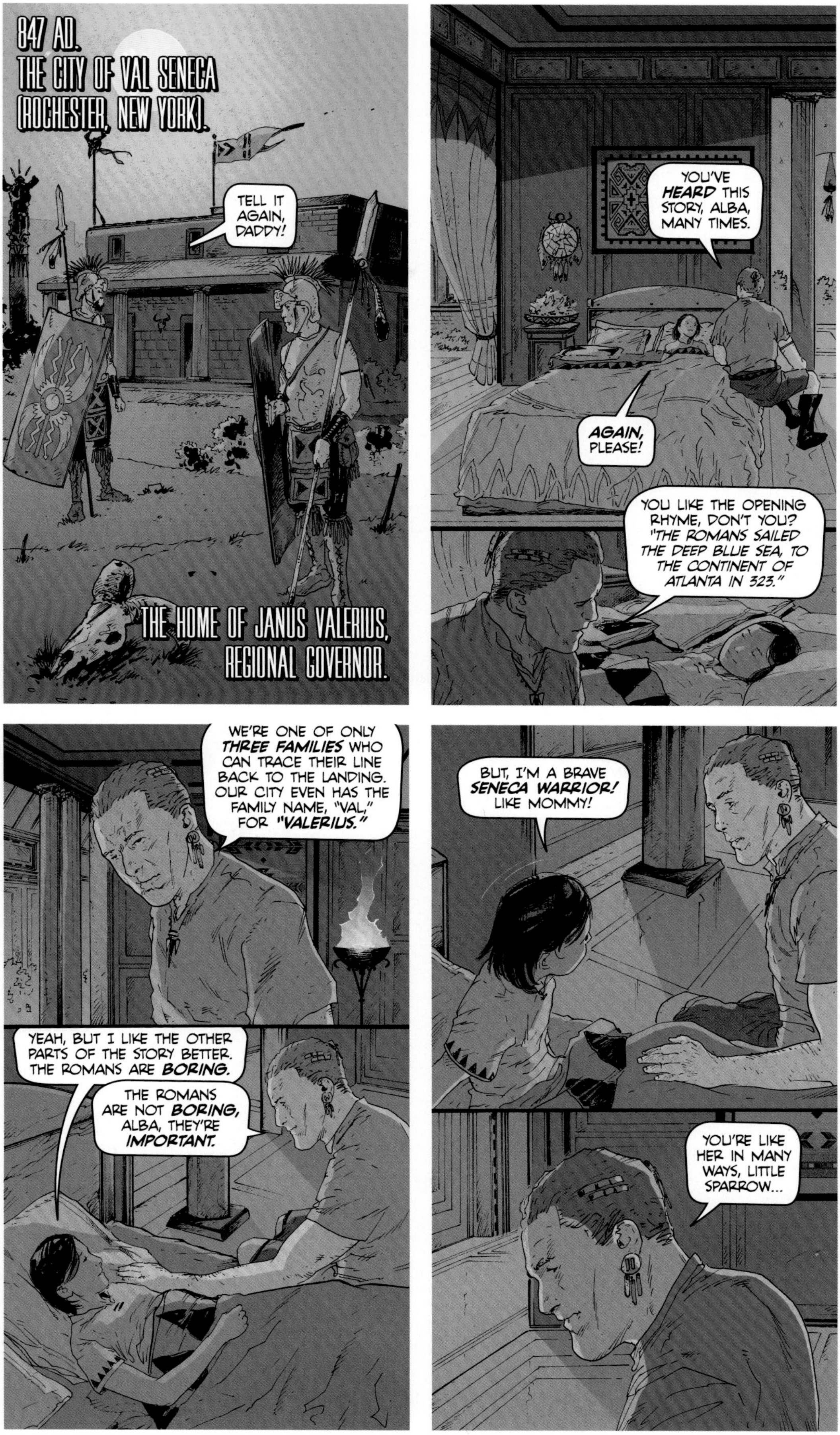

847 AD.
THE CITY OF VAL SENECA
(ROCHESTER, NEW YORK).
TELL IT AGAIN, DADDY!
THE HOME OF JANUS VALERIUS, REGIONAL GOVERNOR.
YOU'VE HEARD THIS STORY, ALBA, MANY TIMES.
AGAIN, PLEASE!
YOU LIKE THE OPENING RHYME, DON'T YOU? "THE ROMANS SAILED THE DEEP BLUE SEA, TO THE CONTINENT OF ATLANTA IN 323."
WE'RE ONE OF ONLY THREE FAMILIES WHO CAN TRACE THEIR LINE BACK TO THE LANDING. OUR CITY EVEN HAS THE FAMILY NAME, "VAL," FOR "VALERIUS."
YEAH, BUT I LIKE THE OTHER PARTS OF THE STORY BETTER. THE ROMANS ARE BORING.
THE ROMANS ARE NOT BORING, ALBA, THEY'RE IMPORTANT.
BUT, I'M A BRAVE SENECA WARRIOR! LIKE MOMMY!
YOU'RE LIKE HER IN MANY WAYS, LITTLE SPARROW...

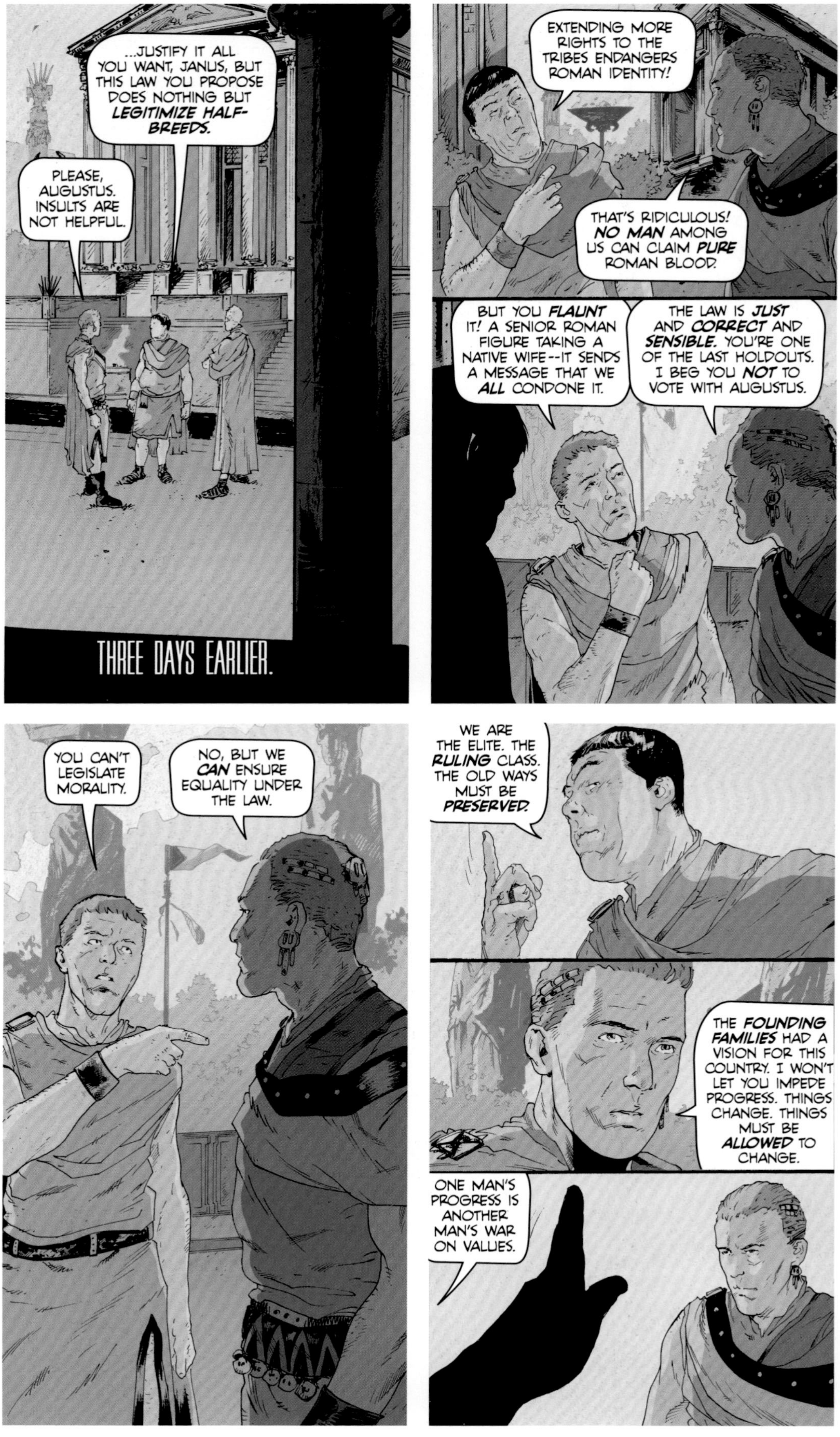
...JUSTIFY IT ALL YOU WANT, JANUS, BUT THIS LAW YOU PROPOSE DOES NOTHING BUT LEGITIMIZE HALF-BREEDS.
PLEASE, AUGUSTUS. INSULTS ARE NOT HELPFUL.
THREE DAYS EARLIER.
EXTENDING MORE RIGHTS TO THE TRIBES ENDANGERS ROMAN IDENTITY!
THAT'S RIDICULOUS! NO MAN AMONG US CAN CLAIM PURE ROMAN BLOOD.
BUT YOU FLAUNT IT! A SENIOR ROMAN FIGURE TAKING A NATIVE WIFE--IT SENDS A MESSAGE THAT WE ALL CONDONE IT.
THE LAW IS JUST AND CORRECT AND SENSIBLE. YOU'RE ONE OF THE LAST HOLDOUTS. I BEG YOU NOT TO VOTE WITH AUGUSTUS.
YOU CAN'T LEGISLATE MORALITY.
NO, BUT WE CAN ENSURE EQUALITY UNDER THE LAW.
WE ARE THE ELITE. THE RULING CLASS. THE OLD WAYS MUST BE PRESERVED.
THE FOUNDING FAMILIES HAD A VISION FOR THIS COUNTRY. I WON'T LET YOU IMPEDE PROGRESS. THINGS CHANGE. THINGS MUST BE ALLOWED TO CHANGE.
ONE MAN'S PROGRESS IS ANOTHER MAN'S WAR ON VALUES.

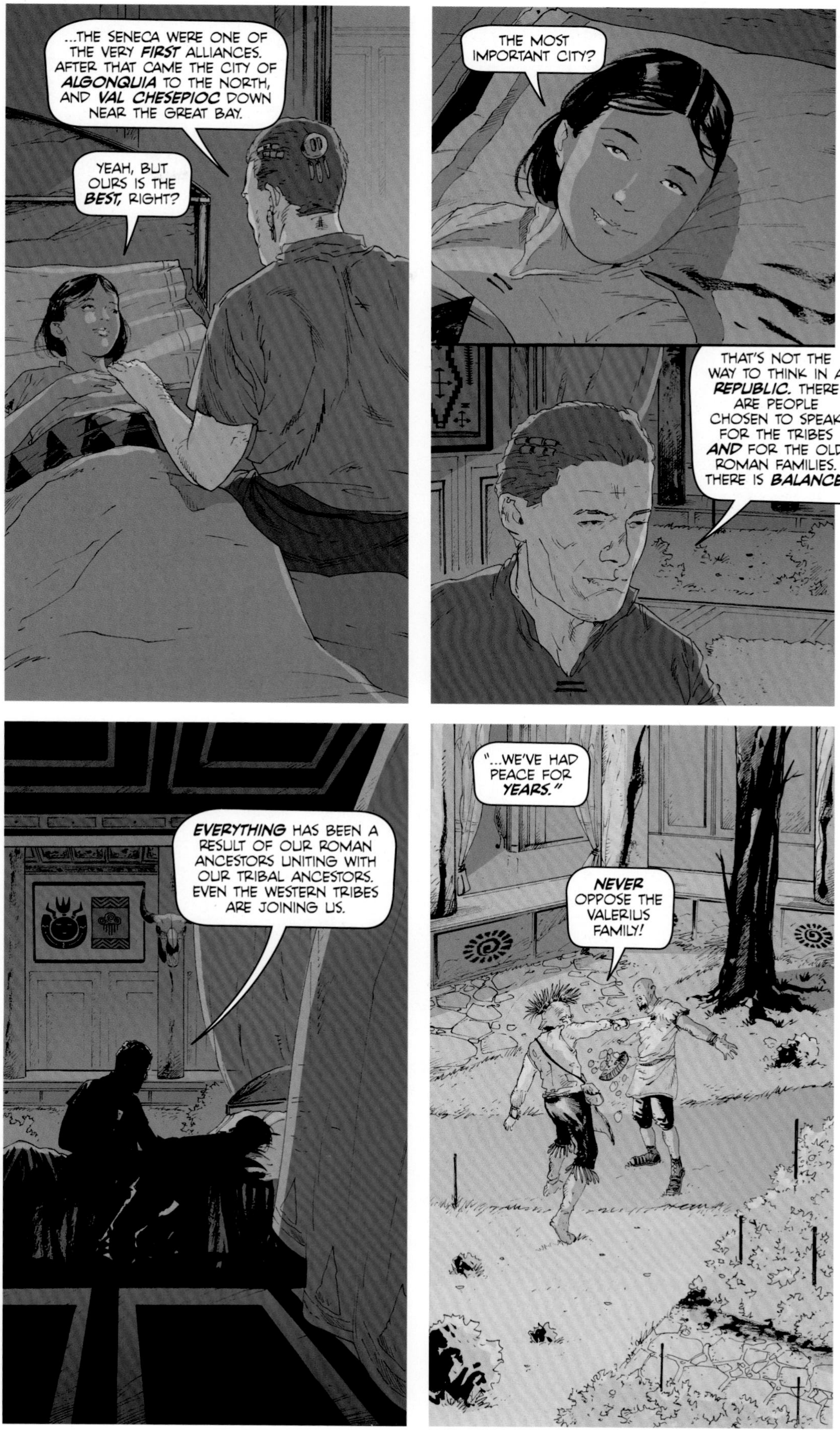
...THE SENECA WERE ONE OF THE VERY FIRST ALLIANCES. AFTER THAT CAME THE CITY OF ALGONQUIA TO THE NORTH, AND VAL CHESEPIOC DOWN NEAR THE GREAT BAY.
YEAH, BUT OURS IS THE BEST, RIGHT?
THE MOST IMPORTANT CITY?
THAT'S NOT THE WAY TO THINK IN A REPUBLIC. THERE ARE PEOPLE CHOSEN TO SPEAK FOR THE TRIBES AND FOR THE OLD ROMAN FAMILIES. THERE IS BALANCE.
EVERYTHING HAS BEEN A RESULT OF OUR ROMAN ANCESTORS UNITING WITH OUR TRIBAL ANCESTORS. EVEN THE WESTERN TRIBES ARE JOINING US.
"...WE'VE HAD PEACE FOR YEARS."
NEVER OPPOSE THE VALERIUS FAMILY!

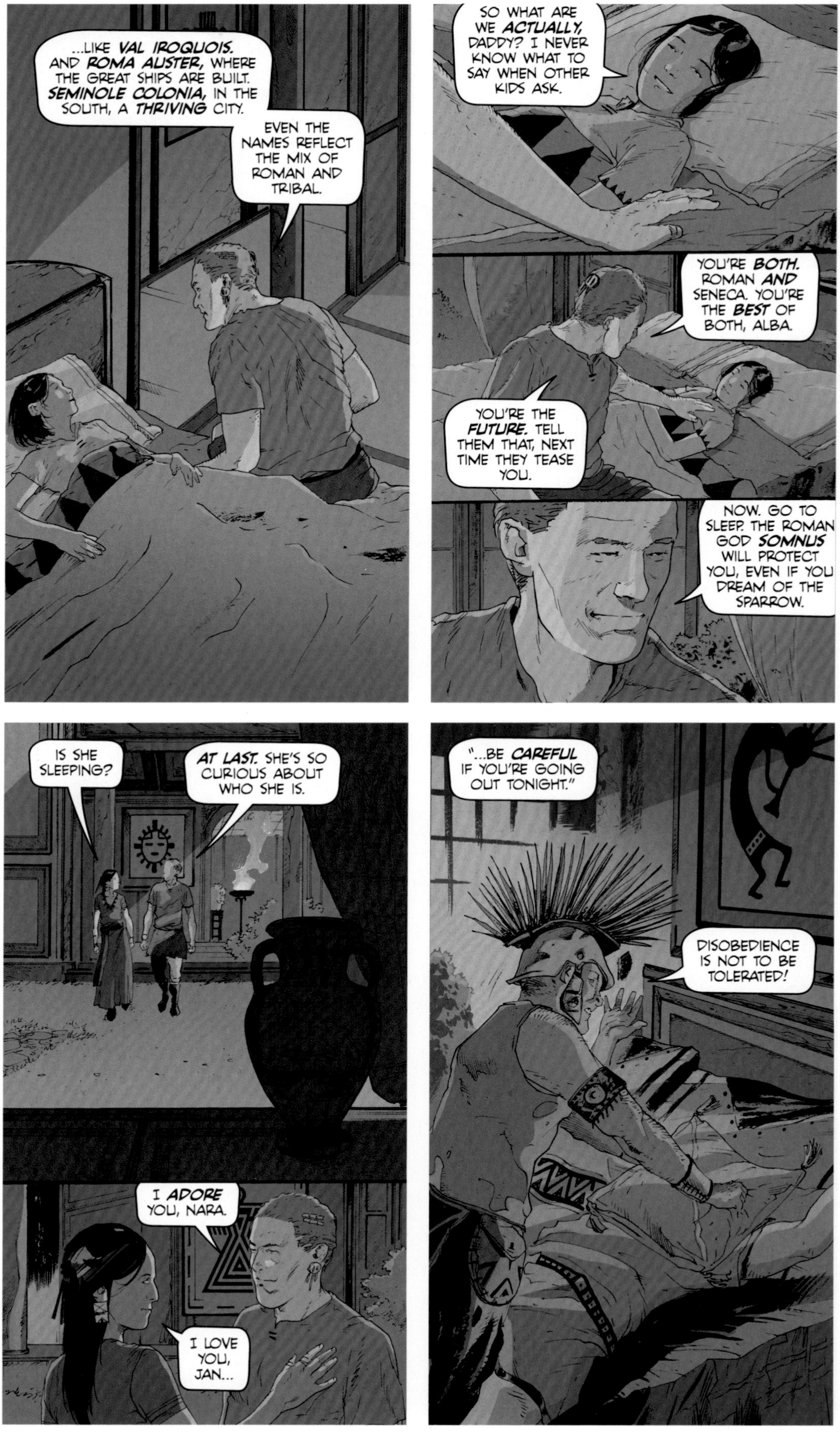
...LIKE VAL IROQUOIS. AND ROMA AUSTER, WHERE THE GREAT SHIPS ARE BUILT. SEMINOLE COLONIA, IN THE SOUTH, A THRIVING CITY.
EVEN THE NAMES REFLECT THE MIX OF ROMAN AND TRIBAL.
SO WHAT ARE WE ACTUALLY, DADDY? I NEVER KNOW WHAT TO SAY WHEN OTHER KIDS ASK.
YOU'RE BOTH. ROMAN AND SENECA. YOU'RE THE BEST OF BOTH, ALBA.
YOU'RE THE FUTURE. TELL THEM THAT, NEXT TIME THEY TEASE YOU.
NOW. GO TO SLEEP. THE ROMAN GOD SOMNUS WILL PROTECT YOU, EVEN IF YOU DREAM OF THE SPARROW.
IS SHE SLEEPING?
AT LAST. SHE'S SO CURIOUS ABOUT WHO SHE IS.
I ADORE YOU, NARA.
I LOVE YOU, JAN...
"...BE CAREFUL IF YOU'RE GOING OUT TONIGHT."
DISOBEDIENCE IS NOT TO BE TOLERATED!

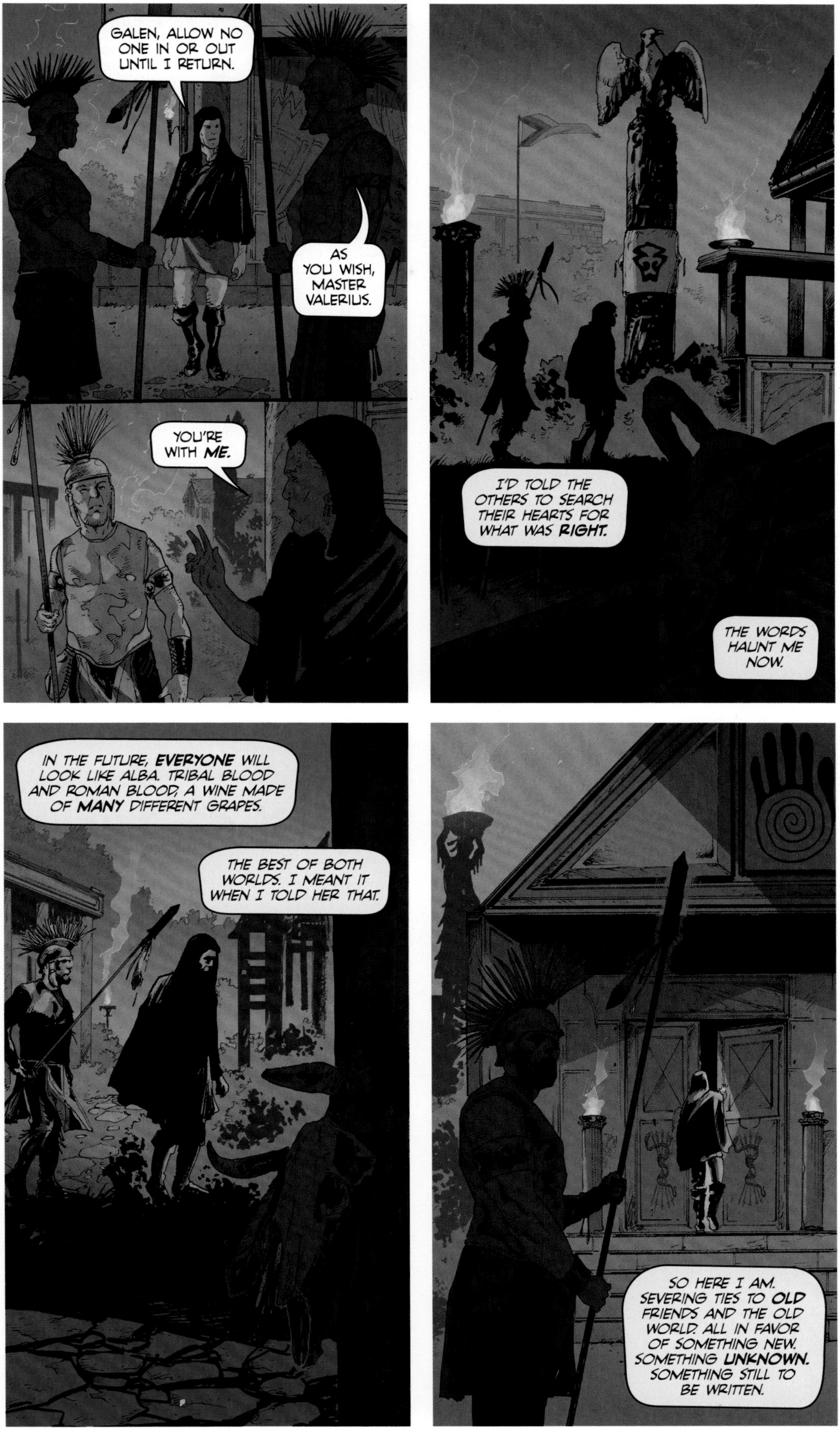
GALEN, ALLOW NO ONE IN OR OUT UNTIL I RETURN.
AS YOU WISH, MASTER VALERIUS.
YOU'RE WITH **ME.**
I'D TOLD THE OTHERS TO SEARCH THEIR HEARTS FOR WHAT WAS **RIGHT.**
THE WORDS HAUNT ME NOW.
IN THE FUTURE, **EVERYONE** WILL LOOK LIKE ALBA. TRIBAL BLOOD AND ROMAN BLOOD; A WINE MADE OF **MANY** DIFFERENT GRAPES.
THE BEST OF BOTH WORLDS. I MEANT IT WHEN I TOLD HER THAT.
SO HERE I AM. SEVERING TIES TO **OLD** FRIENDS AND THE OLD WORLD. ALL IN FAVOR OF SOMETHING NEW. SOMETHING **UNKNOWN.** SOMETHING STILL TO BE WRITTEN.

THE HOUR IS *LATE*, JANUS. HAVE YOU COME TO MAKE ONE FINAL PLEA?

I KNOW I CAN'T SWAY YOU, AUGUSTUS. BUT PROGRESS MARCHES ON, WHETHER YOU WANT IT TO OR NOT.

WE ALL MUST DO WHAT'S RIGHT.

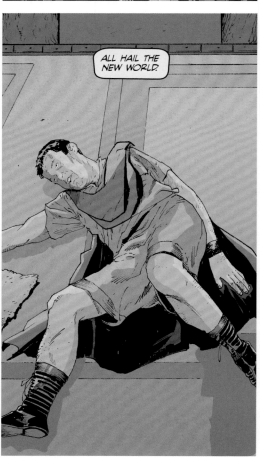

ALL HAIL THE NEW WORLD.

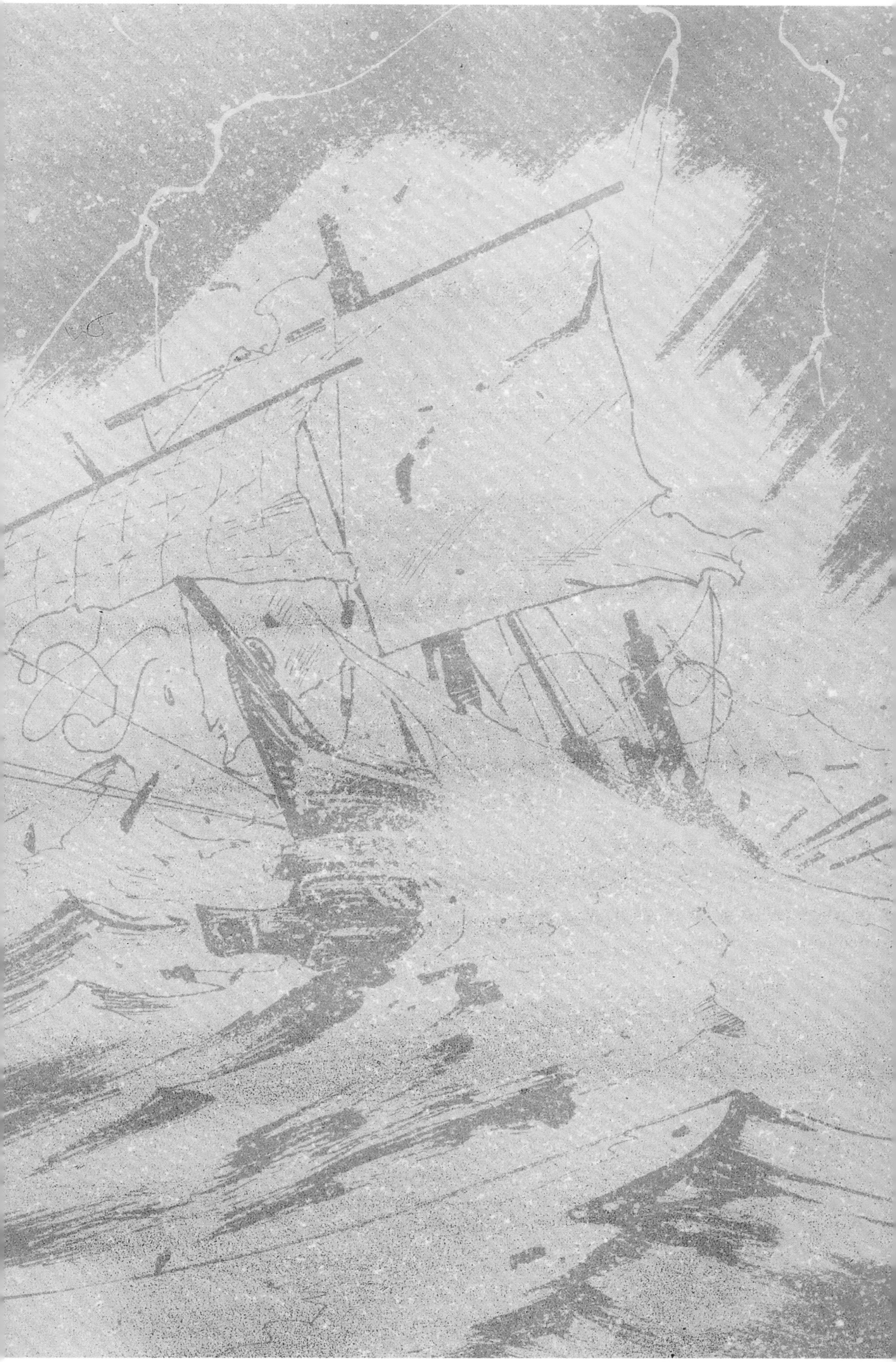

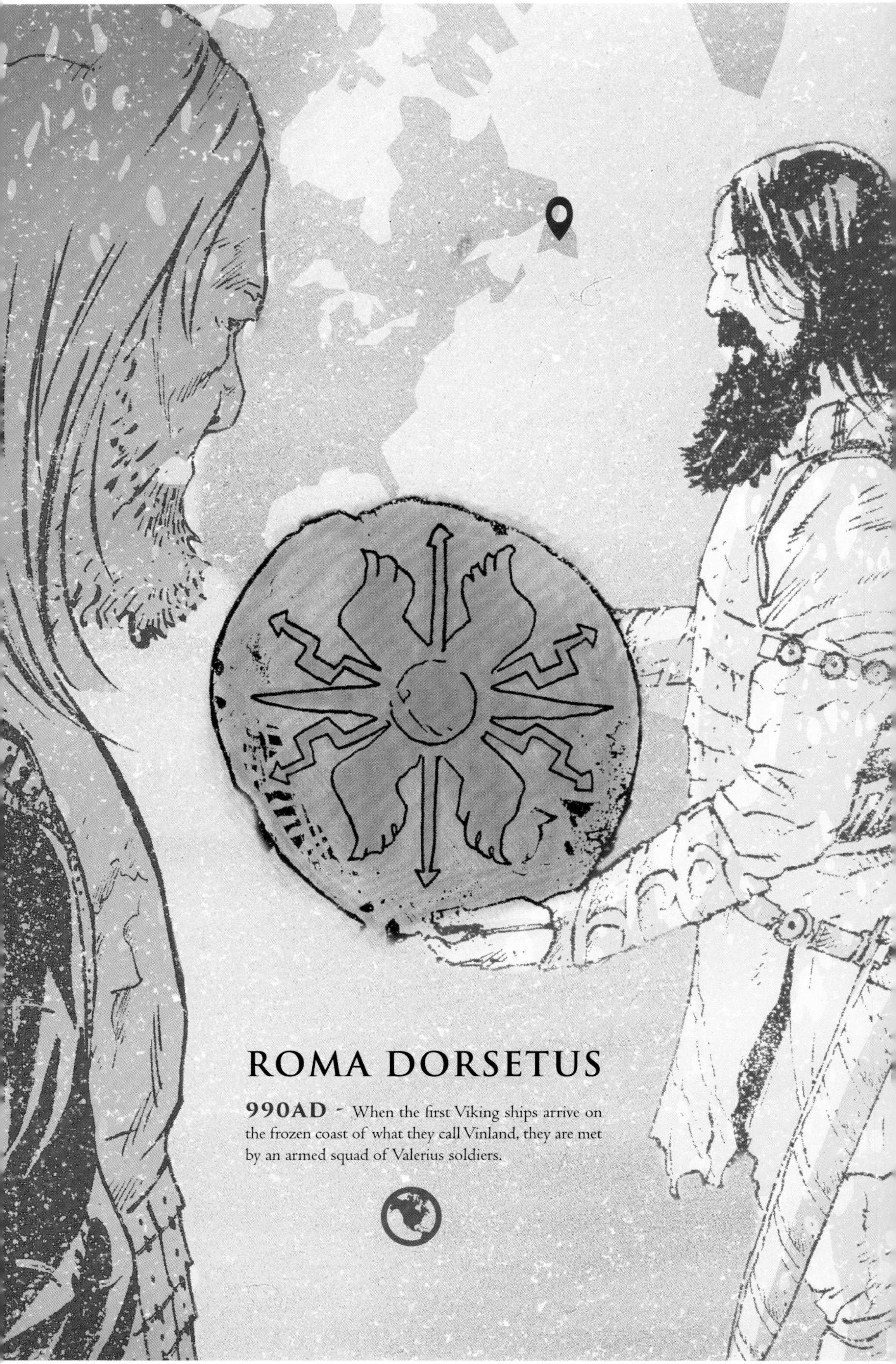

ROMA DORSETUS

990AD - When the first Viking ships arrive on the frozen coast of what they call Vinland, they are met by an armed squad of Valerius soldiers.

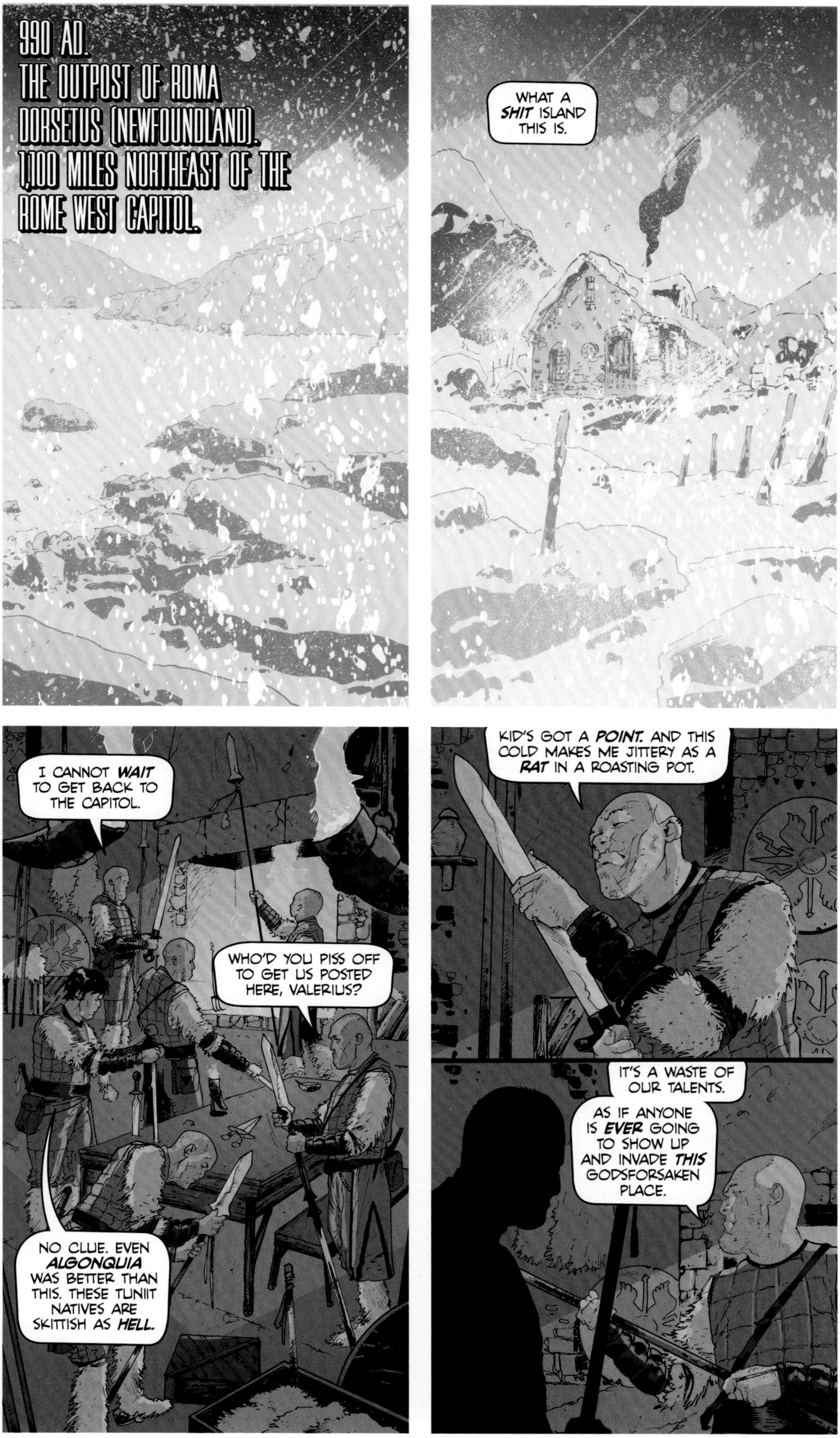
990 AD.
THE OUTPOST OF ROMA DORSETUS (NEWFOUNDLAND).
1,100 MILES NORTHEAST OF THE ROME WEST CAPITOL.
WHAT A SHIT ISLAND THIS IS.
I CANNOT WAIT TO GET BACK TO THE CAPITOL.
WHO'D YOU PISS OFF TO GET US POSTED HERE, VALERIUS?
NO CLUE. EVEN ALGONQUIA WAS BETTER THAN THIS. THESE TUNIIT NATIVES ARE SKITTISH AS HELL.
KID'S GOT A POINT. AND THIS COLD MAKES ME JITTERY AS A RAT IN A ROASTING POT.
IT'S A WASTE OF OUR TALENTS.
AS IF ANYONE IS EVER GOING TO SHOW UP AND INVADE THIS GODSFORSAKEN PLACE.

THUD!
THUD!
THUD!

WHO WOULD DO THAT? WHO WOULD POUND ON OUR DOOR LIKE THAT?

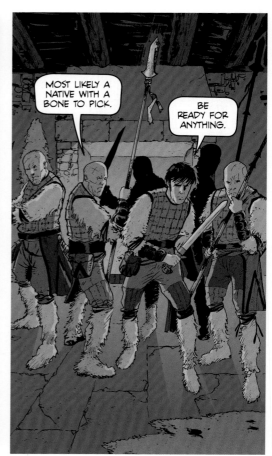

MOST LIKELY A NATIVE WITH A BONE TO PICK.

BE READY FOR ANYTHING.

ON THREE. ONE... TWO...

KRAKK

I LISTENED TO THEIR **BLABBERING** AS LONG AS I COULD STOMACH. THE ICE-SHIRTS? THEIR VOICES SOUNDED LIKE MUSIC.

GAAKKK!

BUT THESE IRON-SHIRTED BASTARDS WERE LIKE HISSING SERPENTS.

FIT ONLY TO BE DRIVEN OUT.

OUT! NOW!

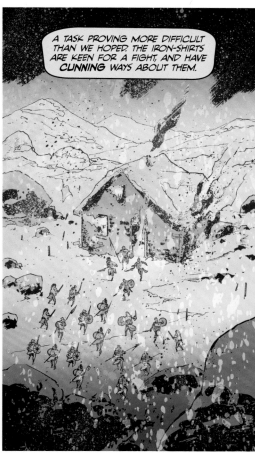

A TASK PROVING MORE DIFFICULT THAN WE HOPED. THE IRON-SHIRTS ARE KEEN FOR A FIGHT, AND HAVE **CUNNING** WAYS ABOUT THEM.

WE'VE BEEN ON A BOAT FOR **WEEKS.** TIME TO STRETCH THE LEGS.

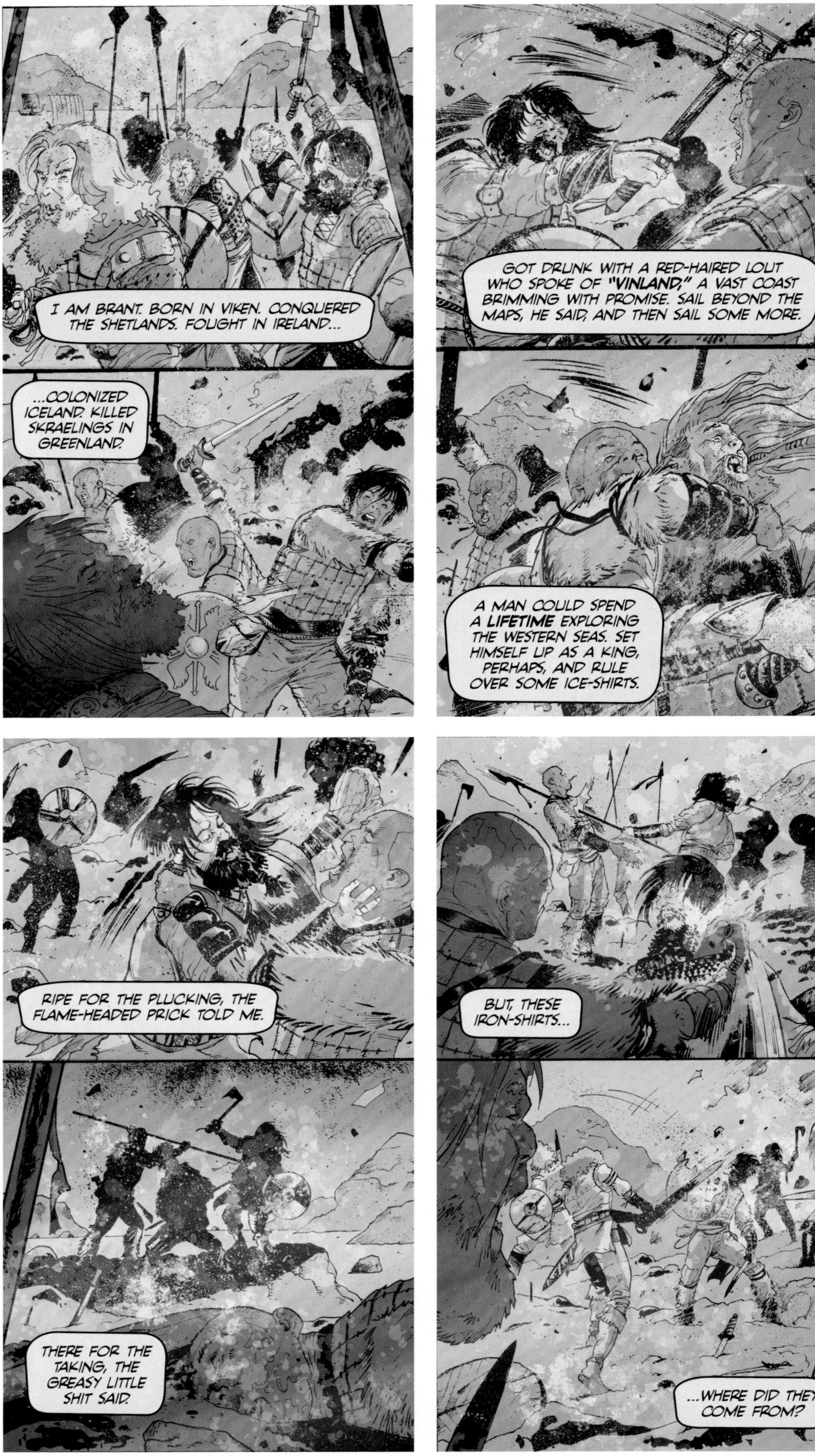
I AM BRANT. BORN IN VIKEN. CONQUERED THE SHETLANDS. FOUGHT IN IRELAND...
GOT DRUNK WITH A RED-HAIRED LOUT WHO SPOKE OF "VINLAND," A VAST COAST BRIMMING WITH PROMISE. SAIL BEYOND THE MAPS, HE SAID, AND THEN SAIL SOME MORE.
...COLONIZED ICELAND. KILLED SKRAELINGS IN GREENLAND.
A MAN COULD SPEND A LIFETIME EXPLORING THE WESTERN SEAS. SET HIMSELF UP AS A KING, PERHAPS, AND RULE OVER SOME ICE-SHIRTS.
RIPE FOR THE PLUCKING, THE FLAME-HEADED PRICK TOLD ME.
BUT, THESE IRON-SHIRTS...
THERE FOR THE TAKING, THE GREASY LITTLE SHIT SAID.
...WHERE DID THEY COME FROM?

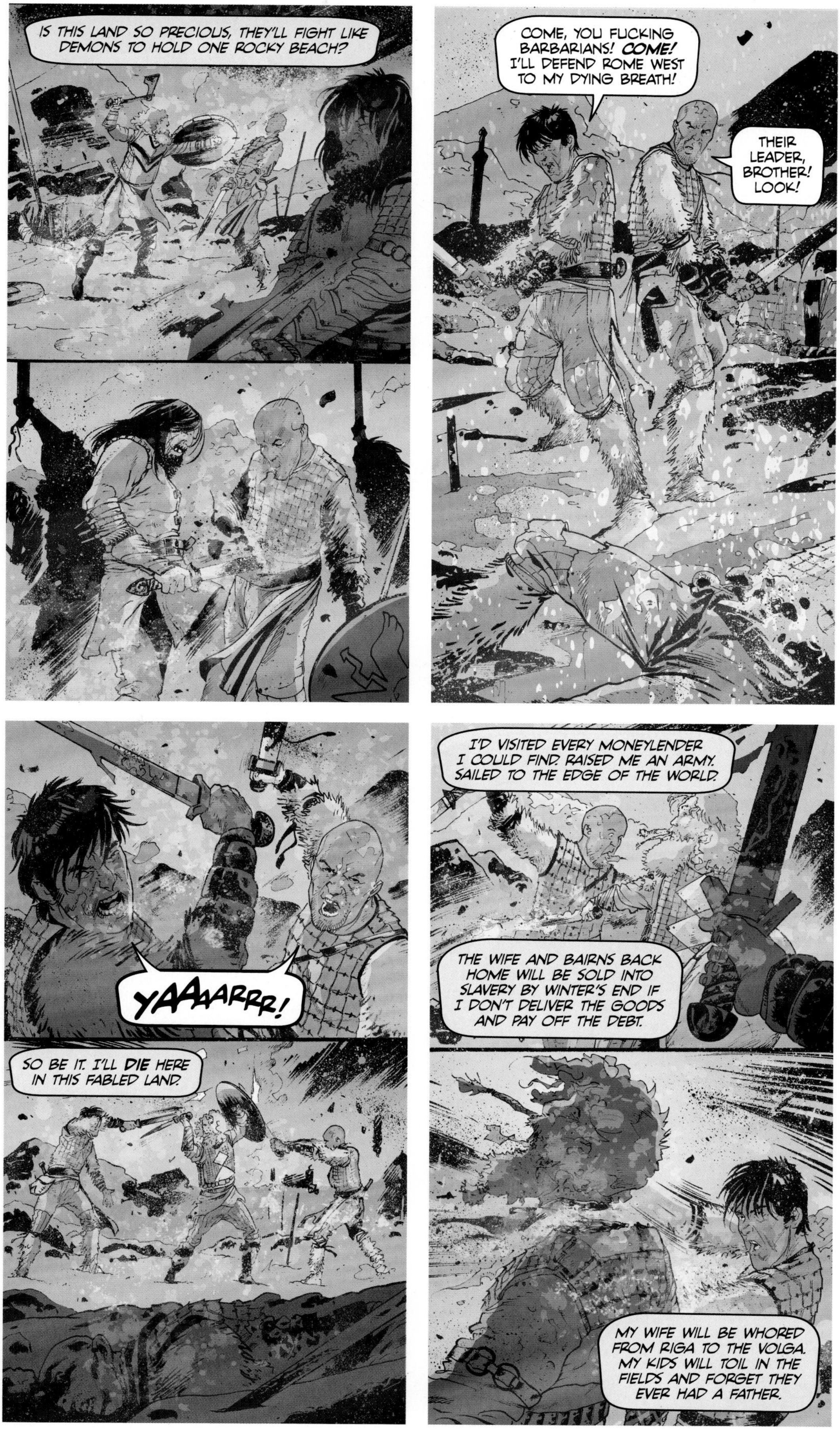
IS THIS LAND SO PRECIOUS, THEY'LL FIGHT LIKE DEMONS TO HOLD ONE ROCKY BEACH?
COME, YOU FUCKING BARBARIANS! COME! I'LL DEFEND ROME WEST TO MY DYING BREATH!
THEIR LEADER, BROTHER! LOOK!
YAAAARRR!
I'D VISITED EVERY MONEYLENDER I COULD FIND. RAISED ME AN ARMY. SAILED TO THE EDGE OF THE WORLD.
THE WIFE AND BAIRNS BACK HOME WILL BE SOLD INTO SLAVERY BY WINTER'S END IF I DON'T DELIVER THE GOODS AND PAY OFF THE DEBT.
SO BE IT. I'LL DIE HERE IN THIS FABLED LAND.
MY WIFE WILL BE WHORED FROM RIGA TO THE VOLGA. MY KIDS WILL TOIL IN THE FIELDS AND FORGET THEY EVER HAD A FATHER.

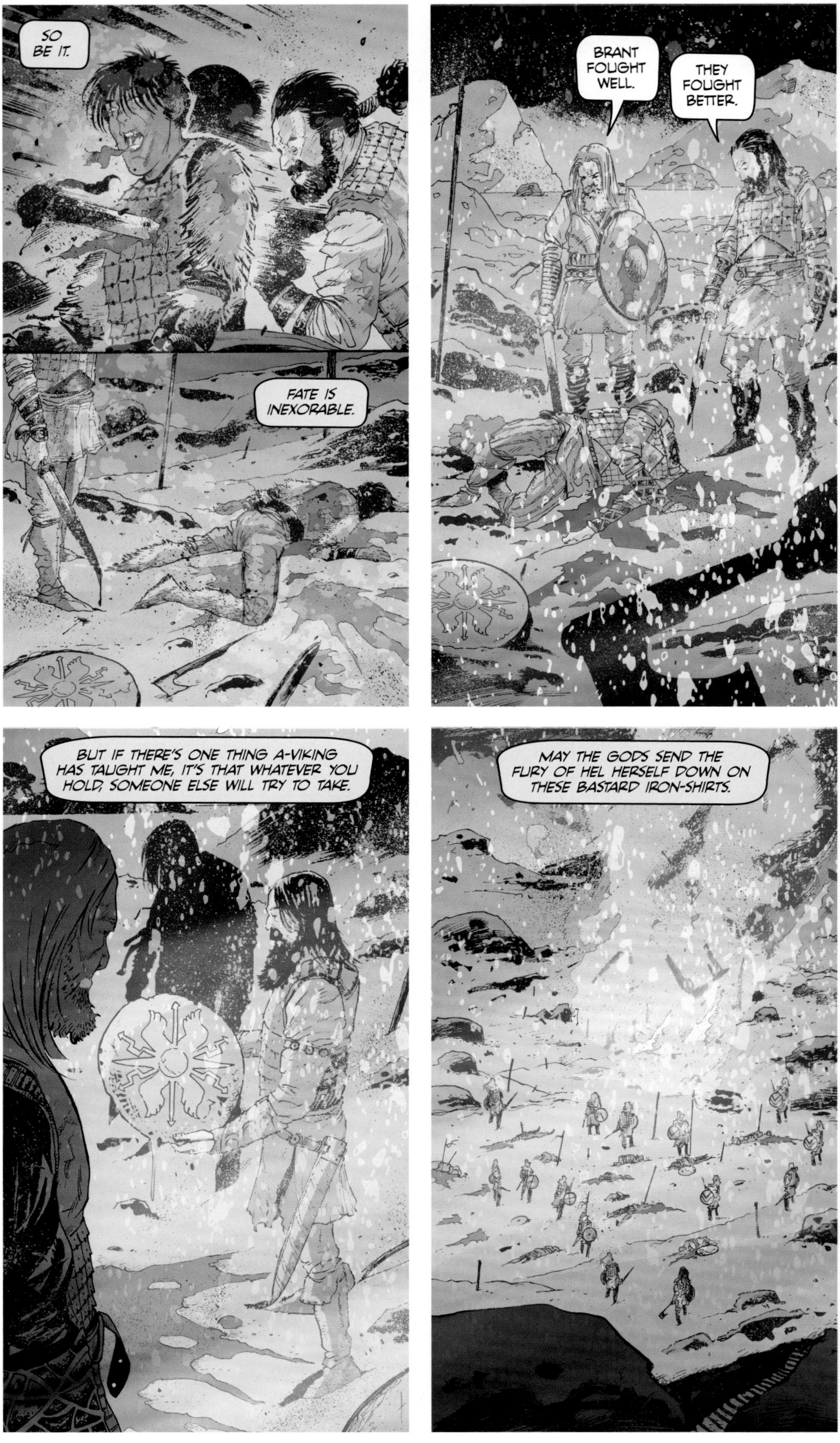
SO BE IT.
FATE IS INEXORABLE.
BRANT FOUGHT WELL.
THEY FOUGHT BETTER.
BUT IF THERE'S ONE THING A-VIKING HAS TAUGHT ME, IT'S THAT WHATEVER YOU HOLD, SOMEONE ELSE WILL TRY TO TAKE.
MAY THE GODS SEND THE FURY OF HEL HERSELF DOWN ON THESE BASTARD IRON-SHIRTS.

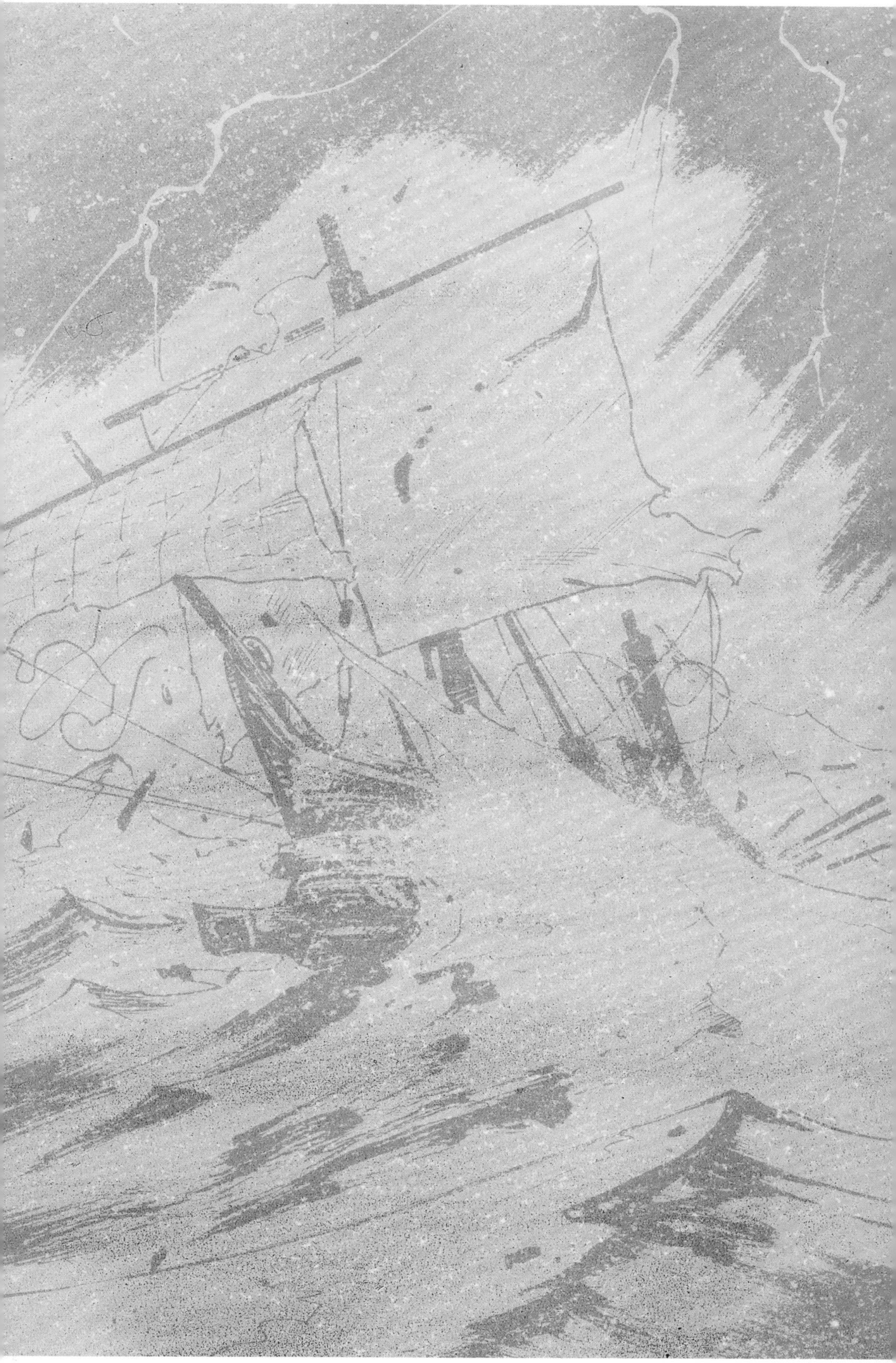

CONCORDIA

IN 1492, Christopher Columbus arrives in the "New World," and realizes he's been beaten by over a thousand years. His shock is compounded when he realizes the natives are speaking Latin.

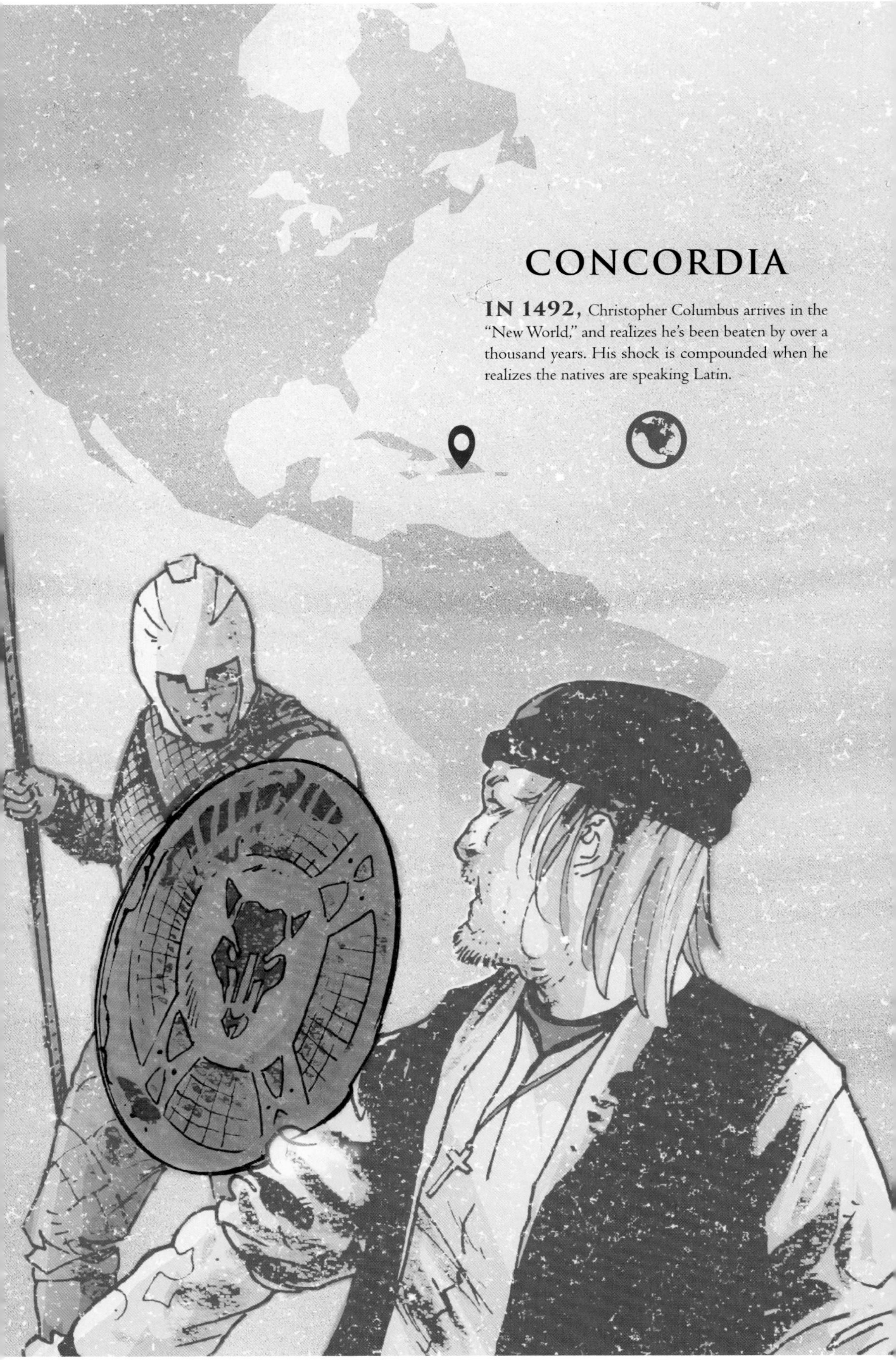

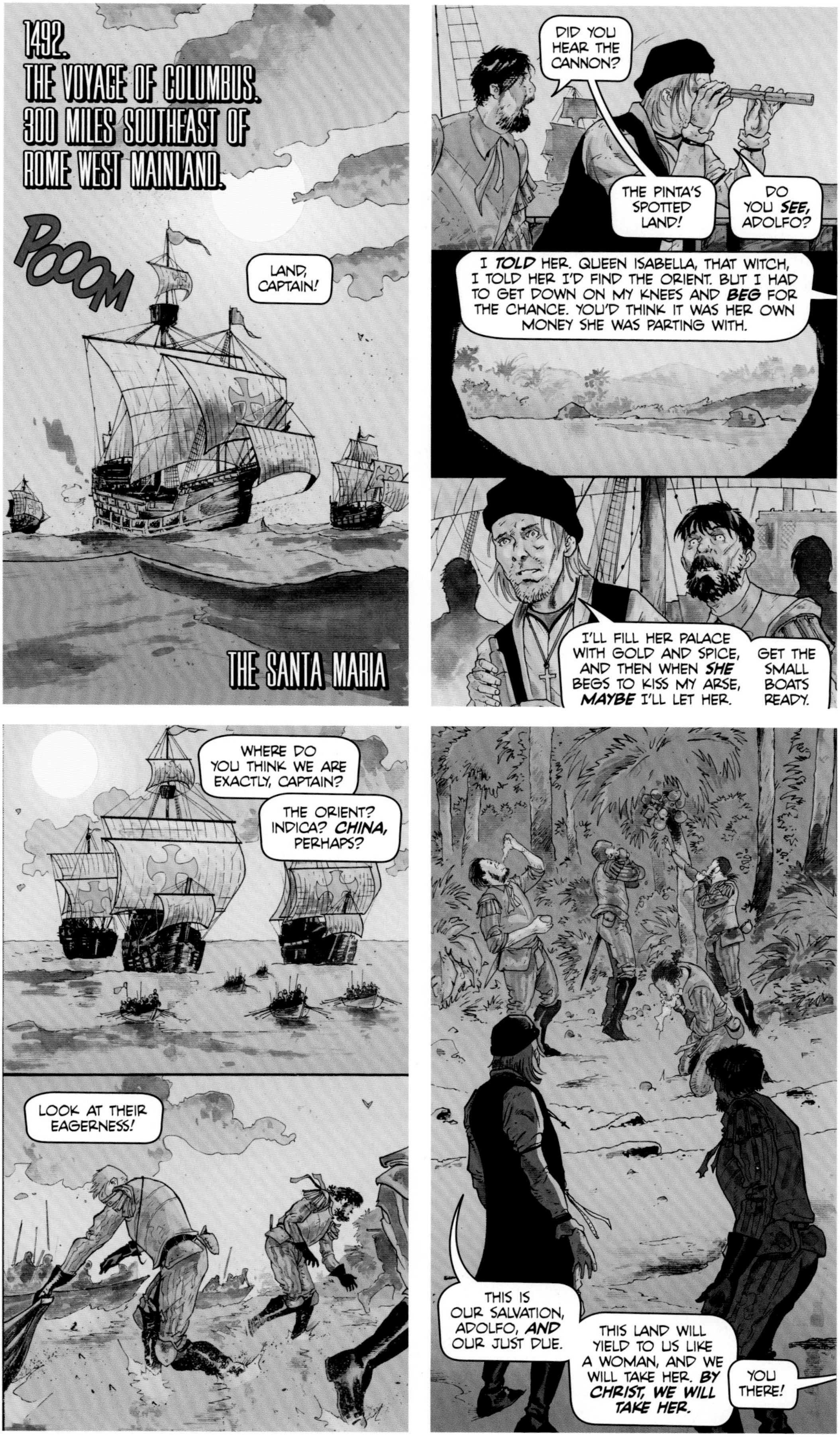
1492.
THE VOYAGE OF COLUMBUS.
300 MILES SOUTHEAST OF ROME WEST MAINLAND.
POOOM
LAND, CAPTAIN!
THE SANTA MARIA
DID YOU HEAR THE CANNON?
THE PINTA'S SPOTTED LAND!
DO YOU SEE, ADOLFO?
I TOLD HER. QUEEN ISABELLA, THAT WITCH, I TOLD HER I'D FIND THE ORIENT. BUT I HAD TO GET DOWN ON MY KNEES AND BEG FOR THE CHANCE. YOU'D THINK IT WAS HER OWN MONEY SHE WAS PARTING WITH.
I'LL FILL HER PALACE WITH GOLD AND SPICE, AND THEN WHEN SHE BEGS TO KISS MY ARSE, MAYBE I'LL LET HER.
GET THE SMALL BOATS READY.
WHERE DO YOU THINK WE ARE EXACTLY, CAPTAIN?
THE ORIENT? INDICA? CHINA, PERHAPS?
LOOK AT THEIR EAGERNESS!
THIS IS OUR SALVATION, ADOLFO, AND OUR JUST DUE.
THIS LAND WILL YIELD TO US LIKE A WOMAN, AND WE WILL TAKE HER. BY CHRIST, WE WILL TAKE HER.
YOU THERE!

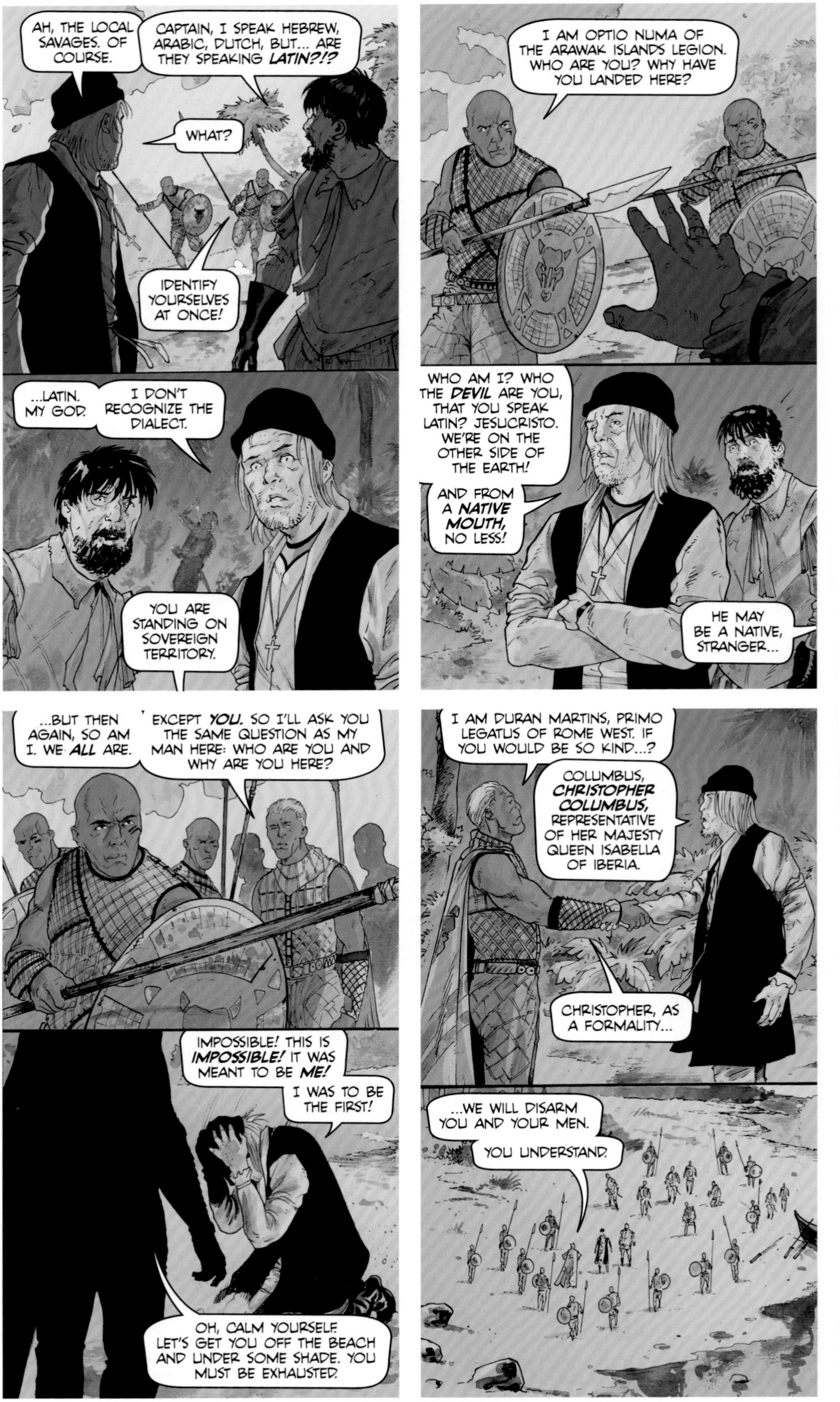
AH, THE LOCAL SAVAGES. OF COURSE.
CAPTAIN, I SPEAK HEBREW, ARABIC, DUTCH, BUT... ARE THEY SPEAKING LATIN?!?
WHAT?
IDENTIFY YOURSELVES AT ONCE!
I AM OPTIO NUMA OF THE ARAWAK ISLANDS LEGION. WHO ARE YOU? WHY HAVE YOU LANDED HERE?
...LATIN. MY GOD.
I DON'T RECOGNIZE THE DIALECT.
YOU ARE STANDING ON SOVEREIGN TERRITORY.
WHO AM I? WHO THE DEVIL ARE YOU, THAT YOU SPEAK LATIN? JESUCRISTO. WE'RE ON THE OTHER SIDE OF THE EARTH!
AND FROM A NATIVE MOUTH, NO LESS!
HE MAY BE A NATIVE, STRANGER...
...BUT THEN AGAIN, SO AM I. WE ALL ARE.
EXCEPT YOU. SO I'LL ASK YOU THE SAME QUESTION AS MY MAN HERE: WHO ARE YOU AND WHY ARE YOU HERE?
IMPOSSIBLE! THIS IS IMPOSSIBLE! IT WAS MEANT TO BE ME!
I WAS TO BE THE FIRST!
OH, CALM YOURSELF. LET'S GET YOU OFF THE BEACH AND UNDER SOME SHADE. YOU MUST BE EXHAUSTED.
I AM DURAN MARTINS, PRIMO LEGATUS OF ROME WEST. IF YOU WOULD BE SO KIND...?
COLUMBUS, CHRISTOPHER COLUMBUS, REPRESENTATIVE OF HER MAJESTY QUEEN ISABELLA OF IBERIA.
CHRISTOPHER, AS A FORMALITY...
...WE WILL DISARM YOU AND YOUR MEN.
YOU UNDERSTAND.

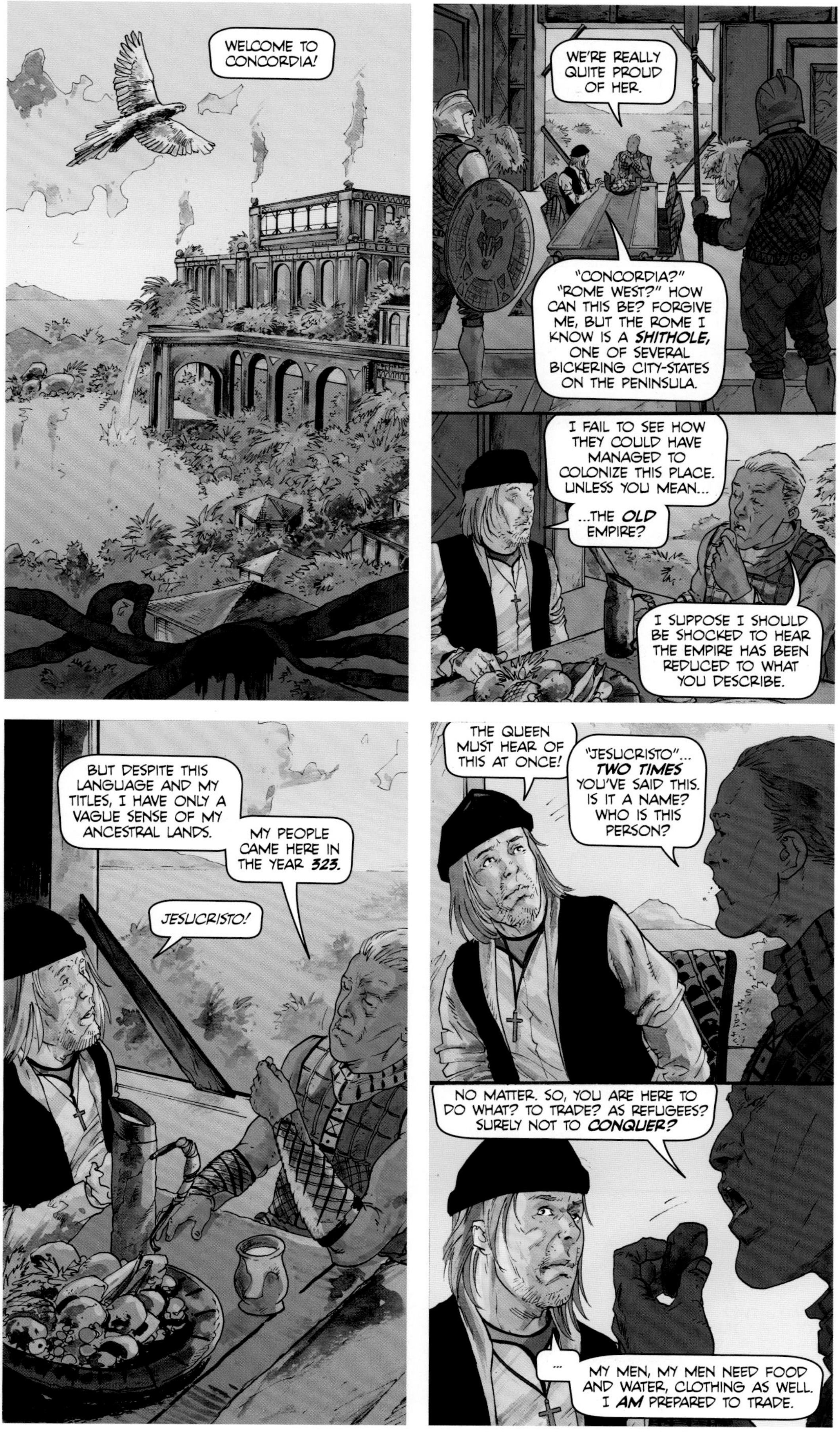
WELCOME TO CONCORDIA!
WE'RE REALLY QUITE PROUD OF HER.
"CONCORDIA?" "ROME WEST?" HOW CAN THIS BE? FORGIVE ME, BUT THE ROME I KNOW IS A ***SHITHOLE,*** ONE OF SEVERAL BICKERING CITY-STATES ON THE PENINSULA.
I FAIL TO SEE HOW THEY COULD HAVE MANAGED TO COLONIZE THIS PLACE. UNLESS YOU MEAN...
...THE ***OLD*** EMPIRE?
I SUPPOSE I SHOULD BE SHOCKED TO HEAR THE EMPIRE HAS BEEN REDUCED TO WHAT YOU DESCRIBE.
BUT DESPITE THIS LANGUAGE AND MY TITLES, I HAVE ONLY A VAGUE SENSE OF MY ANCESTRAL LANDS.
MY PEOPLE CAME HERE IN THE YEAR ***323.***
JESUCRISTO!
THE QUEEN MUST HEAR OF THIS AT ONCE!
"JESUCRISTO"... ***TWO TIMES*** YOU'VE SAID THIS. IS IT A NAME? WHO IS THIS PERSON?
NO MATTER. SO, YOU ARE HERE TO DO WHAT? TO TRADE? AS REFUGEES? SURELY NOT TO ***CONQUER?***
...
MY MEN, MY MEN NEED FOOD AND WATER, CLOTHING AS WELL. I ***AM*** PREPARED TO TRADE.

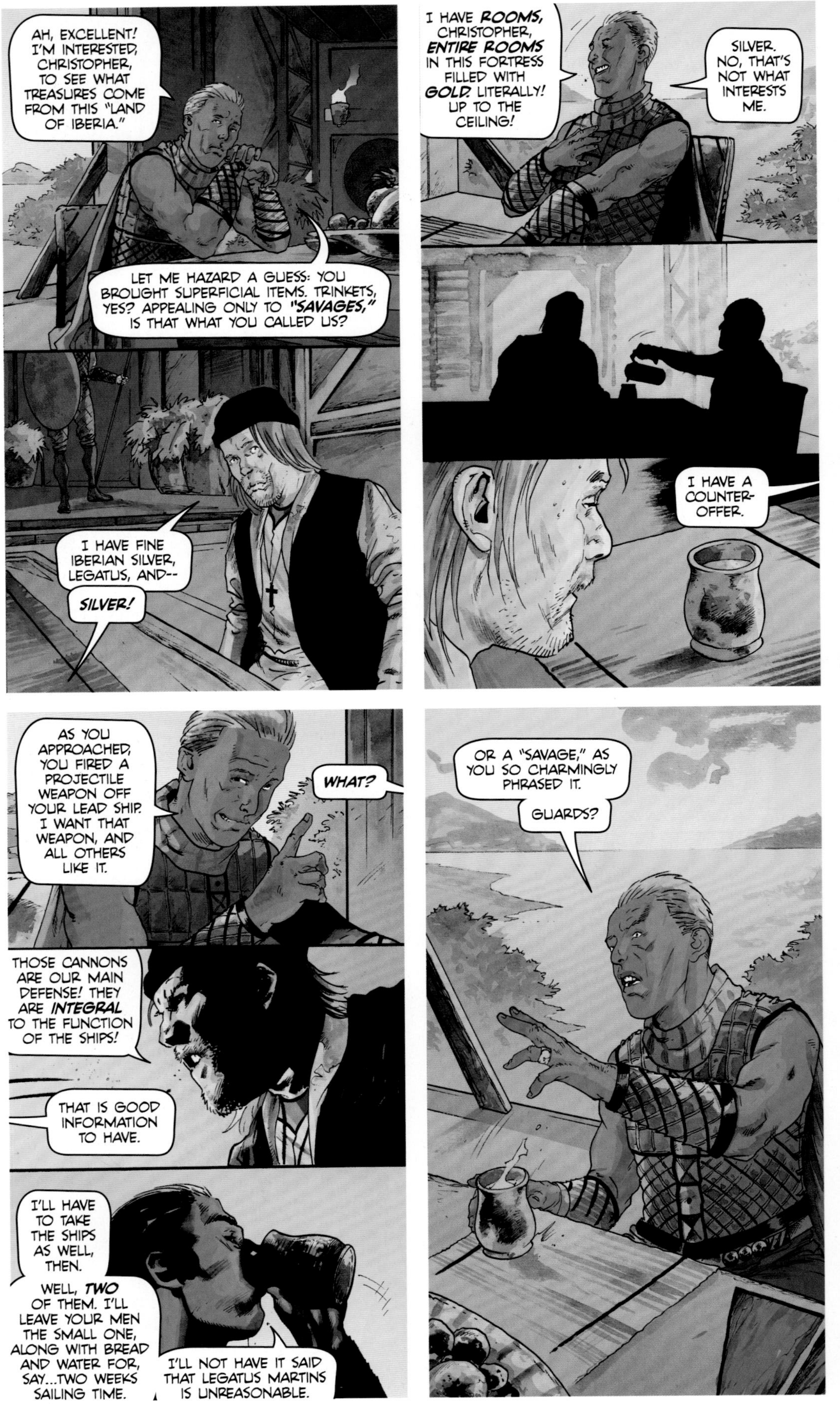

AH, EXCELLENT! I'M INTERESTED, CHRISTOPHER, TO SEE WHAT TREASURES COME FROM THIS "LAND OF IBERIA."
LET ME HAZARD A GUESS: YOU BROUGHT SUPERFICIAL ITEMS. TRINKETS, YES? APPEALING ONLY TO "SAVAGES," IS THAT WHAT YOU CALLED US?
I HAVE FINE IBERIAN SILVER, LEGATUS, AND--
SILVER!
I HAVE ROOMS, CHRISTOPHER, ENTIRE ROOMS IN THIS FORTRESS FILLED WITH GOLD. LITERALLY! UP TO THE CEILING!
SILVER. NO, THAT'S NOT WHAT INTERESTS ME.
I HAVE A COUNTER-OFFER.
AS YOU APPROACHED, YOU FIRED A PROJECTILE WEAPON OFF YOUR LEAD SHIP. I WANT THAT WEAPON, AND ALL OTHERS LIKE IT.
WHAT?
THOSE CANNONS ARE OUR MAIN DEFENSE! THEY ARE INTEGRAL TO THE FUNCTION OF THE SHIPS!
THAT IS GOOD INFORMATION TO HAVE.
I'LL HAVE TO TAKE THE SHIPS AS WELL, THEN.
WELL, TWO OF THEM. I'LL LEAVE YOUR MEN THE SMALL ONE, ALONG WITH BREAD AND WATER FOR, SAY...TWO WEEKS SAILING TIME.
I'LL NOT HAVE IT SAID THAT LEGATUS MARTINS IS UNREASONABLE.
OR A "SAVAGE," AS YOU SO CHARMINGLY PHRASED IT.
GUARDS?

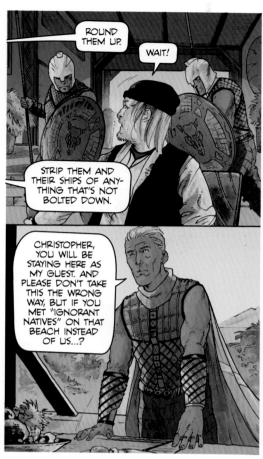

ROUND THEM UP.

WAIT!

STRIP THEM AND THEIR SHIPS OF ANY-THING THAT'S NOT BOLTED DOWN.

CHRISTOPHER, YOU WILL BE STAYING HERE AS MY GUEST. AND PLEASE DON'T TAKE THIS THE WRONG WAY, BUT IF YOU MET "IGNORANT NATIVES" ON THAT BEACH INSTEAD OF US...?

HOW WOULD *THEY* HAVE FARED?

LEGATUS, PLEASE! NO! MY MEN, YOU'VE GIVEN THEM A DEATH SENTENCE!

THIS IS AN OUTRAGE! I AM A ROYAL EMMISSARY! SENT BY A *QUEEN!*

KINGS AND QUEENS, LIKE THE *AZTECS* HAVE? NOW WHO SOUNDS LIKE A SAVAGE?

IF YOU EVER SEE YOUR PRECIOUS QUEEN AGAIN, STRANGER, WHICH IS HIGHLY FUCKING UNLIKELY...

"...TELL HER ROME WEST IS NOT OPEN FOR EXPLOITATION. NOTHING AWAITS HER HERE EXCEPT *DEATH.*"

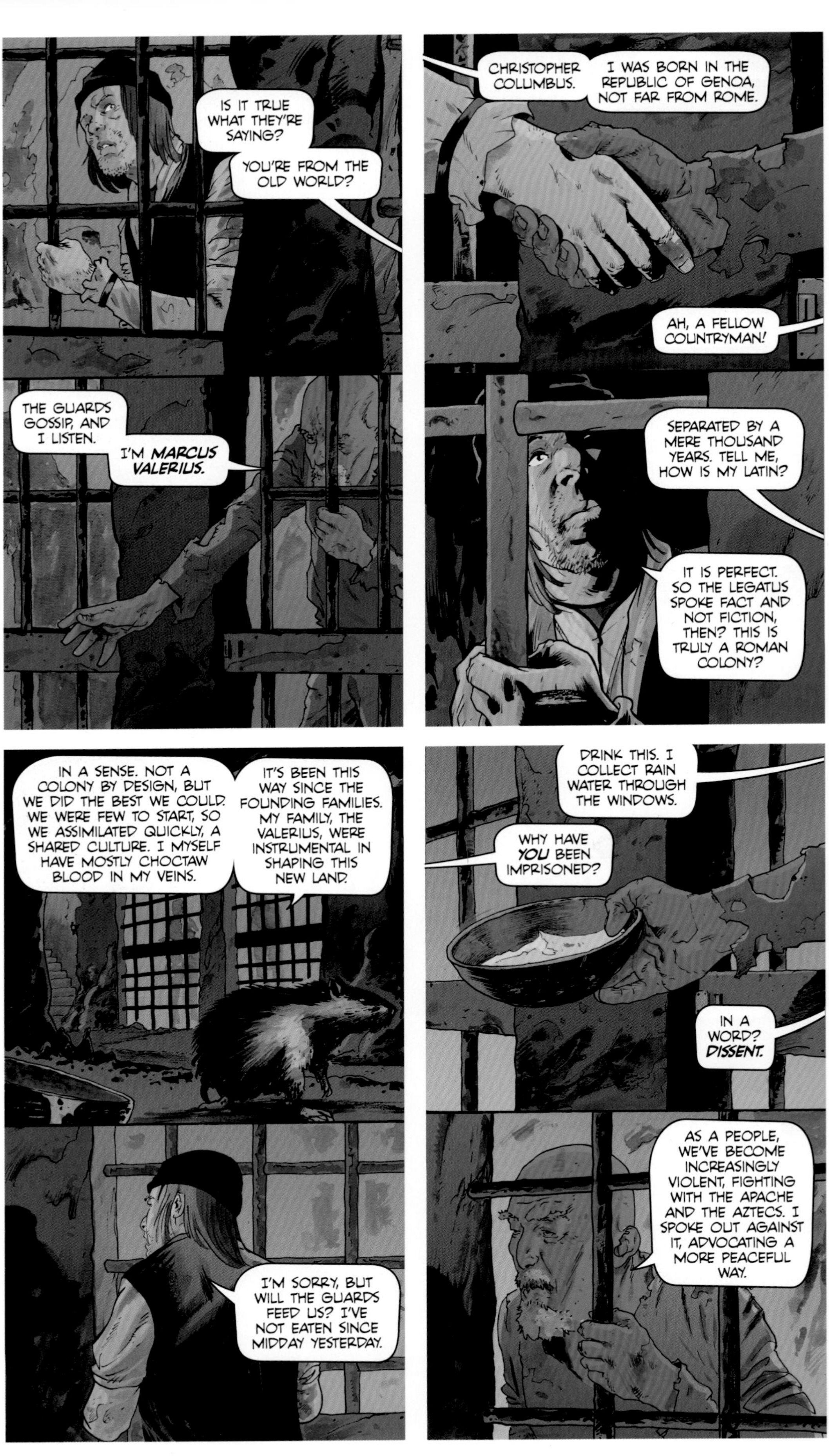
IS IT TRUE WHAT THEY'RE SAYING?
YOU'RE FROM THE OLD WORLD?
CHRISTOPHER COLUMBUS.
I WAS BORN IN THE REPUBLIC OF GENOA, NOT FAR FROM ROME.
AH, A FELLOW COUNTRYMAN!
THE GUARDS GOSSIP, AND I LISTEN.
I'M MARCUS VALERIUS.
SEPARATED BY A MERE THOUSAND YEARS. TELL ME, HOW IS MY LATIN?
IT IS PERFECT. SO THE LEGATUS SPOKE FACT AND NOT FICTION, THEN? THIS IS TRULY A ROMAN COLONY?
IN A SENSE. NOT A COLONY BY DESIGN, BUT WE DID THE BEST WE COULD. WE WERE FEW TO START, SO WE ASSIMILATED QUICKLY, A SHARED CULTURE. I MYSELF HAVE MOSTLY CHOCTAW BLOOD IN MY VEINS.
IT'S BEEN THIS WAY SINCE THE FOUNDING FAMILIES. MY FAMILY, THE VALERIUS, WERE INSTRUMENTAL IN SHAPING THIS NEW LAND.
I'M SORRY, BUT WILL THE GUARDS FEED US? I'VE NOT EATEN SINCE MIDDAY YESTERDAY.
DRINK THIS. I COLLECT RAIN WATER THROUGH THE WINDOWS.
WHY HAVE YOU BEEN IMPRISONED?
IN A WORD? DISSENT.
AS A PEOPLE, WE'VE BECOME INCREASINGLY VIOLENT, FIGHTING WITH THE APACHE AND THE AZTECS. I SPOKE OUT AGAINST IT, ADVOCATING A MORE PEACEFUL WAY.

YOU'RE AN EDUCATED MAN, LIVING UNDER A MONARCH. YOU CAN GUESS WHAT HAPPENS WHEN YOU CHALLENGE THOSE IN POWER.

WAR SPREADS LIKE A DISEASE.

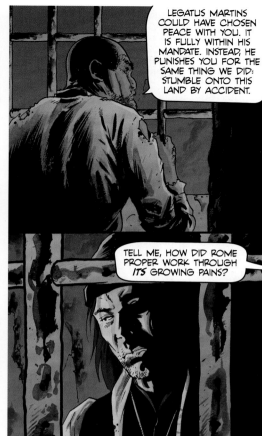

LEGATUS MARTINS COULD HAVE CHOSEN PEACE WITH YOU. IT IS FULLY WITHIN HIS MANDATE. INSTEAD, HE PUNISHES YOU FOR THE SAME THING WE DID: STUMBLE ONTO THIS LAND BY ACCIDENT.

TELL ME, HOW DID ROME PROPER WORK THROUGH *ITS* GROWING PAINS?

THE OLD EMPIRE IS GONE, VALERIUS. WEAKENED BY CORRUPTION AND INFIGHTING. IN THE END, ALL IT TOOK WAS A HANDFUL OF BARBARIANS TO BRING IT DOWN.

ONE OF THE GREAT TRAVESTIES OF HISTORY.

IF THE VALERIUS FAMILY IS AS YOU DESCRIBE, PERHAPS THEY CAN BE AS INSTRUMENTAL IN SHAPING THE FUTURE OF THIS LAND AS THEY DID ITS PAST.

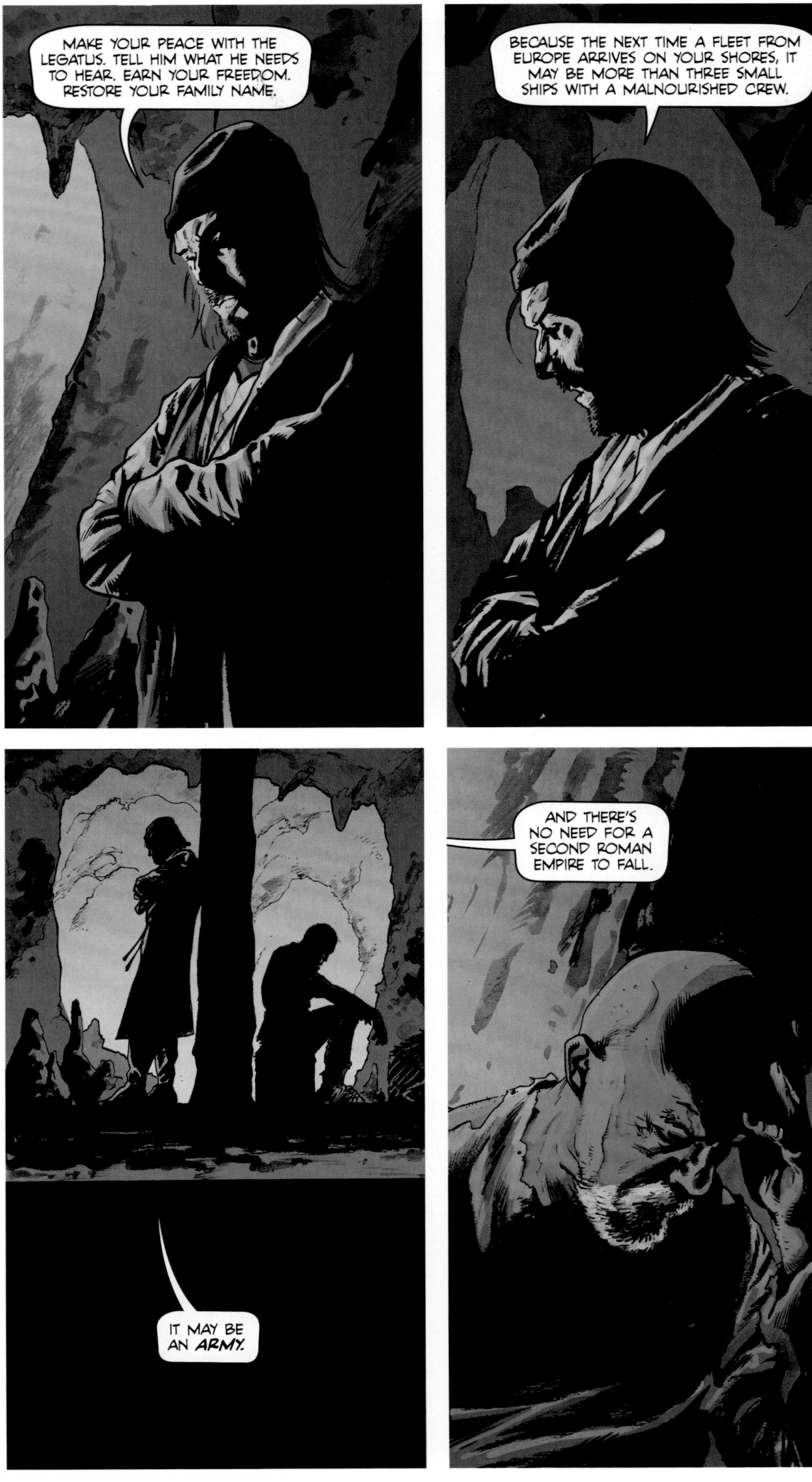
MAKE YOUR PEACE WITH THE LEGATUS. TELL HIM WHAT HE NEEDS TO HEAR. EARN YOUR FREEDOM. RESTORE YOUR FAMILY NAME.
BECAUSE THE NEXT TIME A FLEET FROM EUROPE ARRIVES ON YOUR SHORES, IT MAY BE MORE THAN THREE SMALL SHIPS WITH A MALNOURISHED CREW.
IT MAY BE AN ARMY.
AND THERE'S NO NEED FOR A SECOND ROMAN EMPIRE TO FALL.

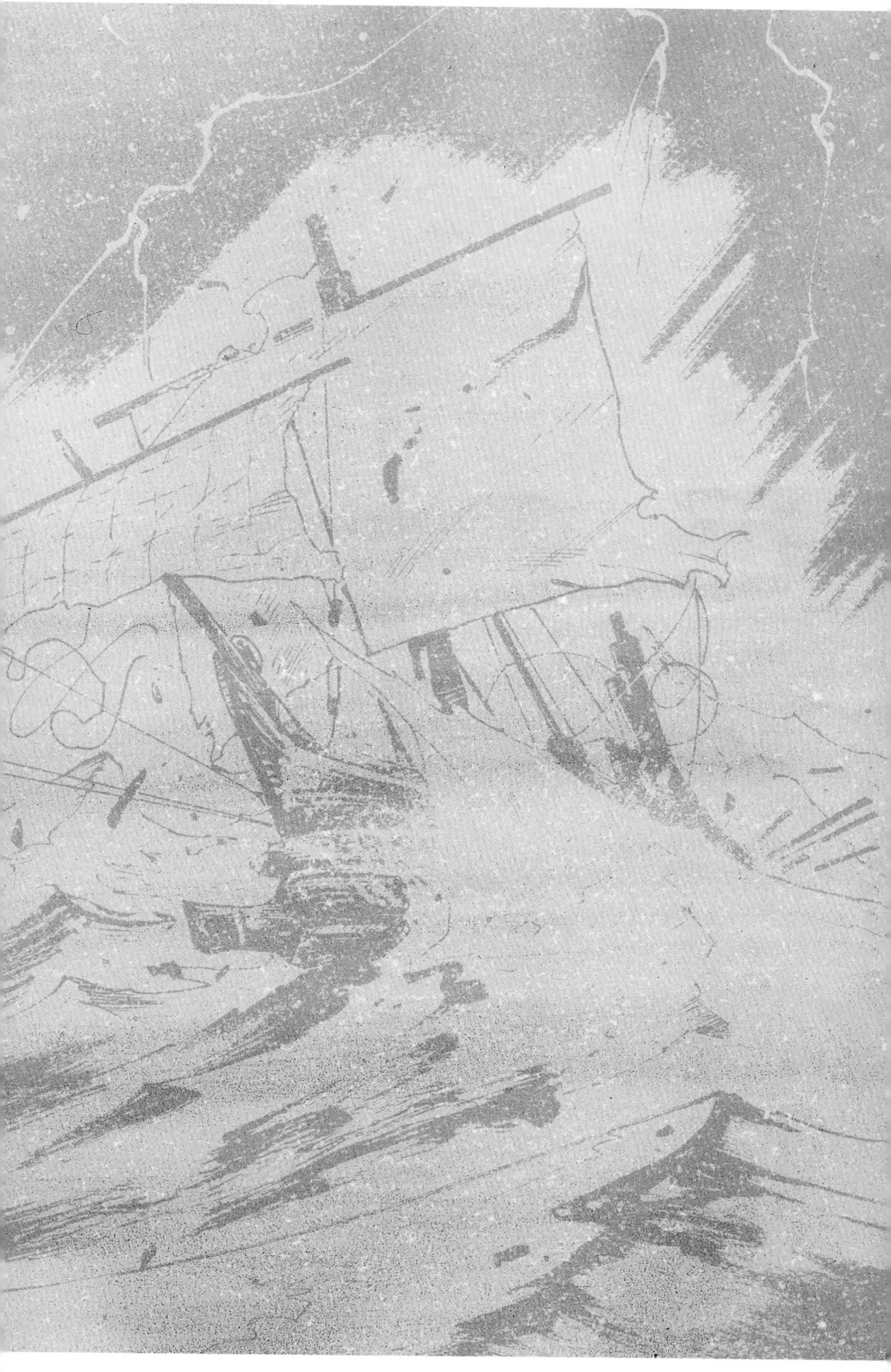

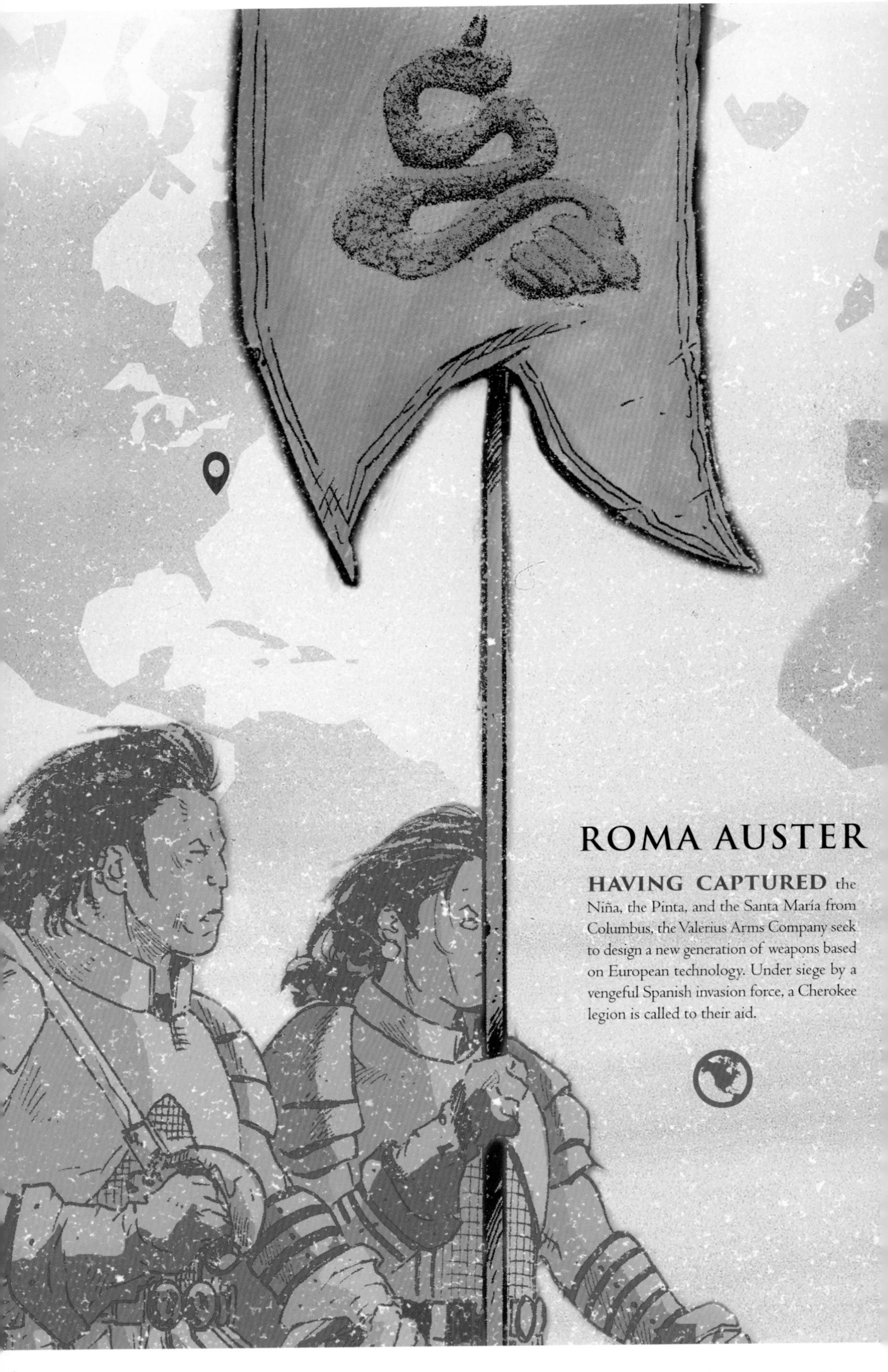

ROMA AUSTER

HAVING CAPTURED the Niña, the Pinta, and the Santa María from Columbus, the Valerius Arms Company seek to design a new generation of weapons based on European technology. Under siege by a vengeful Spanish invasion force, a Cherokee legion is called to their aid.

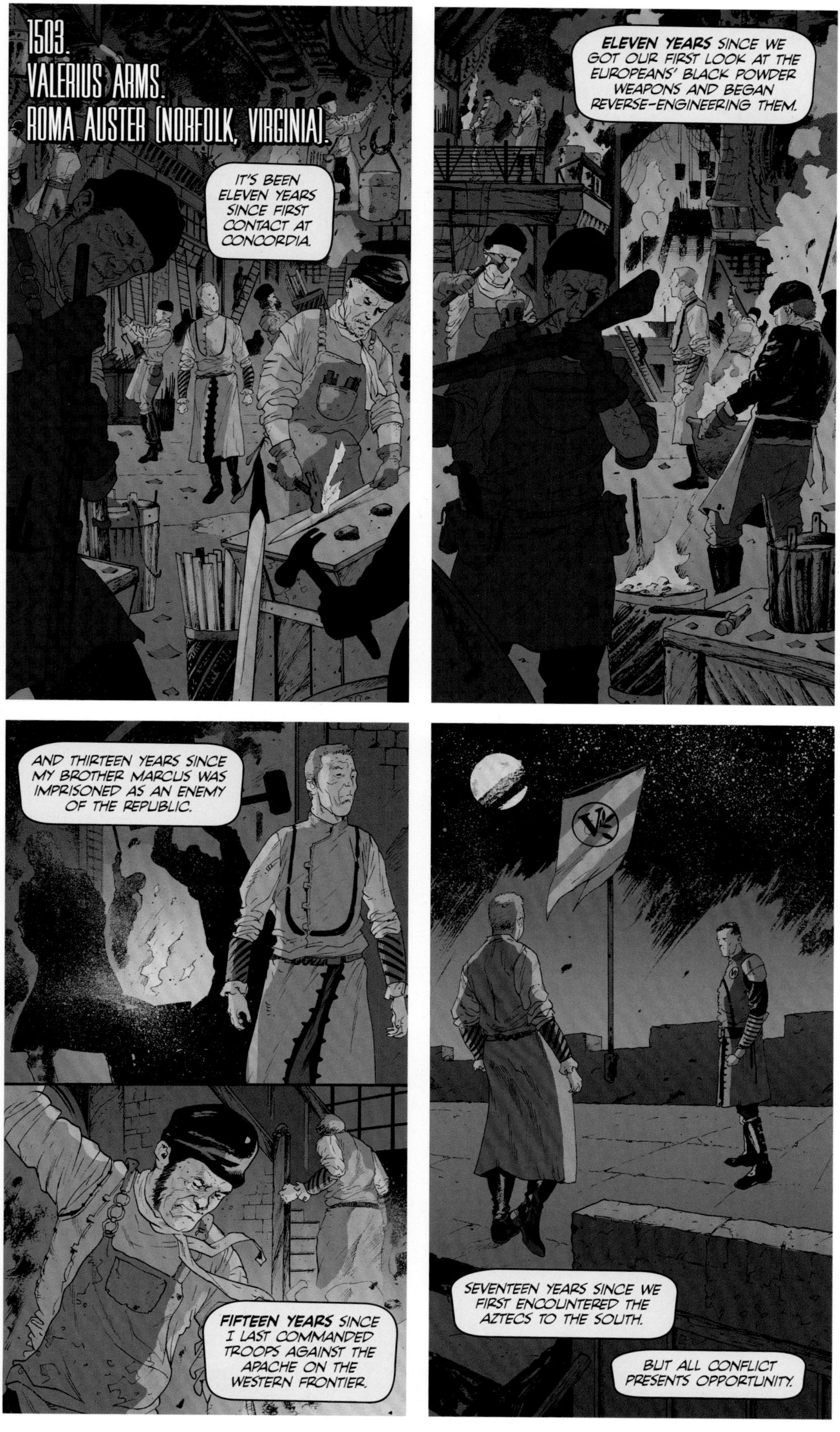
1503.
VALERIUS ARMS.
ROMA AUSTER (NORFOLK, VIRGINIA).
IT'S BEEN ELEVEN YEARS SINCE FIRST CONTACT AT CONCORDIA.
ELEVEN YEARS SINCE WE GOT OUR FIRST LOOK AT THE EUROPEANS' BLACK POWDER WEAPONS AND BEGAN REVERSE-ENGINEERING THEM.
AND THIRTEEN YEARS SINCE MY BROTHER MARCUS WAS IMPRISONED AS AN ENEMY OF THE REPUBLIC.
FIFTEEN YEARS SINCE I LAST COMMANDED TROOPS AGAINST THE APACHE ON THE WESTERN FRONTIER.
SEVENTEEN YEARS SINCE WE FIRST ENCOUNTERED THE AZTECS TO THE SOUTH.
BUT ALL CONFLICT PRESENTS OPPORTUNITY.

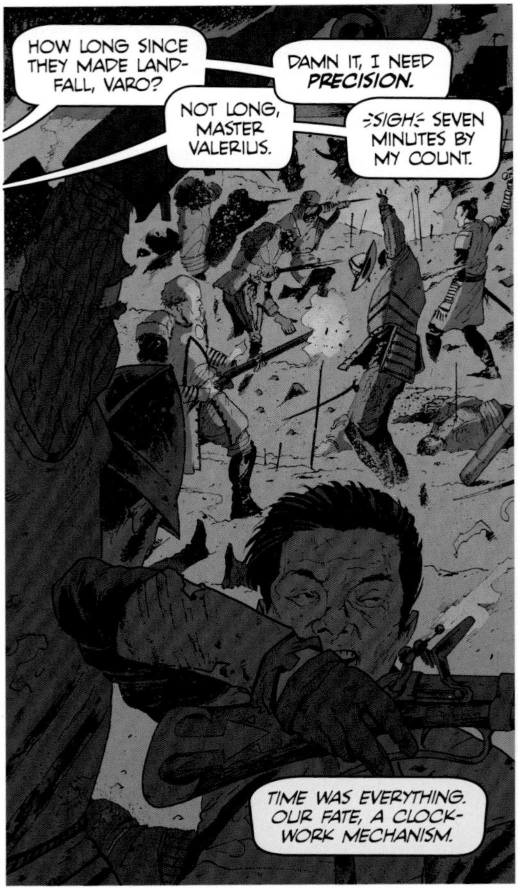
HOW LONG SINCE THEY MADE LAND-FALL, VARO?
NOT LONG, MASTER VALERIUS.
DAMN IT, I NEED PRECISION.
=SIGH= SEVEN MINUTES BY MY COUNT.
TIME WAS EVERYTHING. OUR FATE, A CLOCK-WORK MECHANISM.
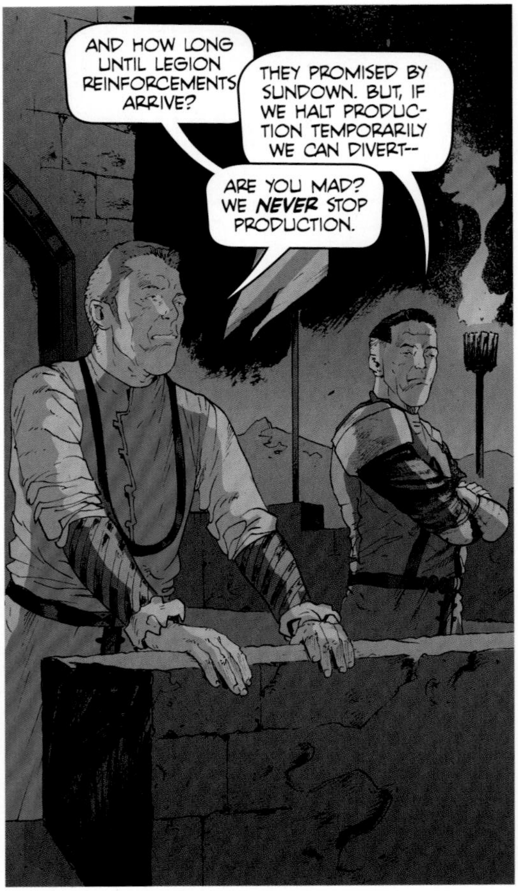
AND HOW LONG UNTIL LEGION REINFORCEMENTS ARRIVE?
THEY PROMISED BY SUNDOWN. BUT, IF WE HALT PRODUCTION TEMPORARILY WE CAN DIVERT--
ARE YOU MAD? WE NEVER STOP PRODUCTION.
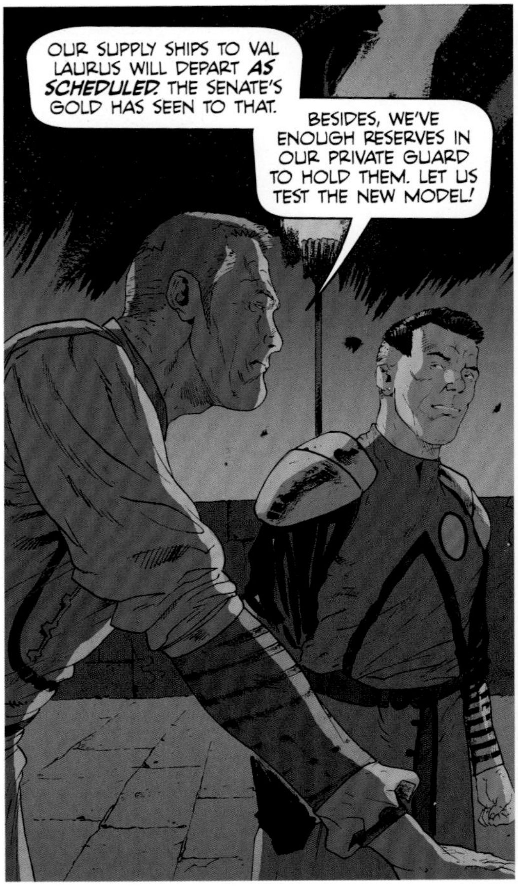
OUR SUPPLY SHIPS TO VAL LAURUS WILL DEPART AS SCHEDULED. THE SENATE'S GOLD HAS SEEN TO THAT.
BESIDES, WE'VE ENOUGH RESERVES IN OUR PRIVATE GUARD TO HOLD THEM. LET US TEST THE NEW MODEL!
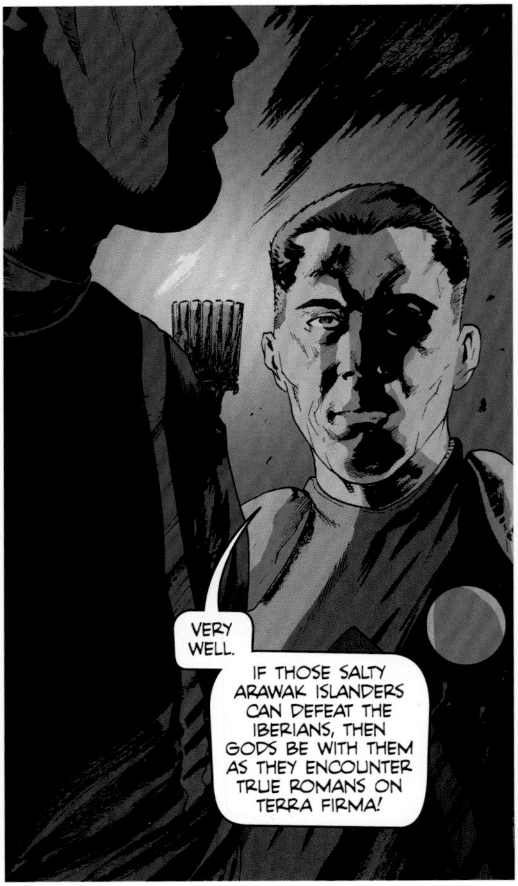
VERY WELL.
IF THOSE SALTY ARAWAK ISLANDERS CAN DEFEAT THE IBERIANS, THEN GODS BE WITH THEM AS THEY ENCOUNTER TRUE ROMANS ON TERRA FIRMA!

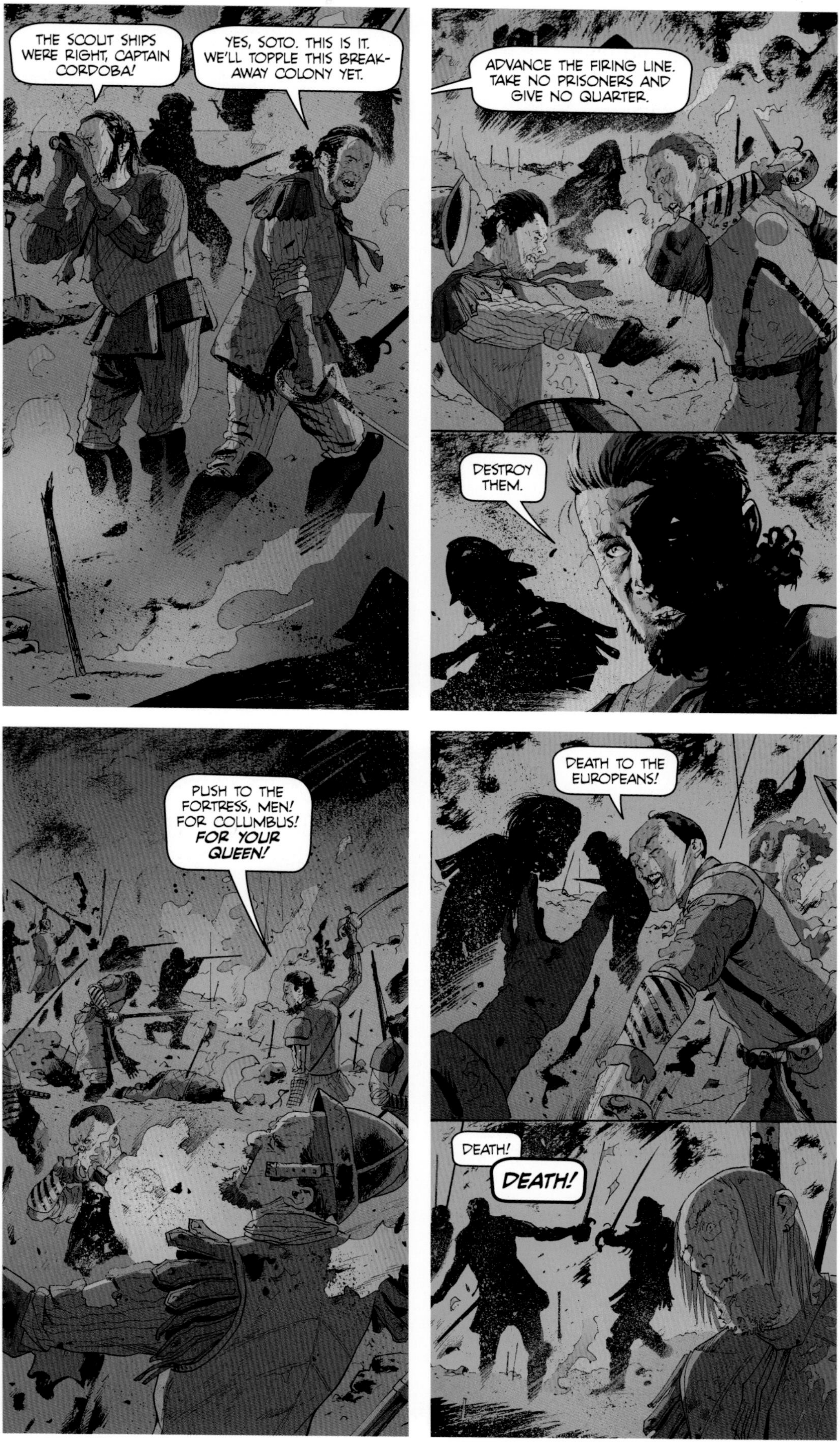
THE SCOUT SHIPS WERE RIGHT, CAPTAIN CORDOBA!
YES, SOTO. THIS IS IT. WE'LL TOPPLE THIS BREAKAWAY COLONY YET.
ADVANCE THE FIRING LINE. TAKE NO PRISONERS AND GIVE NO QUARTER.
DESTROY THEM.
PUSH TO THE FORTRESS, MEN! FOR COLUMBUS! FOR YOUR QUEEN!
DEATH TO THE EUROPEANS!
DEATH!
DEATH!

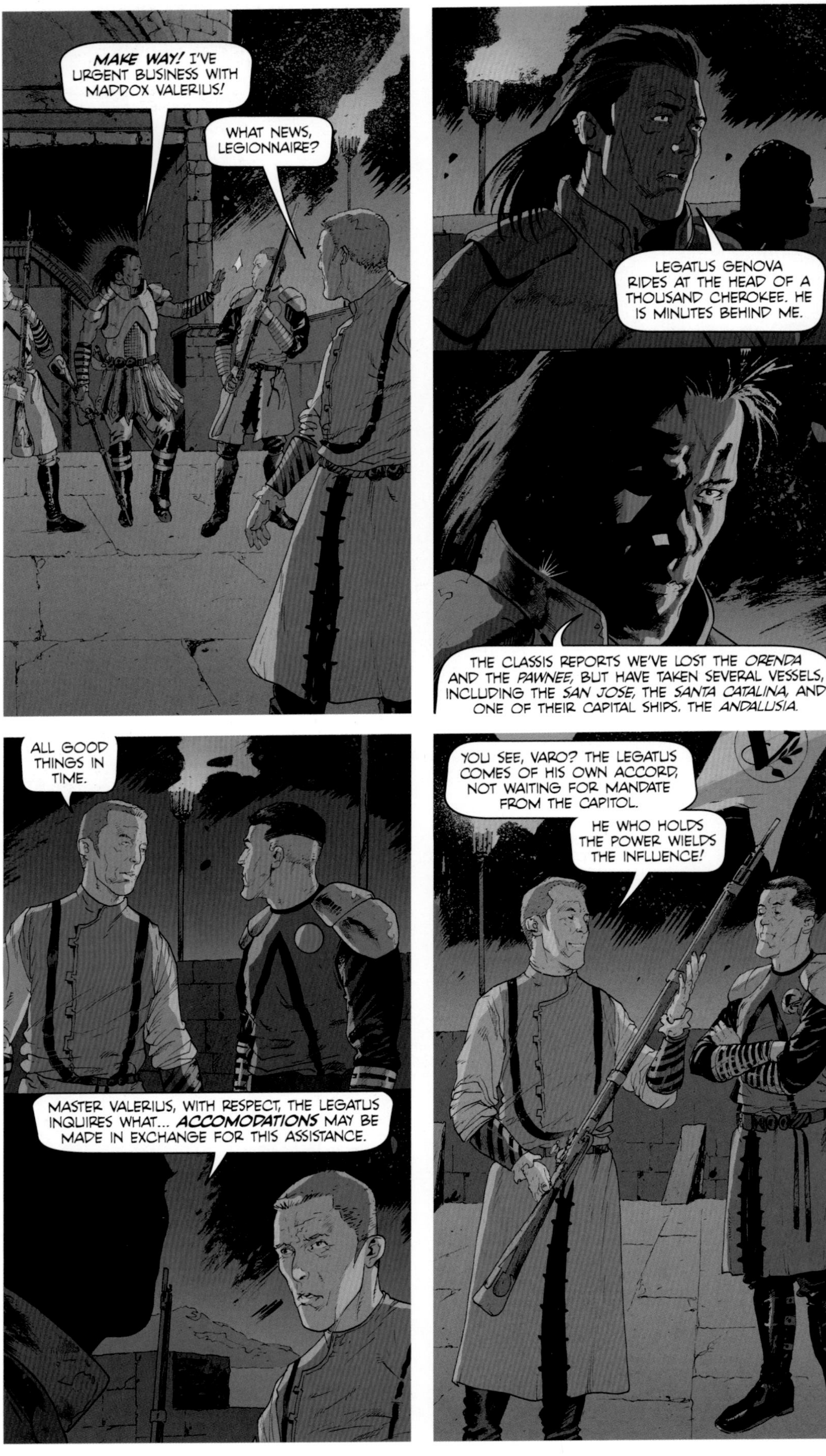
MAKE WAY! I'VE URGENT BUSINESS WITH MADDOX VALERIUS!
WHAT NEWS, LEGIONNAIRE?
LEGATUS GENOVA RIDES AT THE HEAD OF A THOUSAND CHEROKEE. HE IS MINUTES BEHIND ME.
THE CLASSIS REPORTS WE'VE LOST THE ORENDA AND THE PAWNEE, BUT HAVE TAKEN SEVERAL VESSELS, INCLUDING THE SAN JOSE, THE SANTA CATALINA, AND ONE OF THEIR CAPITAL SHIPS, THE ANDALUSIA.
ALL GOOD THINGS IN TIME.
MASTER VALERIUS, WITH RESPECT, THE LEGATUS INQUIRES WHAT... ACCOMODATIONS MAY BE MADE IN EXCHANGE FOR THIS ASSISTANCE.
YOU SEE, VARO? THE LEGATUS COMES OF HIS OWN ACCORD, NOT WAITING FOR MANDATE FROM THE CAPITOL.
HE WHO HOLDS THE POWER WIELDS THE INFLUENCE!

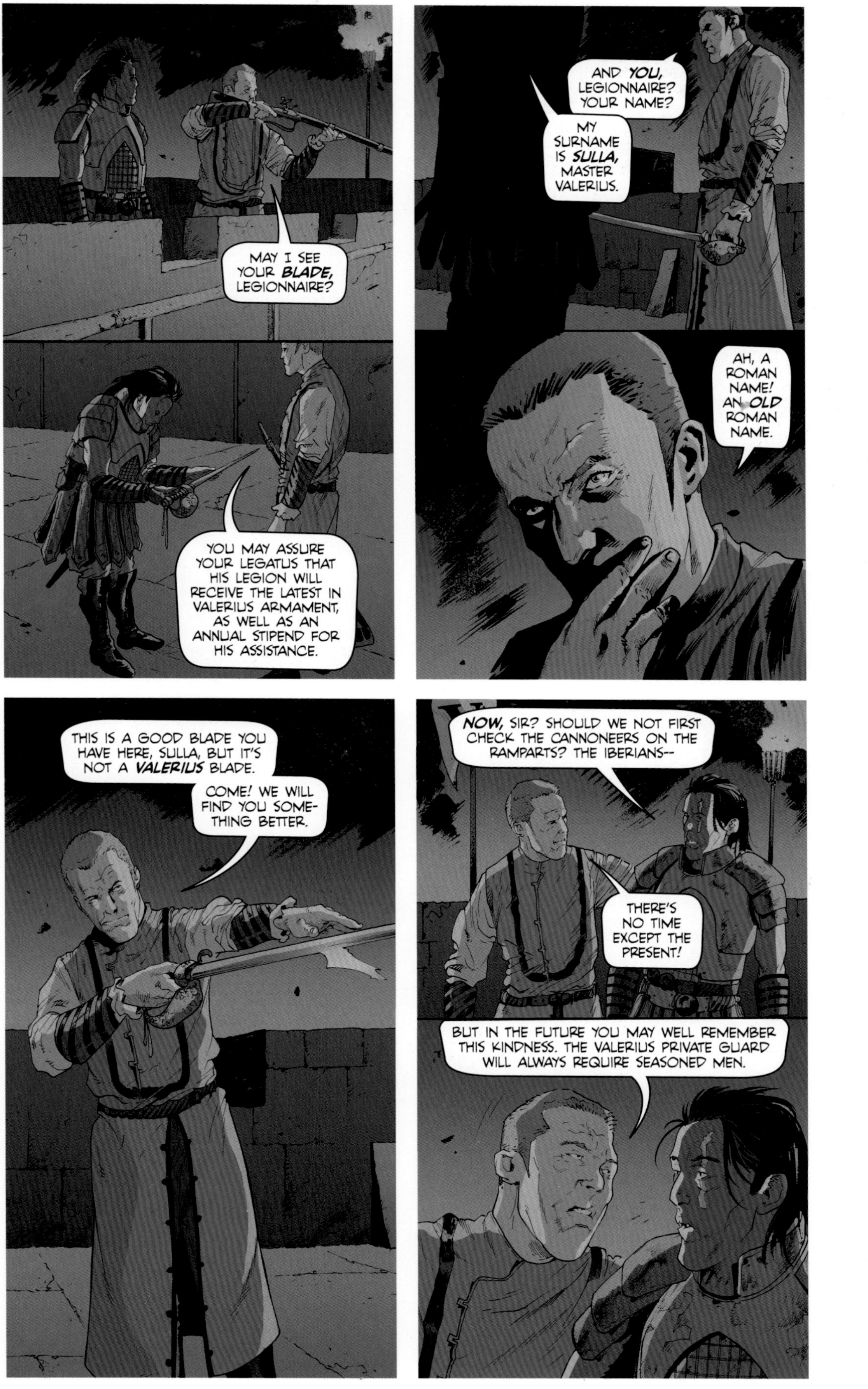
MAY I SEE YOUR BLADE, LEGIONNAIRE?
AND YOU, LEGIONNAIRE? YOUR NAME?
MY SURNAME IS SULLA, MASTER VALERIUS.
YOU MAY ASSURE YOUR LEGATUS THAT HIS LEGION WILL RECEIVE THE LATEST IN VALERIUS ARMAMENT, AS WELL AS AN ANNUAL STIPEND FOR HIS ASSISTANCE.
AH, A ROMAN NAME! AN OLD ROMAN NAME.
THIS IS A GOOD BLADE YOU HAVE HERE, SULLA, BUT IT'S NOT A VALERIUS BLADE.
COME! WE WILL FIND YOU SOME-THING BETTER.
NOW, SIR? SHOULD WE NOT FIRST CHECK THE CANNONEERS ON THE RAMPARTS? THE IBERIANS--
THERE'S NO TIME EXCEPT THE PRESENT!
BUT IN THE FUTURE YOU MAY WELL REMEMBER THIS KINDNESS. THE VALERIUS PRIVATE GUARD WILL ALWAYS REQUIRE SEASONED MEN.

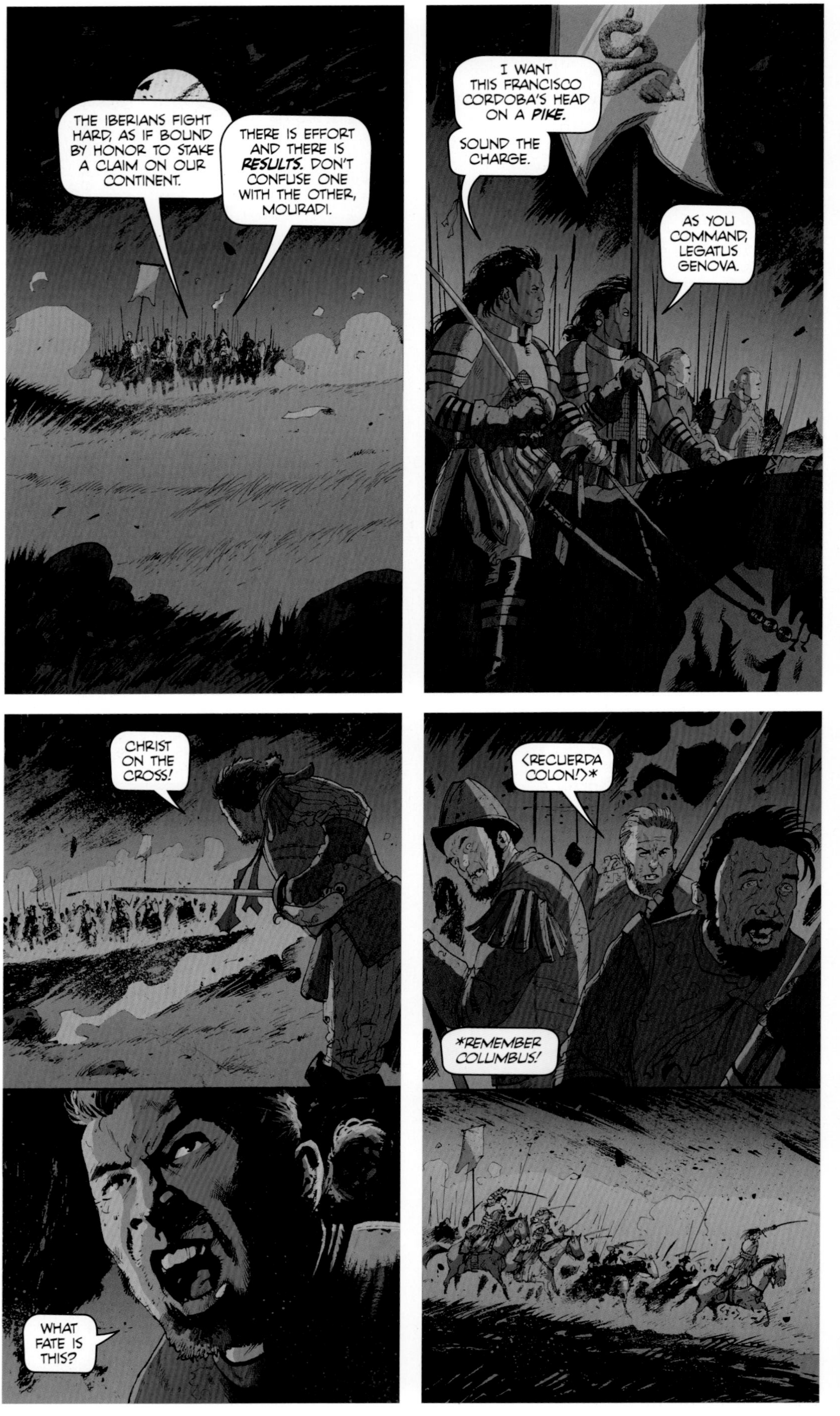
THE IBERIANS FIGHT HARD, AS IF BOUND BY HONOR TO STAKE A CLAIM ON OUR CONTINENT.
THERE IS EFFORT AND THERE IS *RESULTS.* DON'T CONFUSE ONE WITH THE OTHER, MOURADI.
I WANT THIS FRANCISCO CORDOBA'S HEAD ON A *PIKE.*
SOUND THE CHARGE.
AS YOU COMMAND, LEGATUS GENOVA.
CHRIST ON THE CROSS!
WHAT FATE IS THIS?
<RECUERDA COLON!>*
*REMEMBER COLUMBUS!

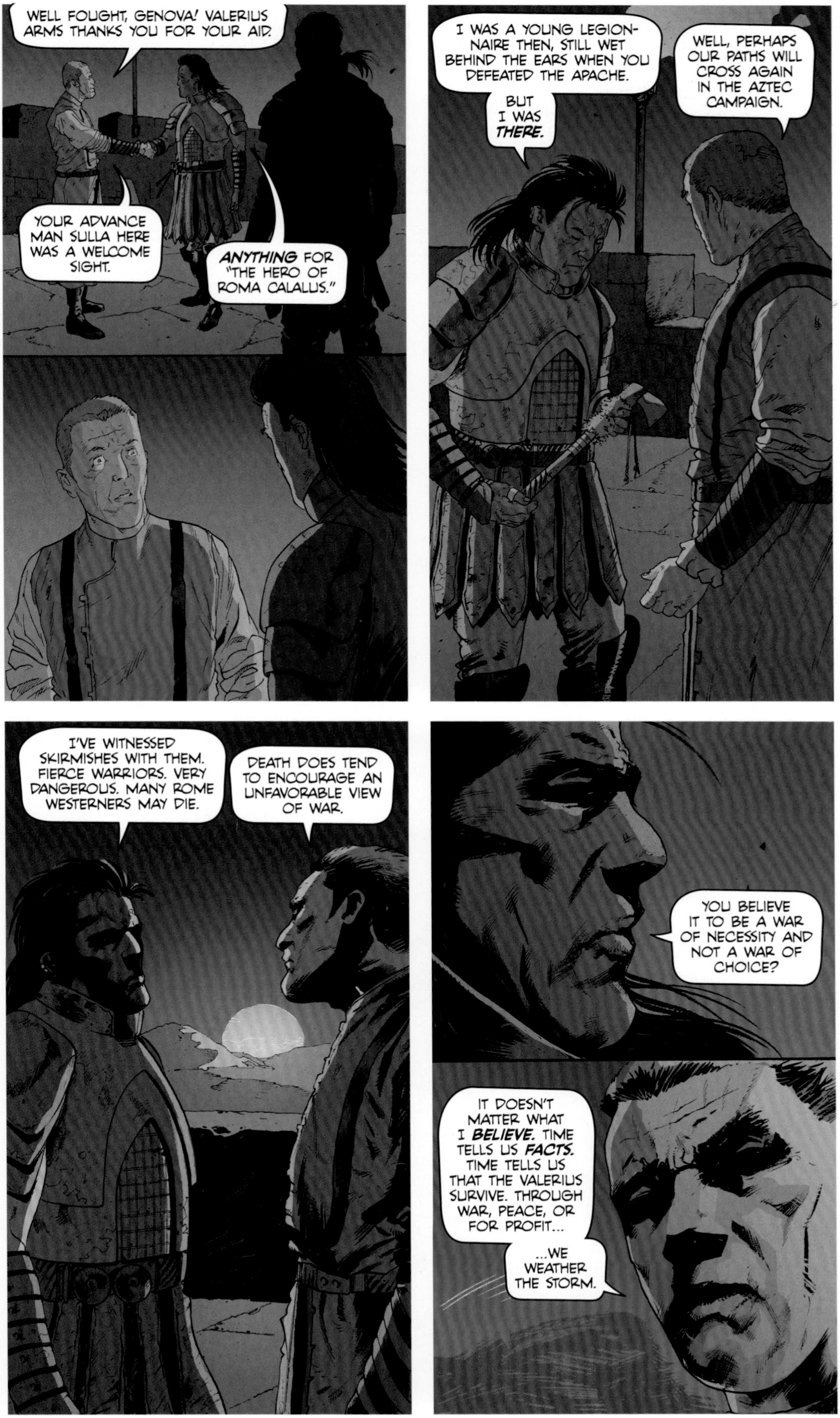
WELL FOUGHT, GENOVA! VALERIUS ARMS THANKS YOU FOR YOUR AID.
YOUR ADVANCE MAN SULLA HERE WAS A WELCOME SIGHT.
ANYTHING FOR "THE HERO OF ROMA CALALUS."
I WAS A YOUNG LEGIONNAIRE THEN, STILL WET BEHIND THE EARS WHEN YOU DEFEATED THE APACHE.
BUT I WAS THERE.
WELL, PERHAPS OUR PATHS WILL CROSS AGAIN IN THE AZTEC CAMPAIGN.
I'VE WITNESSED SKIRMISHES WITH THEM. FIERCE WARRIORS. VERY DANGEROUS. MANY ROME WESTERNERS MAY DIE.
DEATH DOES TEND TO ENCOURAGE AN UNFAVORABLE VIEW OF WAR.
YOU BELIEVE IT TO BE A WAR OF NECESSITY AND NOT A WAR OF CHOICE?
IT DOESN'T MATTER WHAT I BELIEVE. TIME TELLS US FACTS. TIME TELLS US THAT THE VALERIUS SURVIVE. THROUGH WAR, PEACE, OR FOR PROFIT...
...WE WEATHER THE STORM.

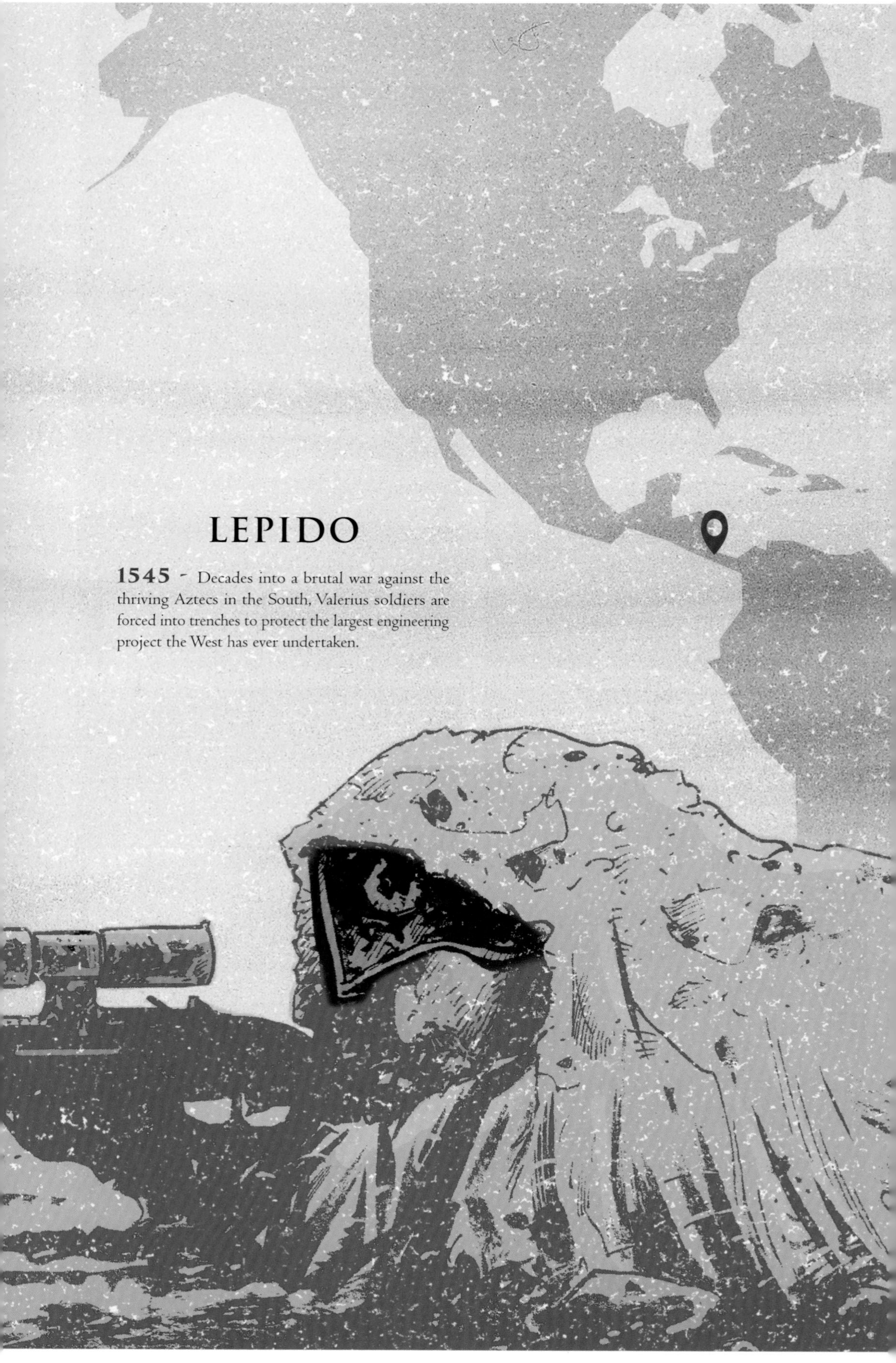

LEPIDO

1545 - Decades into a brutal war against the thriving Aztecs in the South, Valerius soldiers are forced into trenches to protect the largest engineering project the West has ever undertaken.

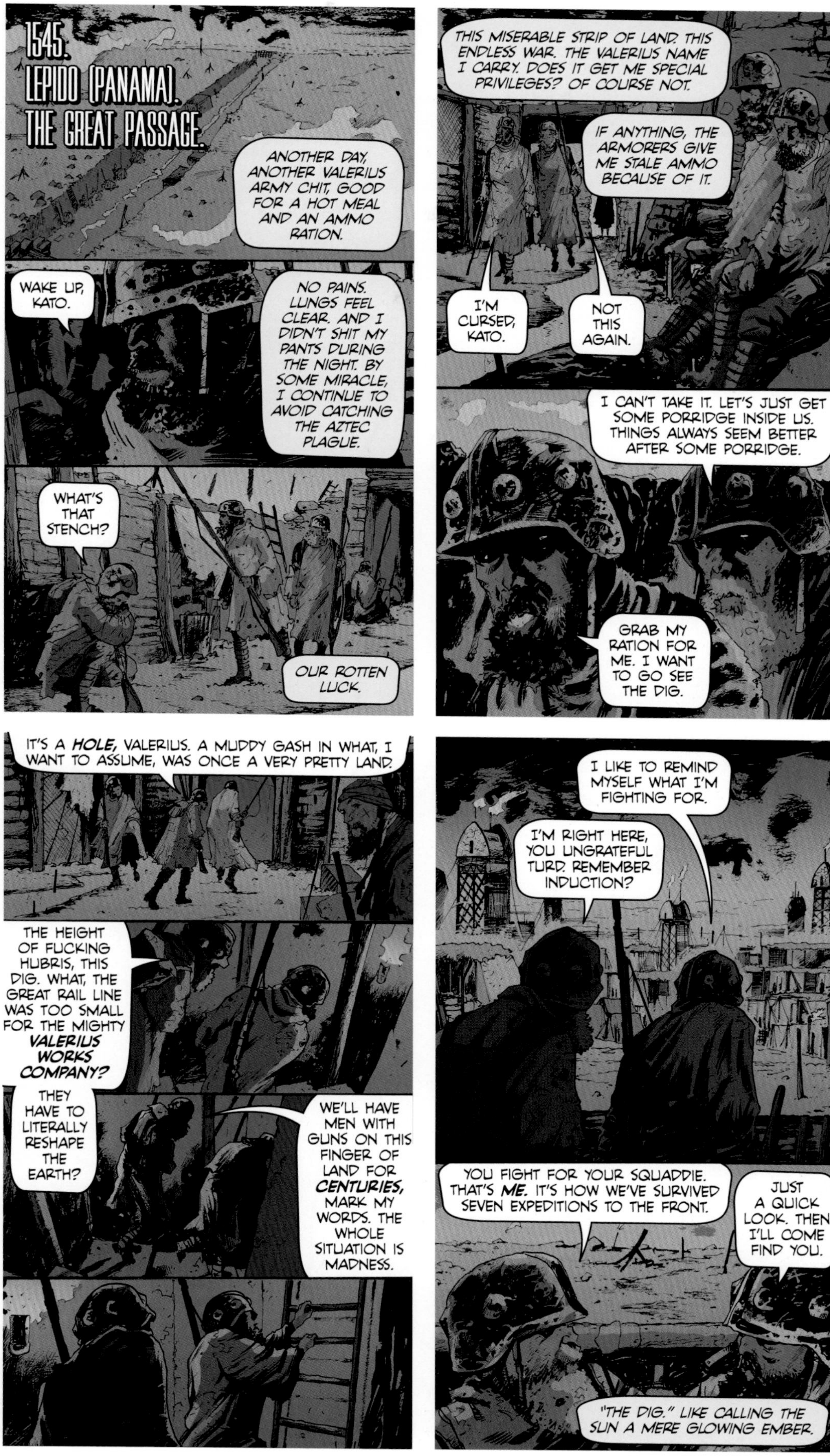
1545. LEPIDO (PANAMA). THE GREAT PASSAGE.
ANOTHER DAY, ANOTHER VALERIUS ARMY CHIT, GOOD FOR A HOT MEAL AND AN AMMO RATION.
WAKE UP, KATO.
NO PAINS. LUNGS FEEL CLEAR. AND I DIDN'T SHIT MY PANTS DURING THE NIGHT. BY SOME MIRACLE, I CONTINUE TO AVOID CATCHING THE AZTEC PLAGUE.
WHAT'S THAT STENCH?
OUR ROTTEN LUCK.
THIS MISERABLE STRIP OF LAND. THIS ENDLESS WAR. THE VALERIUS NAME I CARRY. DOES IT GET ME SPECIAL PRIVILEGES? OF COURSE NOT.
IF ANYTHING, THE ARMORERS GIVE ME STALE AMMO BECAUSE OF IT.
I'M CURSED, KATO.
NOT THIS AGAIN.
I CAN'T TAKE IT. LET'S JUST GET SOME PORRIDGE INSIDE US. THINGS ALWAYS SEEM BETTER AFTER SOME PORRIDGE.
GRAB MY RATION FOR ME. I WANT TO GO SEE THE DIG.
IT'S A HOLE, VALERIUS. A MUDDY GASH IN WHAT, I WANT TO ASSUME, WAS ONCE A VERY PRETTY LAND.
THE HEIGHT OF FUCKING HUBRIS, THIS DIG. WHAT, THE GREAT RAIL LINE WAS TOO SMALL FOR THE MIGHTY VALERIUS WORKS COMPANY?
THEY HAVE TO LITERALLY RESHAPE THE EARTH?
WE'LL HAVE MEN WITH GUNS ON THIS FINGER OF LAND FOR CENTURIES, MARK MY WORDS. THE WHOLE SITUATION IS MADNESS.
I LIKE TO REMIND MYSELF WHAT I'M FIGHTING FOR.
I'M RIGHT HERE, YOU UNGRATEFUL TURD. REMEMBER INDUCTION?
YOU FIGHT FOR YOUR SQUADDIE. THAT'S ME. IT'S HOW WE'VE SURVIVED SEVEN EXPEDITIONS TO THE FRONT.
JUST A QUICK LOOK. THEN I'LL COME FIND YOU.
"THE DIG." LIKE CALLING THE SUN A MERE GLOWING EMBER.

A NAVIGABLE CANAL FROM THE EASTERN SEA TO THE WESTERN OCEAN. RIVALS PATENT A RAIL SYSTEM TO HAUL SHIPS OVERLAND, AND VALERIUS RESPONDS WITH A PLAN TO LITERALLY CLEAVE THE EARTH IN TWO.

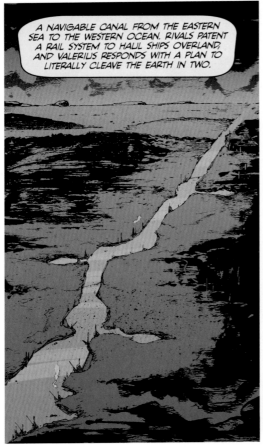

I WAS FOUR YEARS OLD WHEN THEY BROKE GROUND. I WAS SIX WHEN THE AZTECS ATTACKED. AT FOURTEEN THEY CONSCRIPTED ME, AND NOW I'M TWENTY-EIGHT.

MY BEST GUESS IS I'LL BE THIRTY-FIVE WHEN THE DIG IS DUG, WELL PAST MIDDLE AGE. IF THE PLAGUE HASN'T KILLED US ALL BY THEN, MAYBE THE AZTECS WILL FINALLY BACK OFF.

ANYWAY, KATO IS RIGHT. WE MAY TECHNICALLY BE FIGHTING TO PROTECT THE DIG, BUT OUR DUTY IS TO EACH OTHER. WE LOSE THAT TRUST, THIS EXPEDITION WILL BE OUR LAST.

BUT BY THE GODS, IT'S A GRAND VIEW. SURELY THERE'S NOTHING ON EARTH TO RIVAL THIS FEAT OF HUMAN TOIL AND ENGINEERING.

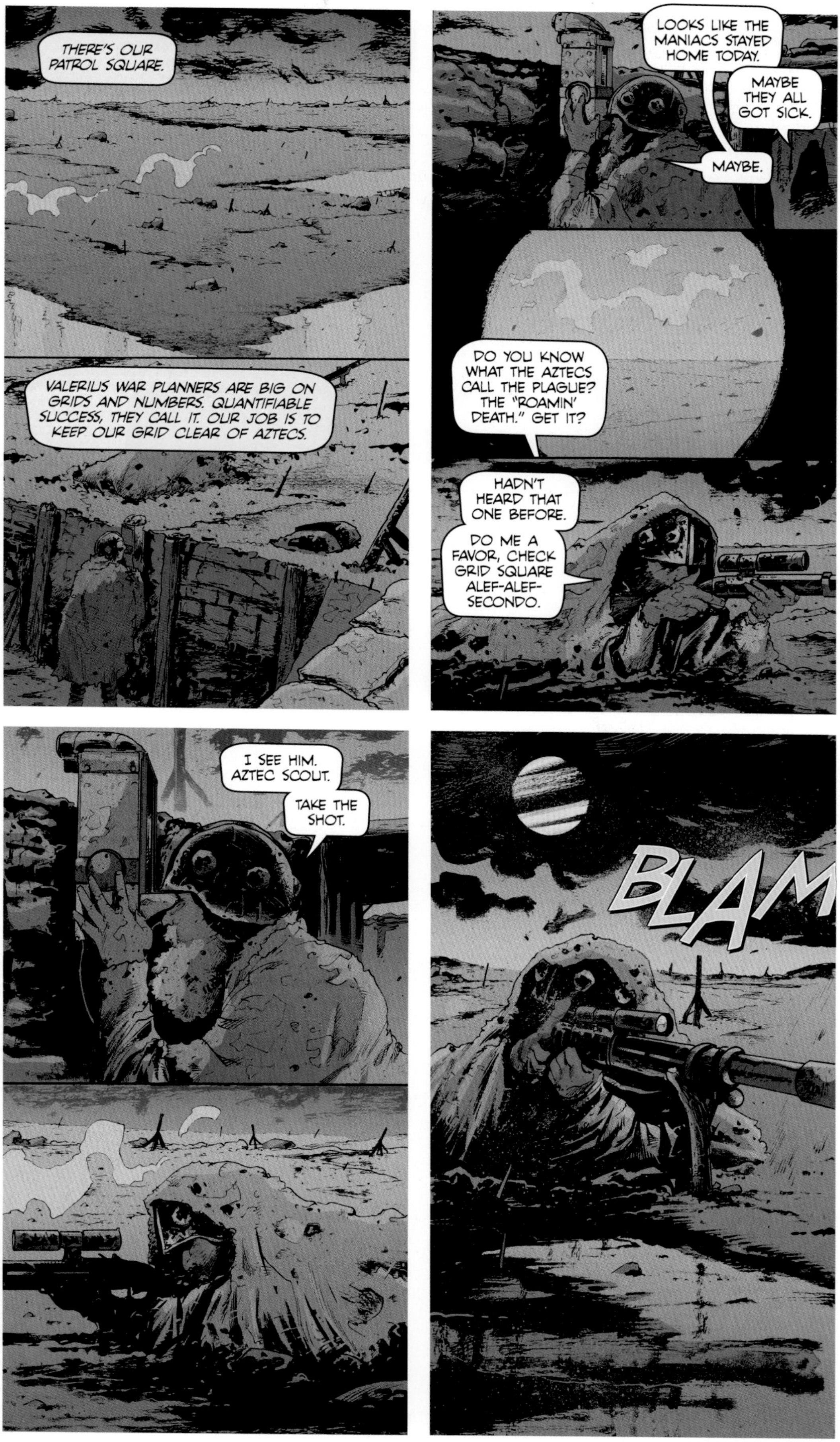
THERE'S OUR PATROL SQUARE.
VALERIUS WAR PLANNERS ARE BIG ON GRIDS AND NUMBERS. QUANTIFIABLE SUCCESS, THEY CALL IT. OUR JOB IS TO KEEP OUR GRID CLEAR OF AZTECS.
LOOKS LIKE THE MANIACS STAYED HOME TODAY.
MAYBE THEY ALL GOT SICK.
MAYBE.
DO YOU KNOW WHAT THE AZTECS CALL THE PLAGUE? THE "ROAMIN' DEATH." GET IT?
HADN'T HEARD THAT ONE BEFORE.
DO ME A FAVOR, CHECK GRID SQUARE ALEF-ALEF-SECONDO.
I SEE HIM. AZTEC SCOUT.
TAKE THE SHOT.
BLAM

THOK

LET'S RELOCATE.

I THINK WE SHOULD RETRIEVE THE BODY.

WHY?

JUST LEAVE HIM FOR THE BIRDS.

YOU HEARD THE MAJORIUS' BRIEF. INTELLIGENCE CAN HELP WIN THE WAR JUST AS WELL AS BULLETS.

I'D LIKE TO SEE IF WE CAN FIND OUT.

DUNNO, KATO. IT'LL TAKE HOURS TO PROPERLY WORK OUR WAY OUT THERE.

YOU HAVE SOMETHING ELSE TO DO TODAY?

THINK OF THE GRAIN FIELDS, VALERIUS. THINK OF THE BUFFALO. THINK OF THE GOLDEN HOUR.

THE FIRST DECADE OF THE WAR WAS BRUTAL. HUNDREDS OF THOUSANDS OF MEN SENT IN WAVES TO THEIR DEATHS. MEN FOUGHT KNEE DEEP IN CORPSES.

THE WAR EVOLVED IN THE SECOND DECADE, AS VALERIUS INTRODUCED RANGED WEAPONS, MASSIVE GUNS THAT COULD FIRE OVER THE HORIZON. THE AZTECS COUNTERED WITH BOMBS THAT LITERALLY FLEW.

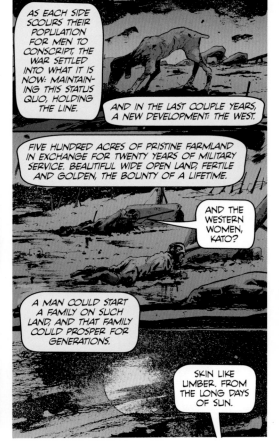

AS EACH SIDE SCOURS THEIR POPULATION FOR MEN TO CONSCRIPT, THE WAR SETTLED INTO WHAT IT IS NOW: MAINTAINING THIS STATUS QUO, HOLDING THE LINE.

AND IN THE LAST COUPLE YEARS, A NEW DEVELOPMENT: THE WEST.

FIVE HUNDRED ACRES OF PRISTINE FARMLAND IN EXCHANGE FOR TWENTY YEARS OF MILITARY SERVICE. BEAUTIFUL WIDE OPEN LAND, FERTILE AND GOLDEN, THE BOUNTY OF A LIFETIME.

AND THE WESTERN WOMEN, KATO?

A MAN COULD START A FAMILY ON SUCH LAND, AND THAT FAMILY COULD PROSPER FOR GENERATIONS.

SKIN LIKE UMBER. FROM THE LONG DAYS OF SUN.

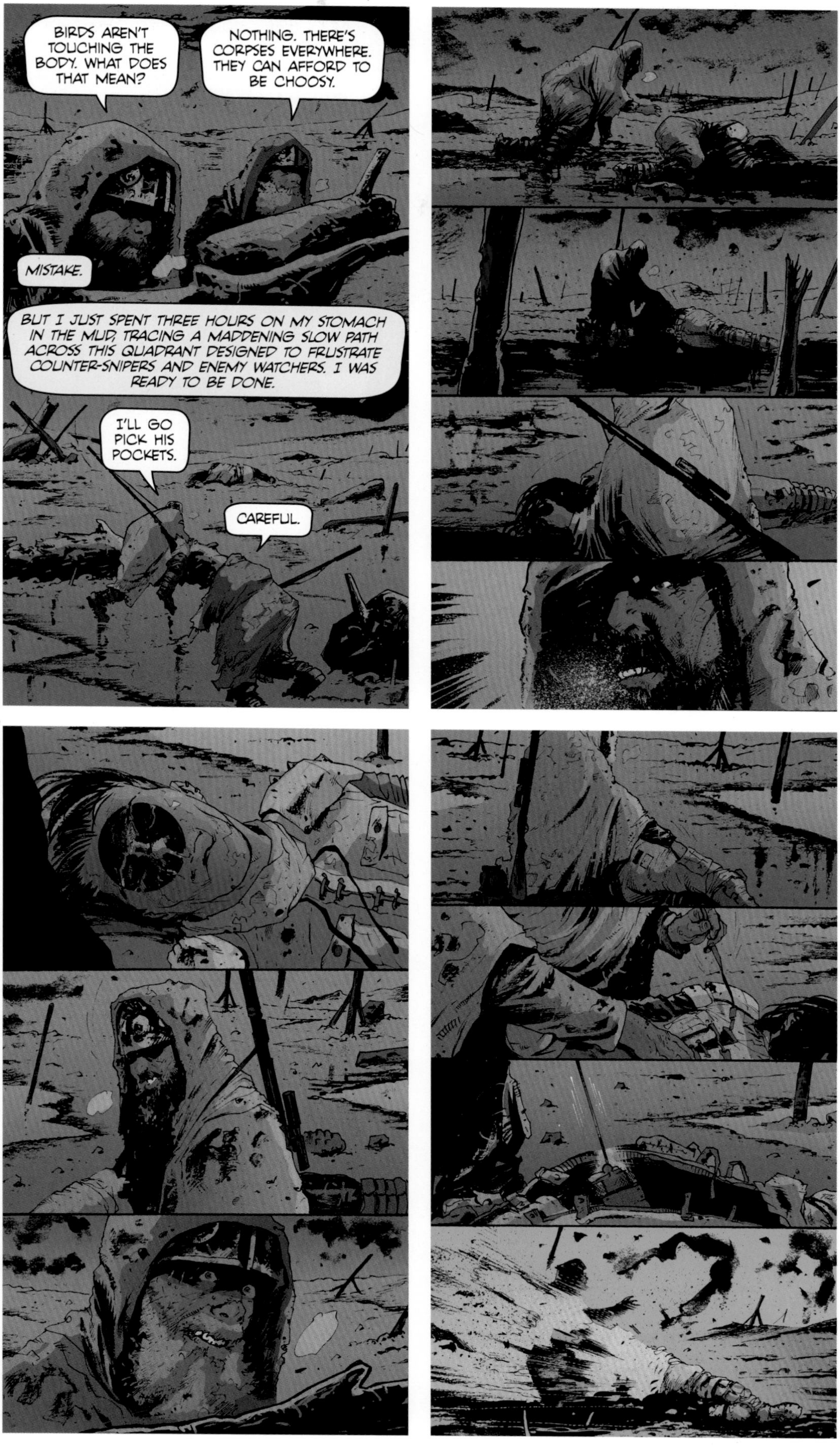
BIRDS AREN'T TOUCHING THE BODY. WHAT DOES THAT MEAN?
NOTHING. THERE'S CORPSES EVERYWHERE. THEY CAN AFFORD TO BE CHOOSY.
MISTAKE.
BUT I JUST SPENT THREE HOURS ON MY STOMACH IN THE MUD, TRACING A MADDENING SLOW PATH ACROSS THIS QUADRANT DESIGNED TO FRUSTRATE COUNTER-SNIPERS AND ENEMY WATCHERS. I WAS READY TO BE DONE.
I'LL GO PICK HIS POCKETS.
CAREFUL.

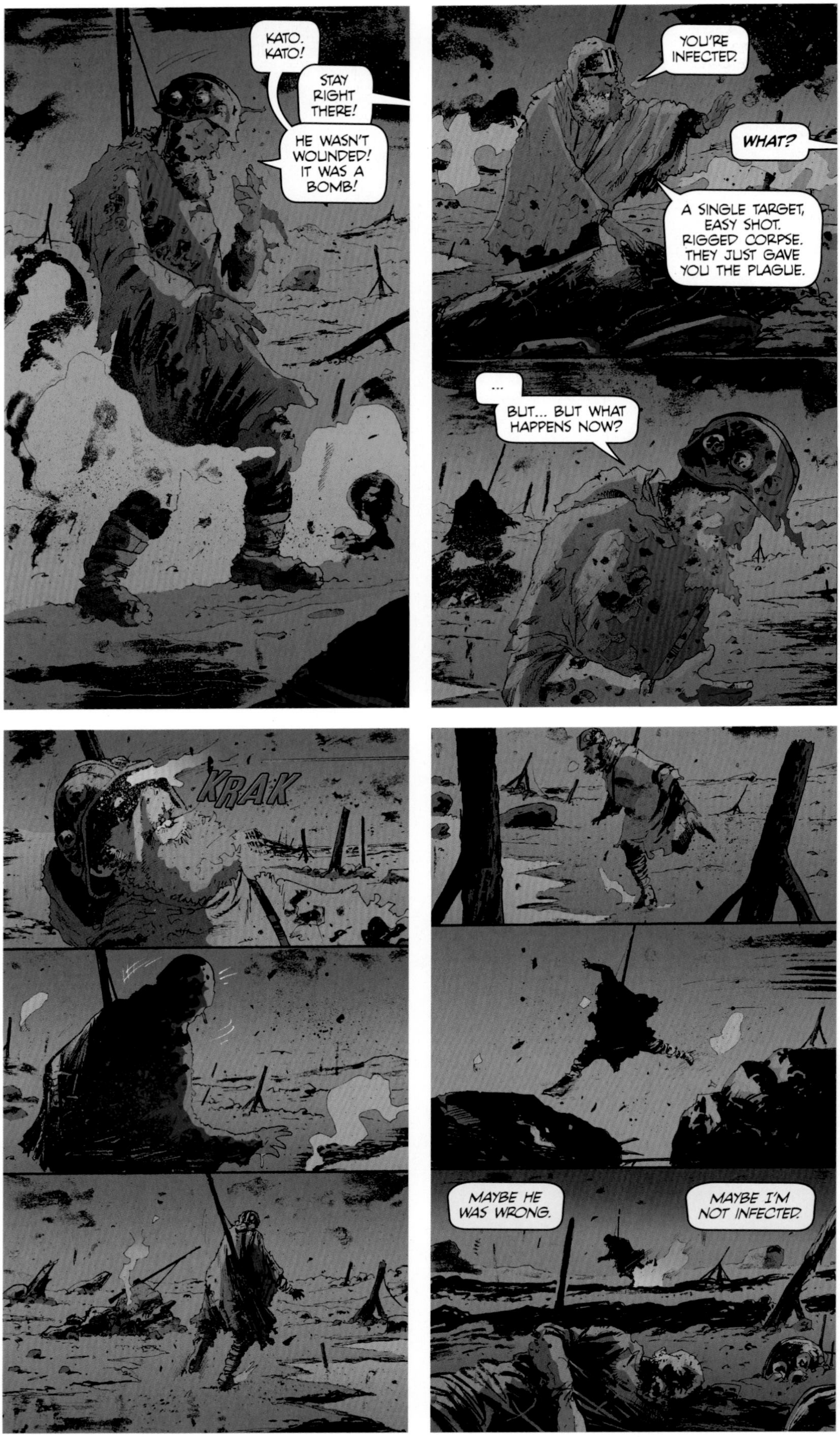
KATO. KATO!
STAY RIGHT THERE!
HE WASN'T WOUNDED! IT WAS A BOMB!
YOU'RE INFECTED.
WHAT?
A SINGLE TARGET, EASY SHOT. RIGGED CORPSE. THEY JUST GAVE YOU THE PLAGUE.
...
BUT... BUT WHAT HAPPENS NOW?
KRAK
MAYBE HE WAS WRONG.
MAYBE I'M NOT INFECTED.

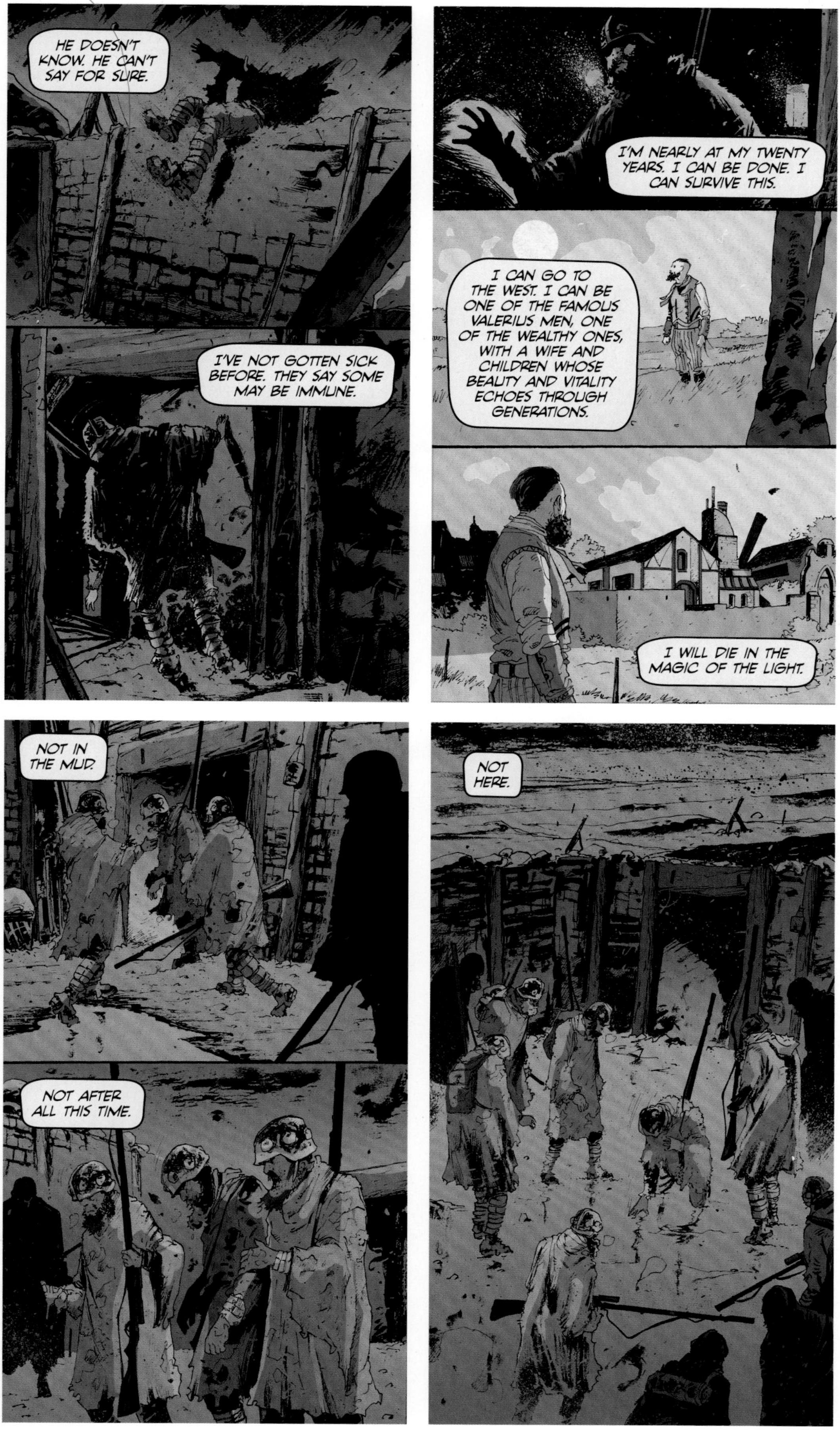
HE DOESN'T KNOW. HE CAN'T SAY FOR SURE.
I'M NEARLY AT MY TWENTY YEARS. I CAN BE DONE. I CAN SURVIVE THIS.
I'VE NOT GOTTEN SICK BEFORE. THEY SAY SOME MAY BE IMMUNE.
I CAN GO TO THE WEST. I CAN BE ONE OF THE FAMOUS VALERIUS MEN, ONE OF THE WEALTHY ONES, WITH A WIFE AND CHILDREN WHOSE BEAUTY AND VITALITY ECHOES THROUGH GENERATIONS.
I WILL DIE IN THE MAGIC OF THE LIGHT.
NOT IN THE MUD.
NOT AFTER ALL THIS TIME.
NOT HERE.

SAUKAGO

IT'S A RARE PERIOD OF PEACE and prosperity as Alameda Valerius travels through the Republic of Rome West, from Saukago, through Sioux Colonia, to the bustling Dutch city-state, The Port of Barentsland.

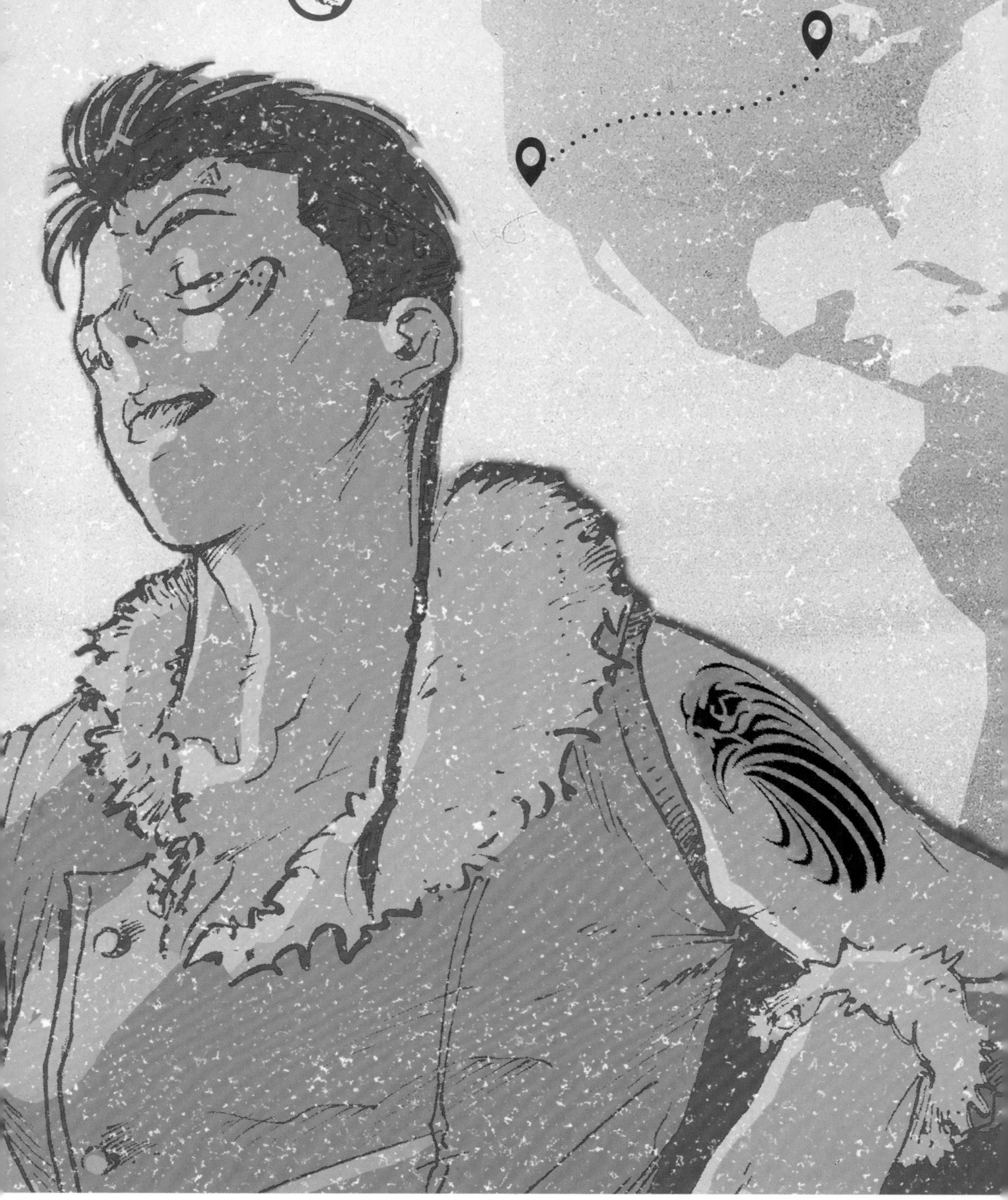

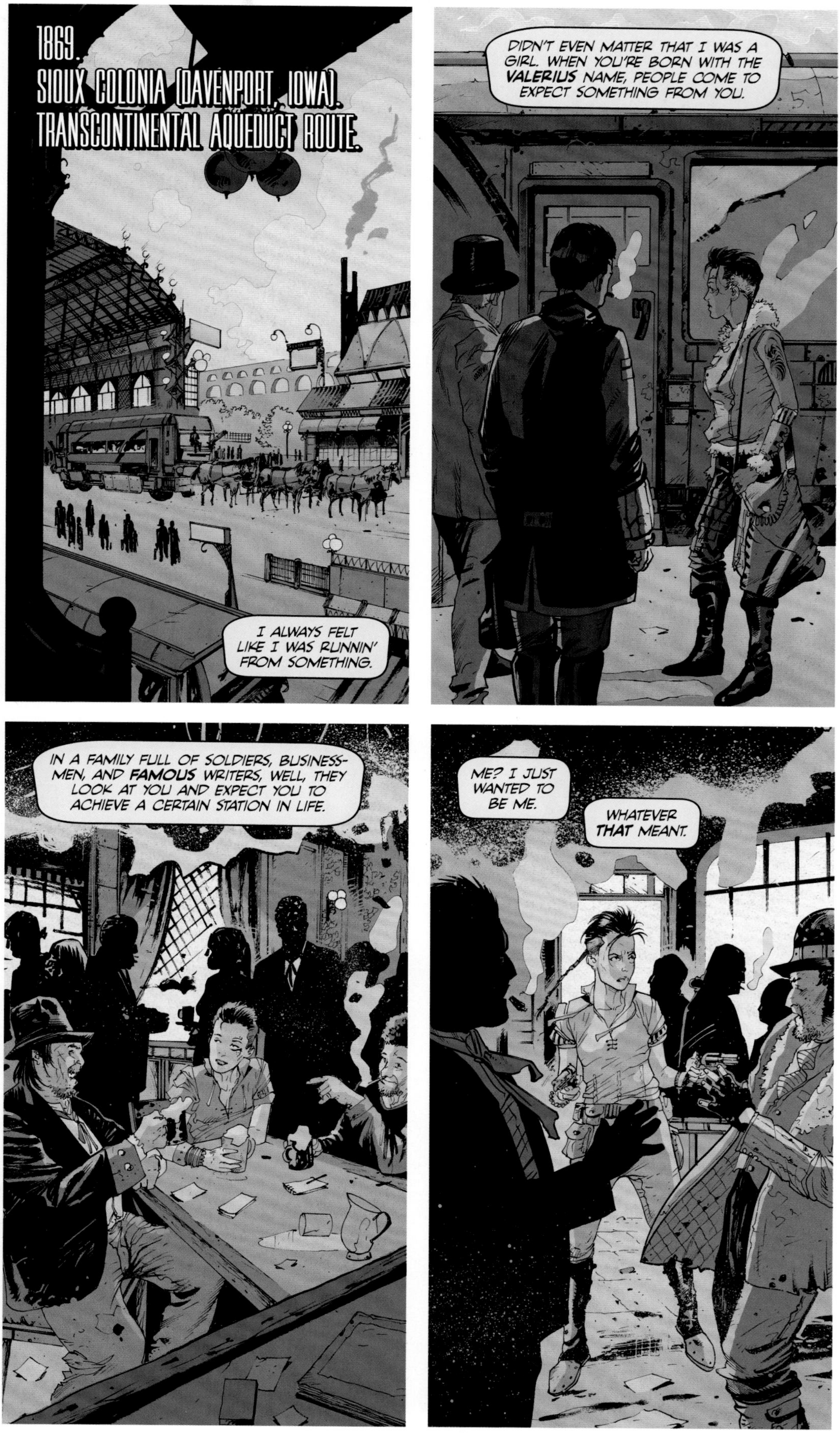
1869.
SIOUX COLONIA (DAVENPORT, IOWA).
TRANSCONTINENTAL AQUEDUCT ROUTE.
I ALWAYS FELT LIKE I WAS RUNNIN' FROM SOMETHING.
DIDN'T EVEN MATTER THAT I WAS A GIRL. WHEN YOU'RE BORN WITH THE **VALERIUS** NAME, PEOPLE COME TO EXPECT SOMETHING FROM YOU.
IN A FAMILY FULL OF SOLDIERS, BUSINESS-MEN, AND **FAMOUS** WRITERS, WELL, THEY LOOK AT YOU AND EXPECT YOU TO ACHIEVE A CERTAIN STATION IN LIFE.
ME? I JUST WANTED TO BE ME.
WHATEVER **THAT** MEANT.

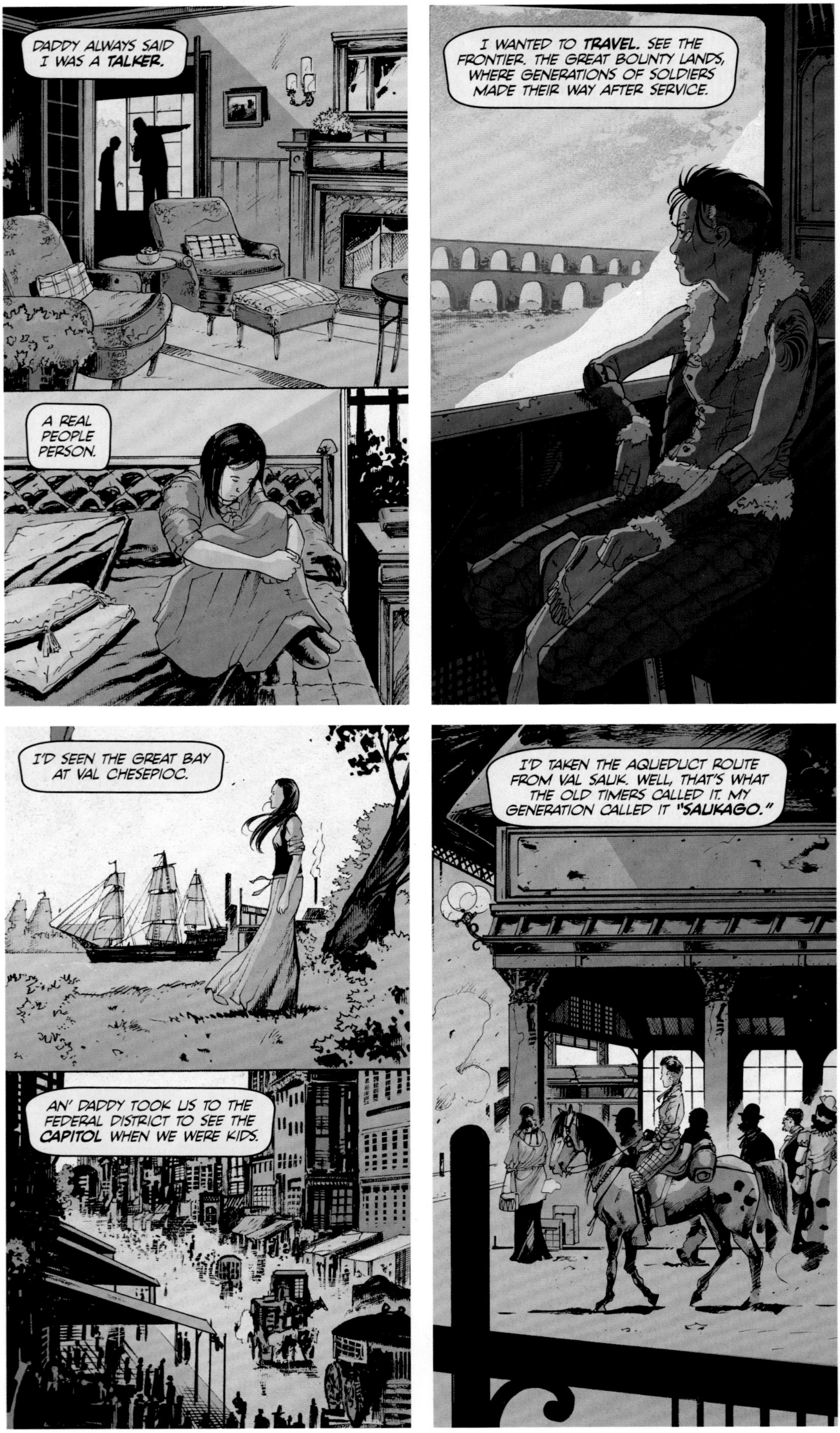
DADDY ALWAYS SAID I WAS A TALKER.
A REAL PEOPLE PERSON.
I WANTED TO TRAVEL. SEE THE FRONTIER. THE GREAT BOUNTY LANDS, WHERE GENERATIONS OF SOLDIERS MADE THEIR WAY AFTER SERVICE.
I'D SEEN THE GREAT BAY AT VAL CHESEPIOC.
AN' DADDY TOOK US TO THE FEDERAL DISTRICT TO SEE THE CAPITOL WHEN WE WERE KIDS.
I'D TAKEN THE AQUEDUCT ROUTE FROM VAL SAUK. WELL, THAT'S WHAT THE OLD TIMERS CALLED IT. MY GENERATION CALLED IT "SAUKAGO."

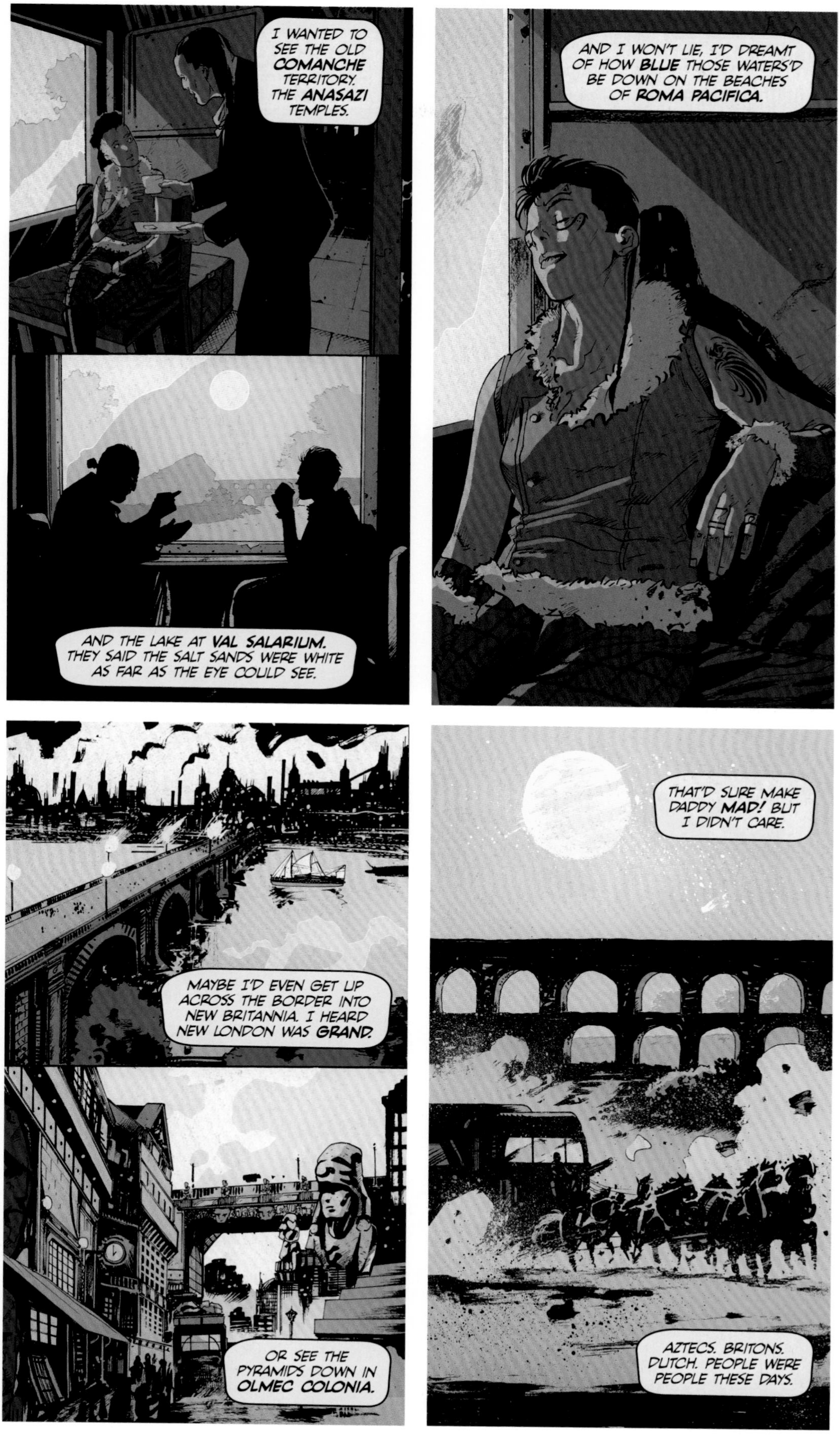
I WANTED TO SEE THE OLD COMANCHE TERRITORY. THE ANASAZI TEMPLES.
AND THE LAKE AT VAL SALARIUM. THEY SAID THE SALT SANDS WERE WHITE AS FAR AS THE EYE COULD SEE.
AND I WON'T LIE, I'D DREAMT OF HOW BLUE THOSE WATERS'D BE DOWN ON THE BEACHES OF ROMA PACIFICA.
MAYBE I'D EVEN GET UP ACROSS THE BORDER INTO NEW BRITANNIA. I HEARD NEW LONDON WAS GRAND.
OR SEE THE PYRAMIDS DOWN IN OLMEC COLONIA.
THAT'D SURE MAKE DADDY MAD! BUT I DIDN'T CARE.
AZTECS. BRITONS. DUTCH. PEOPLE WERE PEOPLE THESE DAYS.

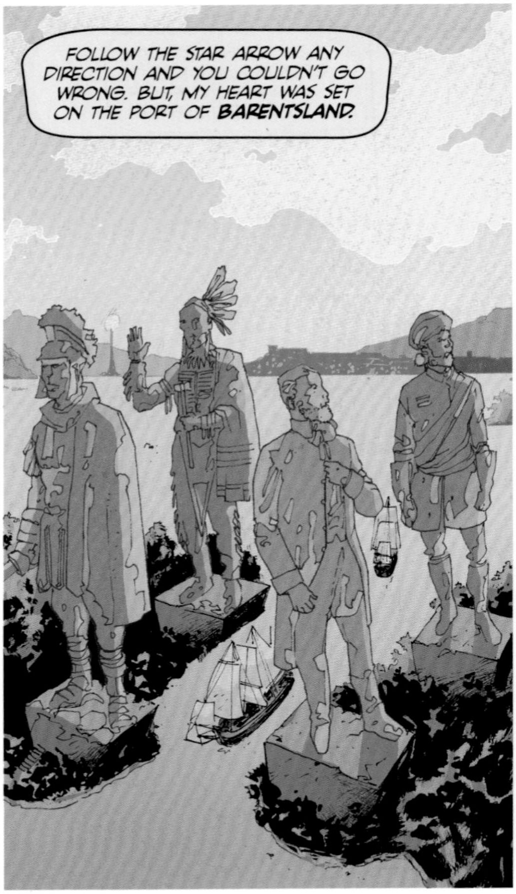
FOLLOW THE STAR ARROW ANY DIRECTION AND YOU COULDN'T GO WRONG. BUT, MY HEART WAS SET ON THE PORT OF **BARENTSLAND**.

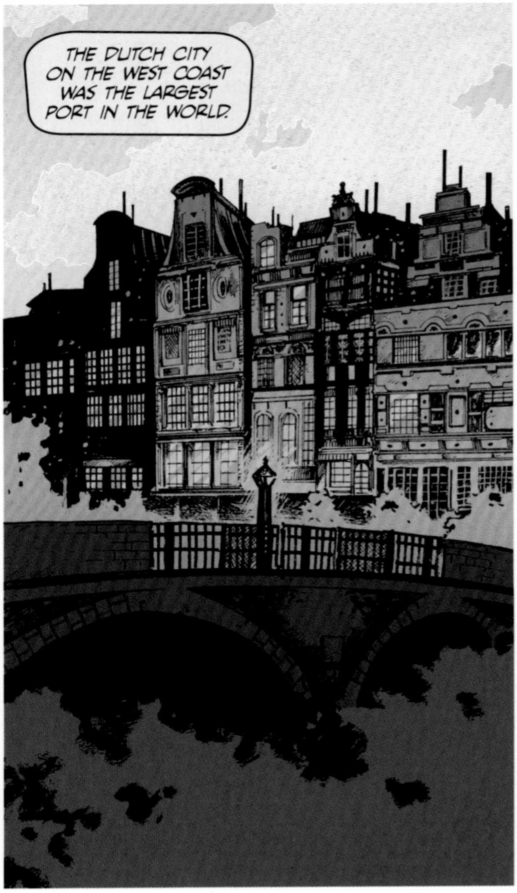
THE DUTCH CITY ON THE WEST COAST WAS THE LARGEST PORT IN THE WORLD.

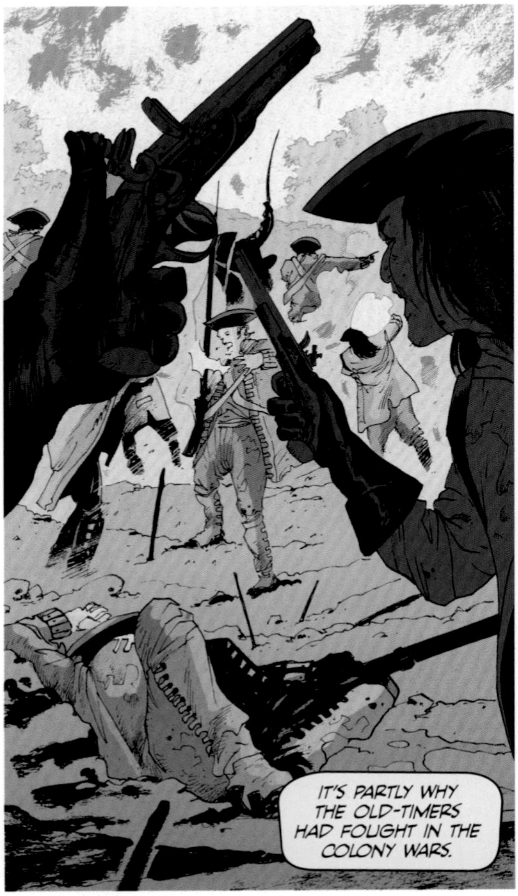
IT'S PARTLY WHY THE OLD-TIMERS HAD FOUGHT IN THE COLONY WARS.

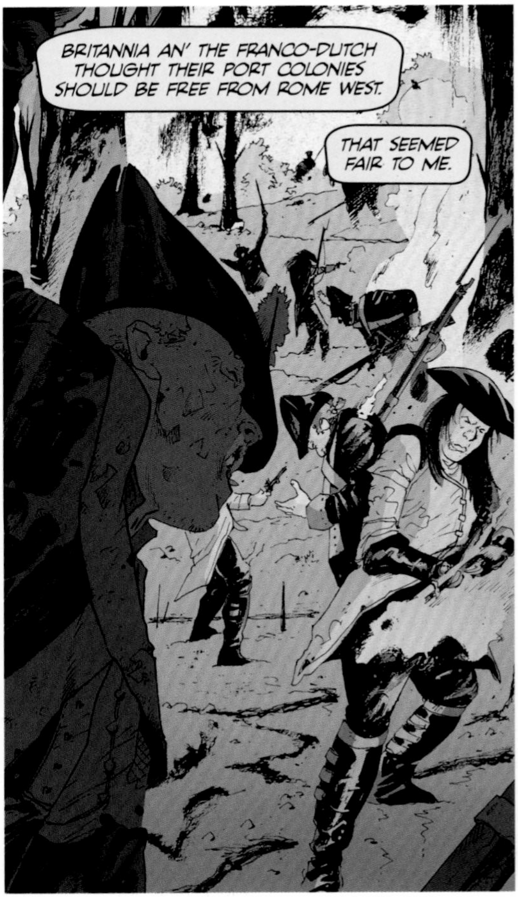
BRITANNIA AN' THE FRANCO-DUTCH THOUGHT THEIR PORT COLONIES SHOULD BE FREE FROM ROME WEST.
THAT SEEMED FAIR TO ME.

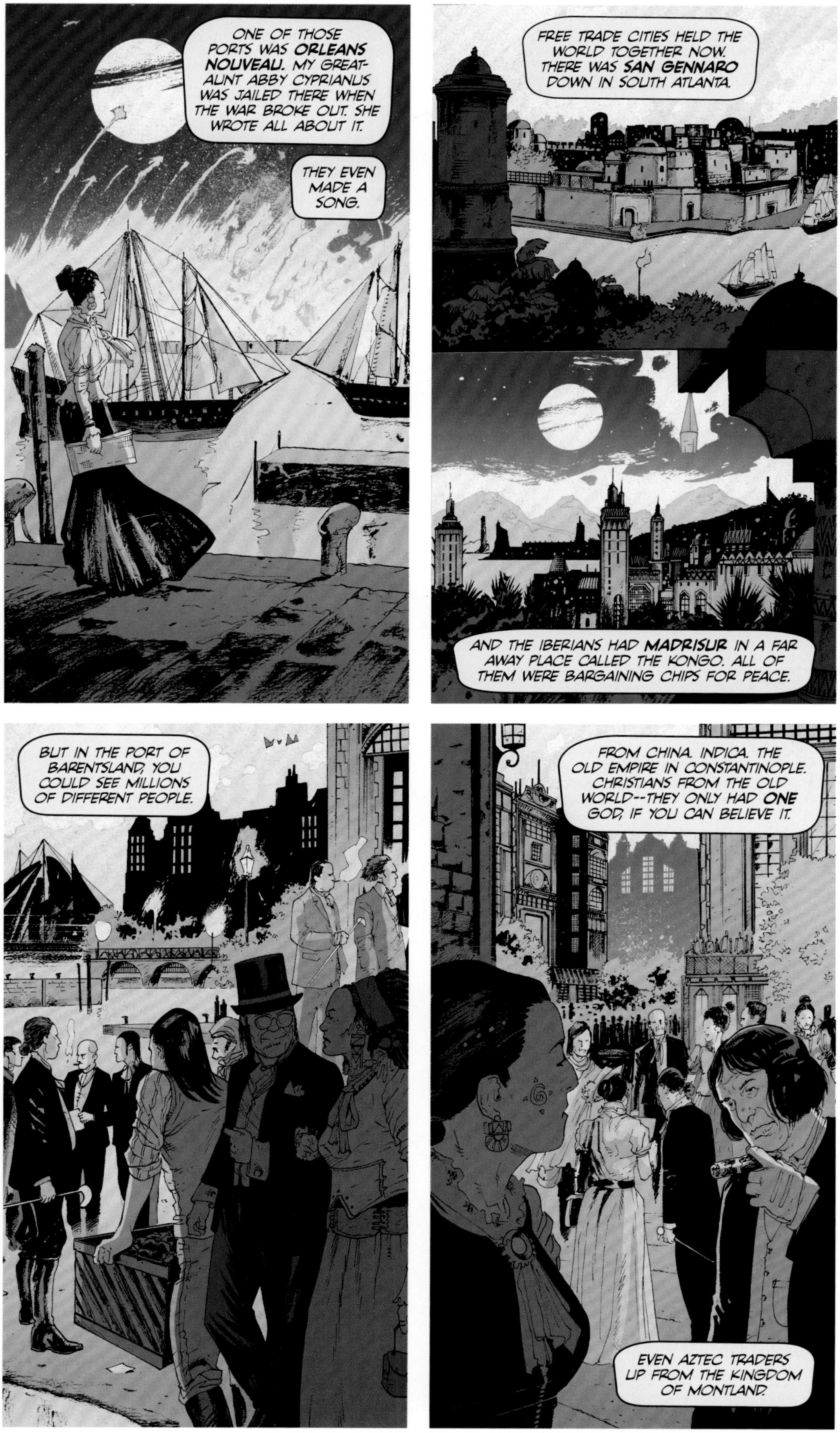
ONE OF THOSE PORTS WAS **ORLEANS NOUVEAU.** MY GREAT-AUNT ABBY CYPRIANUS WAS JAILED THERE WHEN THE WAR BROKE OUT. SHE WROTE ALL ABOUT IT.
THEY EVEN MADE A SONG.
FREE TRADE CITIES HELD THE WORLD TOGETHER NOW. THERE WAS **SAN GENNARO** DOWN IN SOUTH ATLANTA.
AND THE IBERIANS HAD **MADRISUR** IN A FAR AWAY PLACE CALLED THE KONGO. ALL OF THEM WERE BARGAINING CHIPS FOR PEACE.
BUT IN THE PORT OF BARENTSLAND, YOU COULD SEE MILLIONS OF DIFFERENT PEOPLE.
FROM CHINA. INDICA. THE OLD EMPIRE IN CONSTANTINOPLE. CHRISTIANS FROM THE OLD WORLD--THEY ONLY HAD **ONE** GOD, IF YOU CAN BELIEVE IT.
EVEN AZTEC TRADERS UP FROM THE KINGDOM OF MONTLAND.

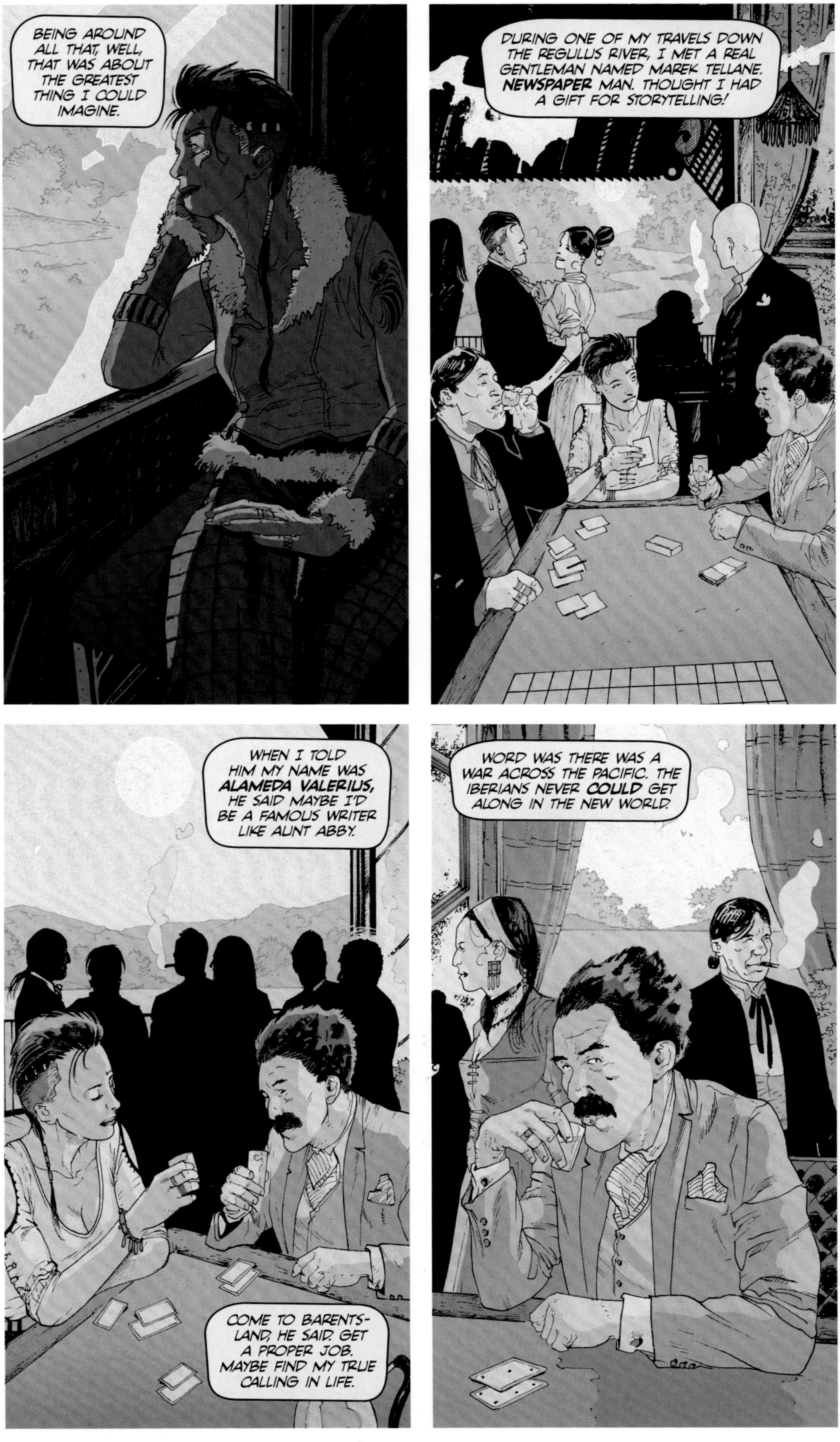
BEING AROUND ALL THAT, WELL, THAT WAS ABOUT THE GREATEST THING I COULD IMAGINE.
DURING ONE OF MY TRAVELS DOWN THE REGULUS RIVER, I MET A REAL GENTLEMAN NAMED MAREK TELLANE. NEWSPAPER MAN. THOUGHT I HAD A GIFT FOR STORYTELLING!
WHEN I TOLD HIM MY NAME WAS ALAMEDA VALERIUS, HE SAID MAYBE I'D BE A FAMOUS WRITER LIKE AUNT ABBY.
COME TO BARENTS-LAND, HE SAID. GET A PROPER JOB. MAYBE FIND MY TRUE CALLING IN LIFE.
WORD WAS THERE WAS A WAR ACROSS THE PACIFIC. THE IBERIANS NEVER COULD GET ALONG IN THE NEW WORLD.

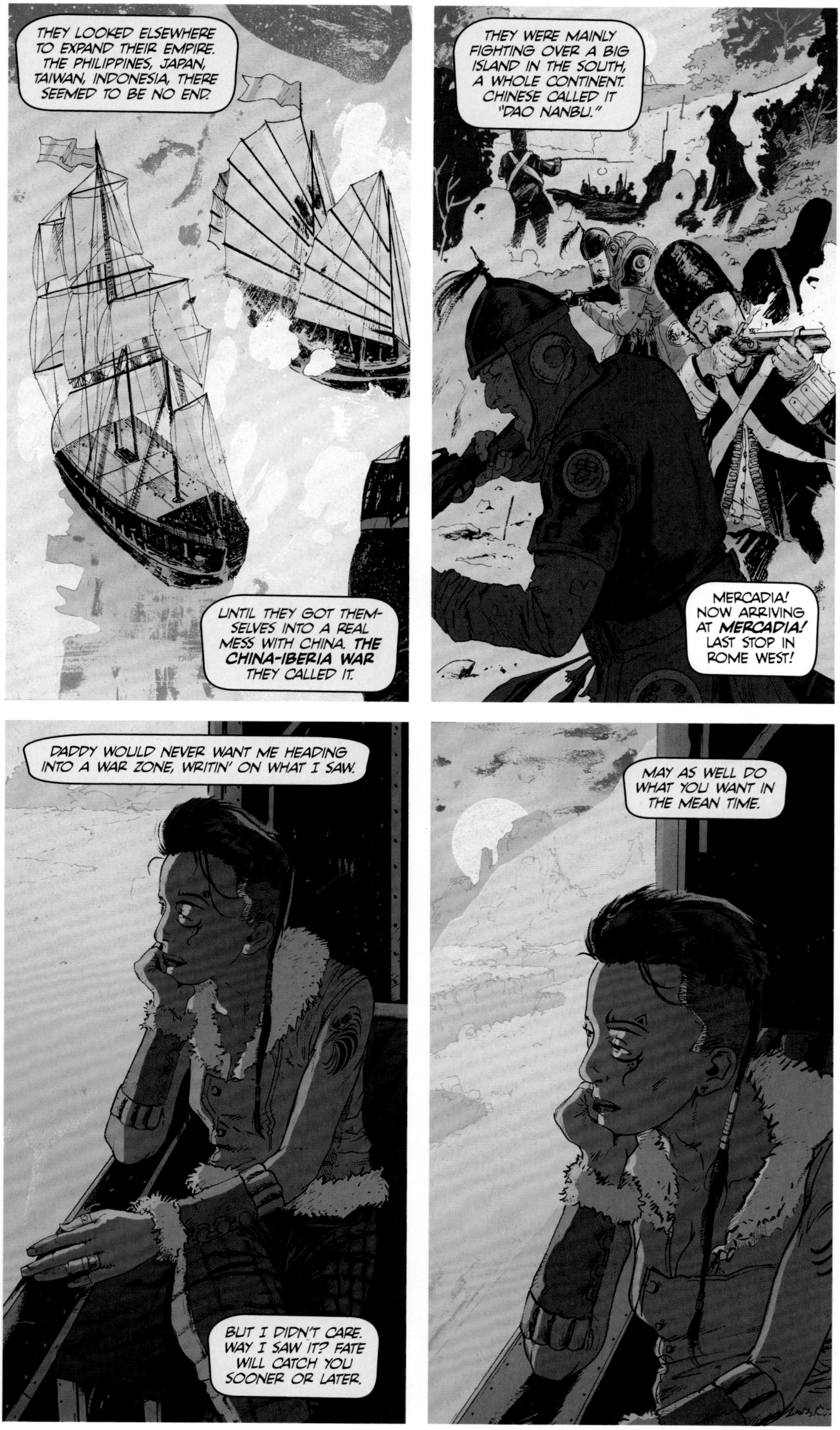
THEY LOOKED ELSEWHERE TO EXPAND THEIR EMPIRE. THE PHILIPPINES, JAPAN, TAIWAN, INDONESIA, THERE SEEMED TO BE NO END.
UNTIL THEY GOT THEM-SELVES INTO A REAL MESS WITH CHINA. **THE CHINA-IBERIA WAR** THEY CALLED IT.
THEY WERE MAINLY FIGHTING OVER A BIG ISLAND IN THE SOUTH, A WHOLE CONTINENT. CHINESE CALLED IT "DAO NANBU."
MERCADIA! NOW ARRIVING AT **MERCADIA!** LAST STOP IN ROME WEST!
DADDY WOULD NEVER WANT ME HEADING INTO A WAR ZONE, WRITIN' ON WHAT I SAW.
BUT I DIDN'T CARE. WAY I SAW IT? FATE WILL CATCH YOU SOONER OR LATER.
MAY AS WELL DO WHAT YOU WANT IN THE MEAN TIME.

THE PORT OF BARENTSLAND

IN 1939, a long-lost Valerius descendant and veteran of the Great War investigates a series of bizarre killings at the hands of a terror sect in the great multicultural metropolis named after Dutch explorer William Barents.

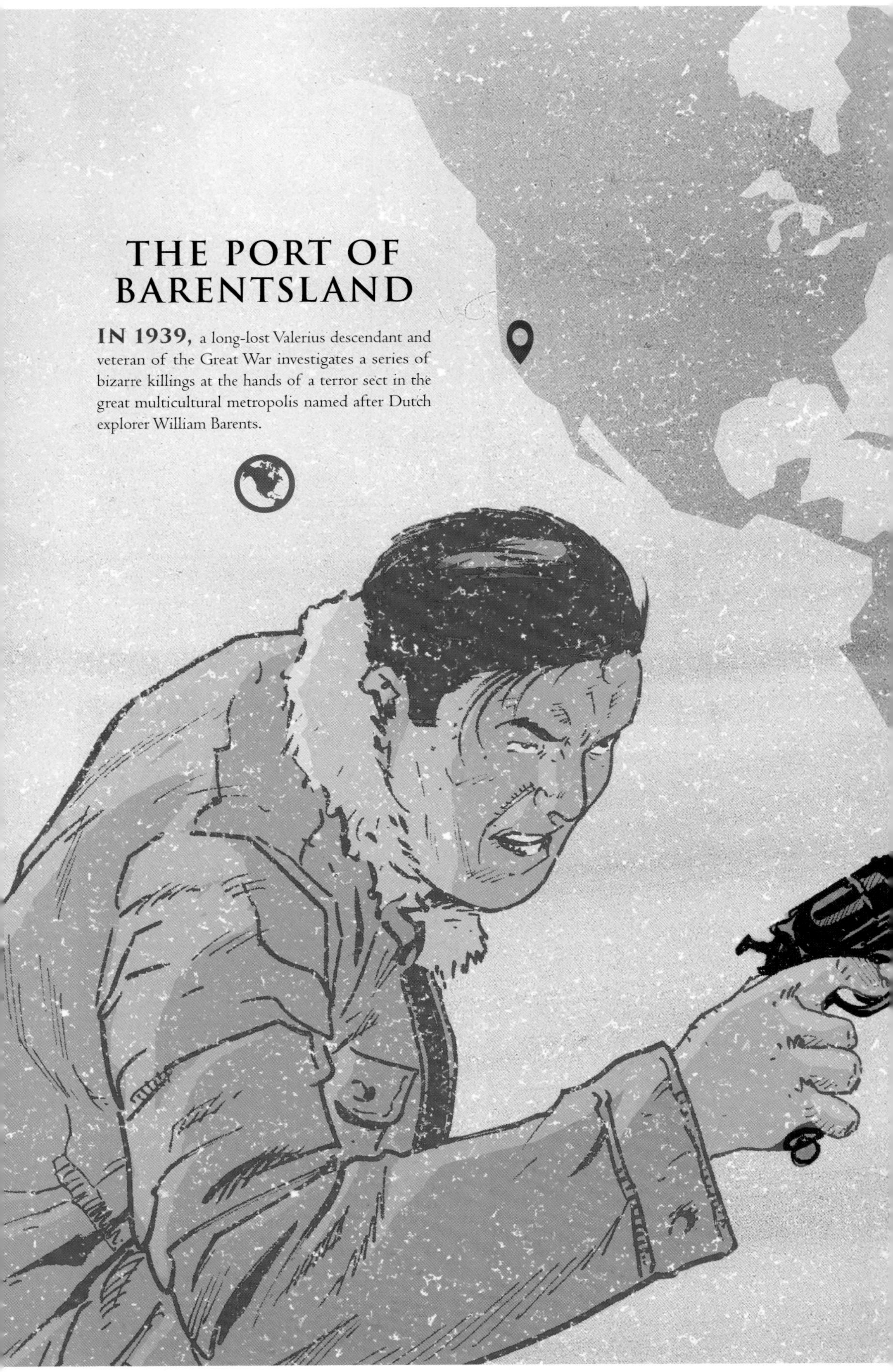

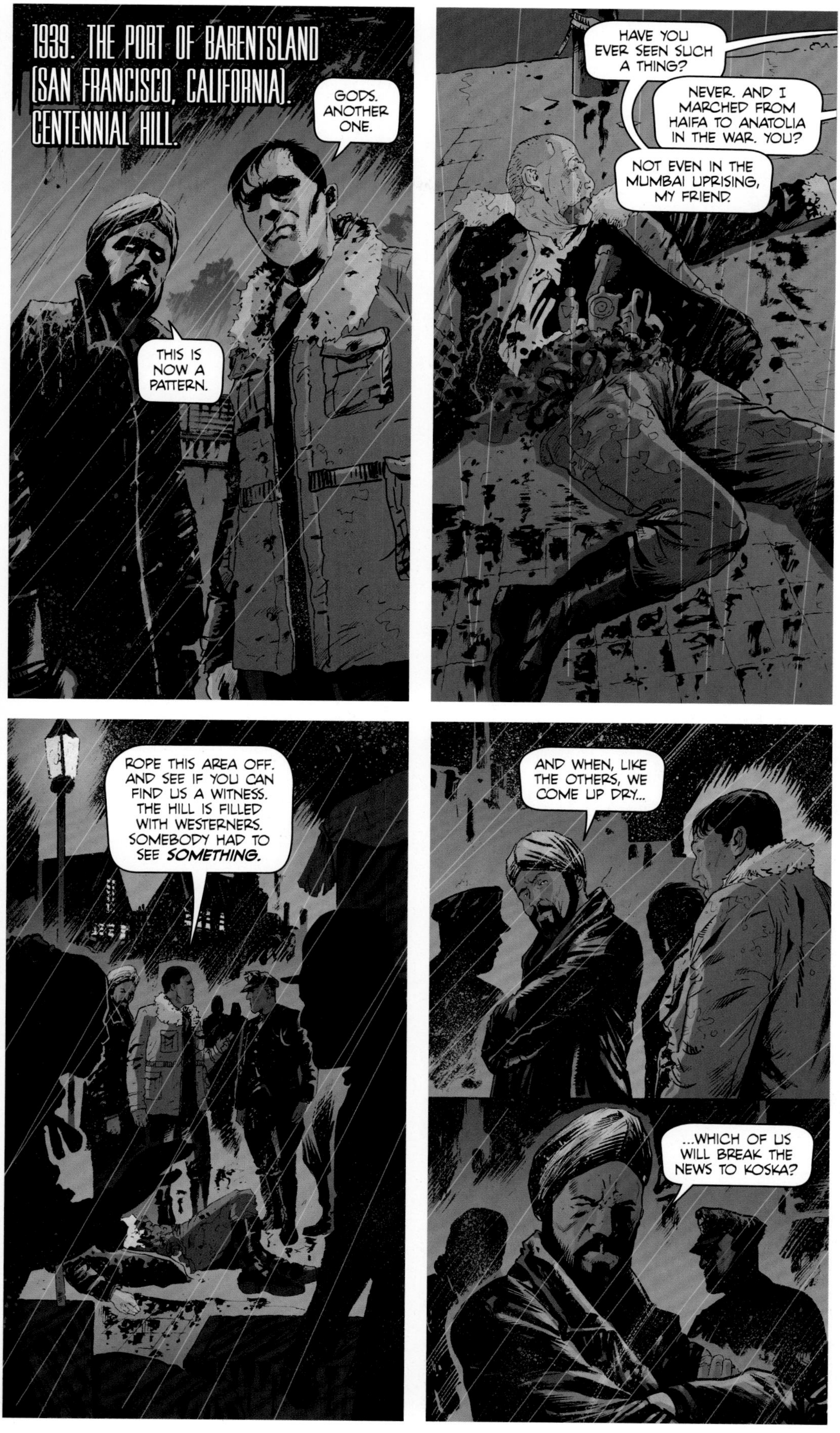
1939. THE PORT OF BARENTSLAND (SAN FRANCISCO, CALIFORNIA). CENTENNIAL HILL.
GODS. ANOTHER ONE.
THIS IS NOW A PATTERN.
HAVE YOU EVER SEEN SUCH A THING?
NEVER. AND I MARCHED FROM HAIFA TO ANATOLIA IN THE WAR. YOU?
NOT EVEN IN THE MUMBAI UPRISING, MY FRIEND.
ROPE THIS AREA OFF. AND SEE IF YOU CAN FIND US A WITNESS. THE HILL IS FILLED WITH WESTERNERS. SOMEBODY HAD TO SEE *SOMETHING.*
AND WHEN, LIKE THE OTHERS, WE COME UP DRY...
...WHICH OF US WILL BREAK THE NEWS TO KOSKA?

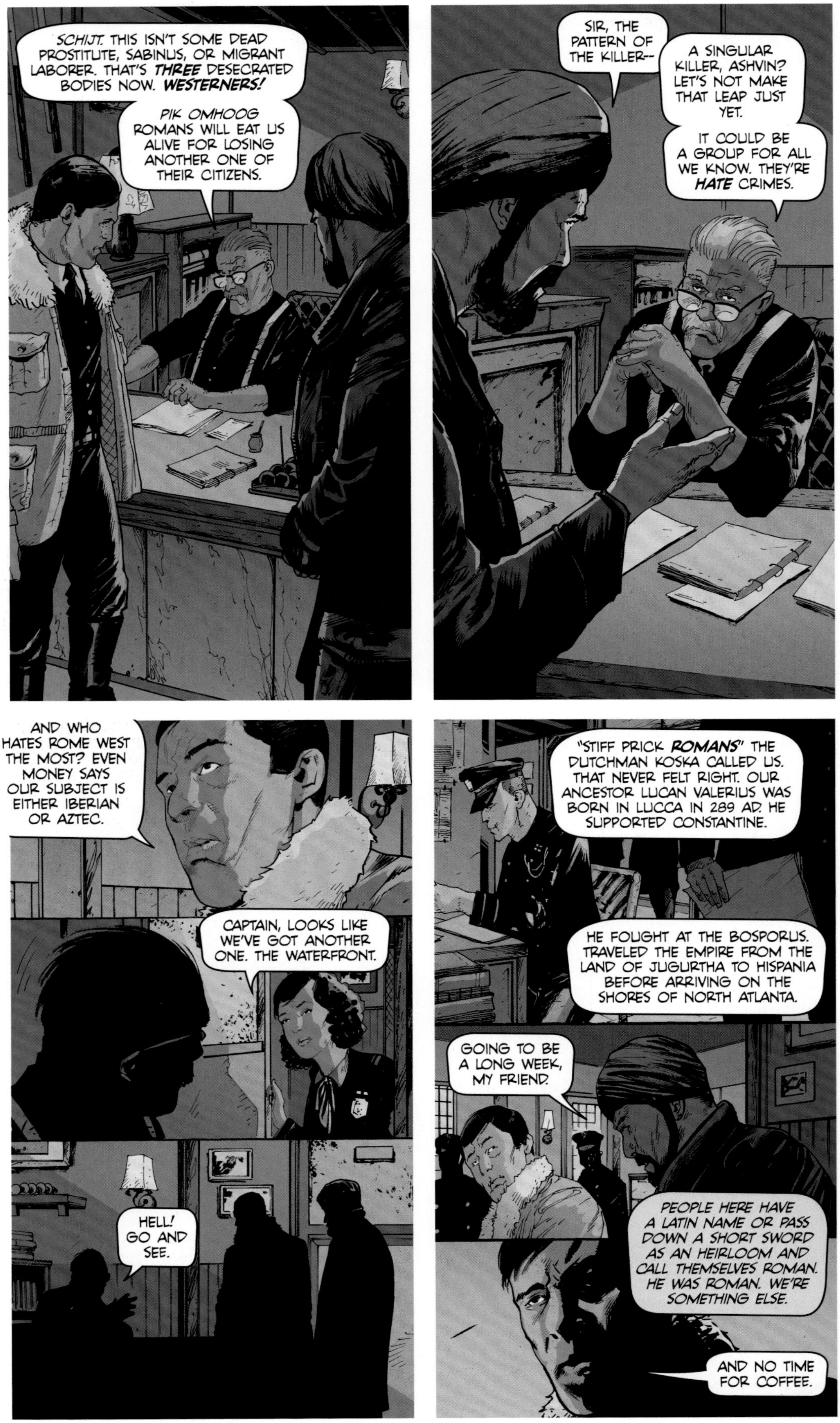

SCHIJT. THIS ISN'T SOME DEAD PROSTITUTE, SABINUS, OR MIGRANT LABORER. THAT'S THREE DESECRATED BODIES NOW. WESTERNERS!
PIK OMHOOG ROMANS WILL EAT US ALIVE FOR LOSING ANOTHER ONE OF THEIR CITIZENS.
SIR, THE PATTERN OF THE KILLER--
A SINGULAR KILLER, ASHVIN? LET'S NOT MAKE THAT LEAP JUST YET.
IT COULD BE A GROUP FOR ALL WE KNOW. THEY'RE HATE CRIMES.
AND WHO HATES ROME WEST THE MOST? EVEN MONEY SAYS OUR SUBJECT IS EITHER IBERIAN OR AZTEC.
CAPTAIN, LOOKS LIKE WE'VE GOT ANOTHER ONE. THE WATERFRONT.
HELL! GO AND SEE.
"STIFF PRICK ROMANS" THE DUTCHMAN KOSKA CALLED US. THAT NEVER FELT RIGHT. OUR ANCESTOR LUCAN VALERIUS WAS BORN IN LUCCA IN 289 AD. HE SUPPORTED CONSTANTINE.
HE FOUGHT AT THE BOSPORUS. TRAVELED THE EMPIRE FROM THE LAND OF JUGURTHA TO HISPANIA BEFORE ARRIVING ON THE SHORES OF NORTH ATLANTA.
GOING TO BE A LONG WEEK, MY FRIEND.
PEOPLE HERE HAVE A LATIN NAME OR PASS DOWN A SHORT SWORD AS AN HEIRLOOM AND CALL THEMSELVES ROMAN. HE WAS ROMAN. WE'RE SOMETHING ELSE.
AND NO TIME FOR COFFEE.

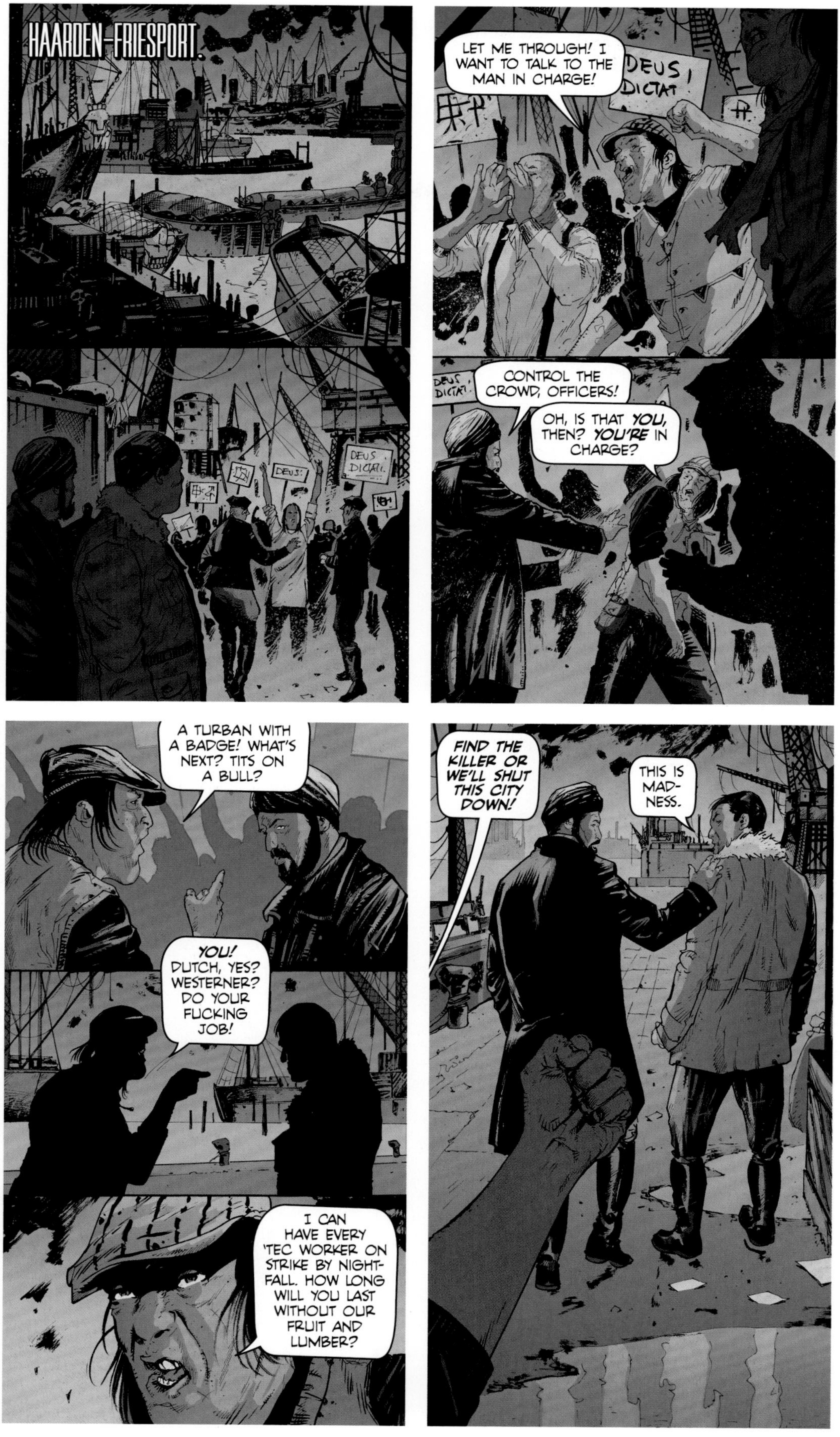
HAARDEN-FRIESPORT.
LET ME THROUGH! I WANT TO TALK TO THE MAN IN CHARGE!
DEUS DICTAT!
CONTROL THE CROWD, OFFICERS!
OH, IS THAT YOU, THEN? YOU'RE IN CHARGE?
A TURBAN WITH A BADGE! WHAT'S NEXT? TITS ON A BULL?
YOU! DUTCH, YES? WESTERNER? DO YOUR FUCKING JOB!
I CAN HAVE EVERY 'TEC WORKER ON STRIKE BY NIGHT-FALL. HOW LONG WILL YOU LAST WITHOUT OUR FRUIT AND LUMBER?
FIND THE KILLER OR WE'LL SHUT THIS CITY DOWN!
THIS IS MAD-NESS.

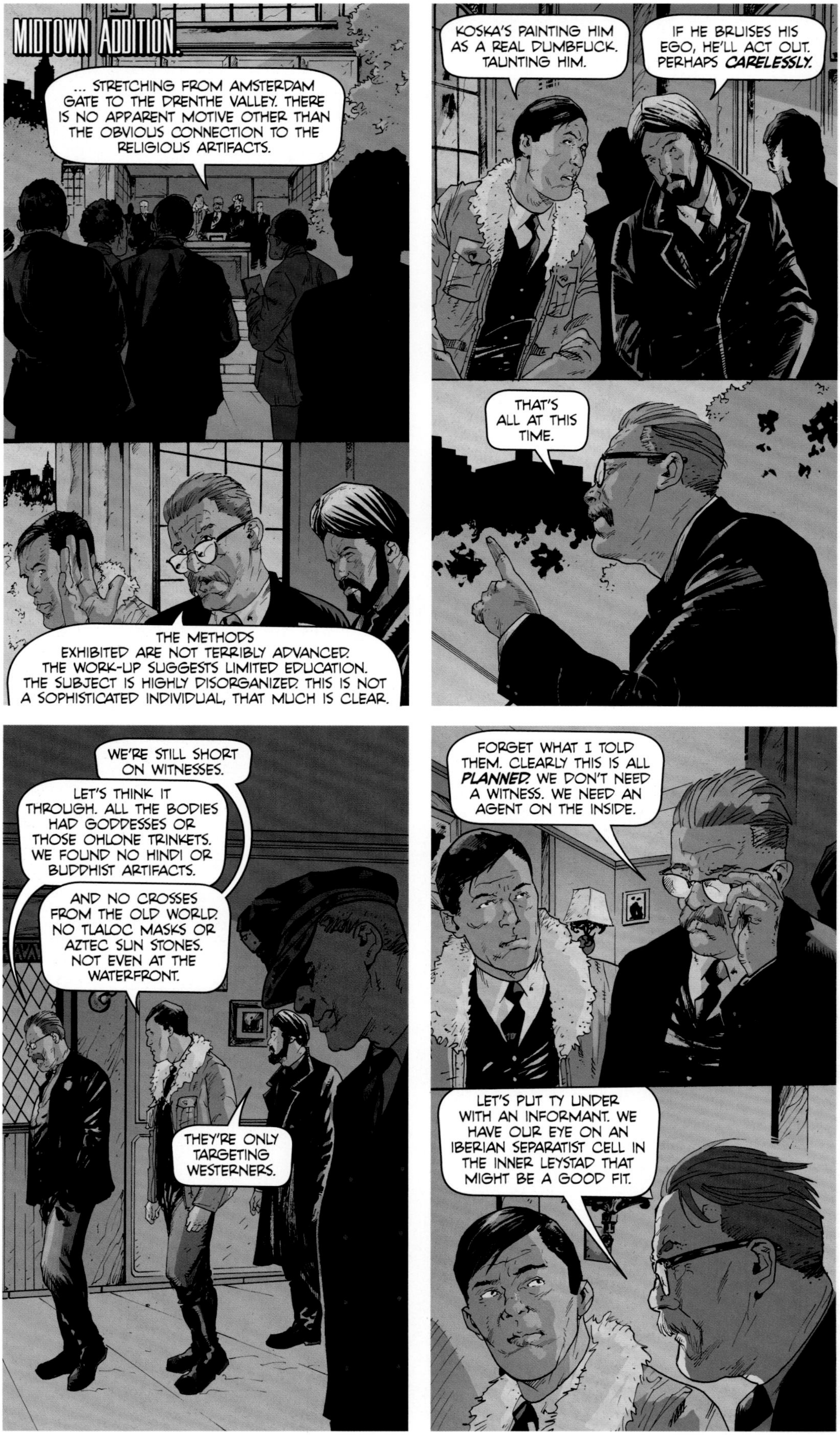
MIDTOWN ADDITION.
... STRETCHING FROM AMSTERDAM GATE TO THE DRENTHE VALLEY. THERE IS NO APPARENT MOTIVE OTHER THAN THE OBVIOUS CONNECTION TO THE RELIGIOUS ARTIFACTS.
THE METHODS EXHIBITED ARE NOT TERRIBLY ADVANCED. THE WORK-UP SUGGESTS LIMITED EDUCATION. THE SUBJECT IS HIGHLY DISORGANIZED. THIS IS NOT A SOPHISTICATED INDIVIDUAL, THAT MUCH IS CLEAR.
KOSKA'S PAINTING HIM AS A REAL DUMBFUCK. TAUNTING HIM.
IF HE BRUISES HIS EGO, HE'LL ACT OUT. PERHAPS CARELESSLY.
THAT'S ALL AT THIS TIME.
WE'RE STILL SHORT ON WITNESSES.
LET'S THINK IT THROUGH. ALL THE BODIES HAD GODDESSES OR THOSE OHLONE TRINKETS. WE FOUND NO HINDI OR BUDDHIST ARTIFACTS.
AND NO CROSSES FROM THE OLD WORLD. NO TLALOC MASKS OR AZTEC SUN STONES. NOT EVEN AT THE WATERFRONT.
THEY'RE ONLY TARGETING WESTERNERS.
FORGET WHAT I TOLD THEM. CLEARLY THIS IS ALL PLANNED. WE DON'T NEED A WITNESS. WE NEED AN AGENT ON THE INSIDE.
LET'S PUT TY UNDER WITH AN INFORMANT. WE HAVE OUR EYE ON AN IBERIAN SEPARATIST CELL IN THE INNER LEYSTAD THAT MIGHT BE A GOOD FIT.

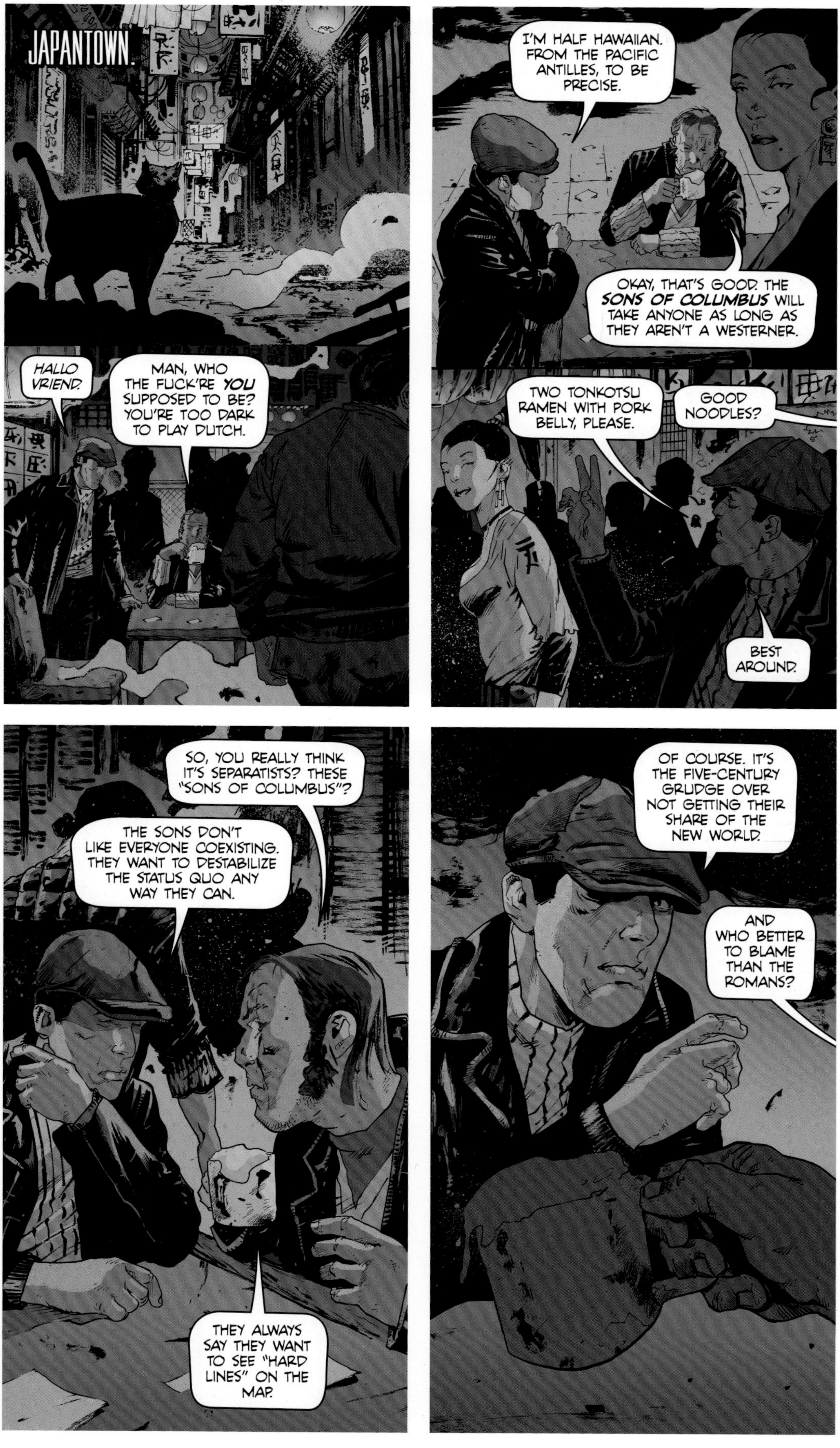
JAPANTOWN.
I'M HALF HAWAIIAN. FROM THE PACIFIC ANTILLES, TO BE PRECISE.
OKAY, THAT'S GOOD. THE SONS OF COLUMBUS WILL TAKE ANYONE AS LONG AS THEY AREN'T A WESTERNER.
HALLO VRIEND.
MAN, WHO THE FUCK'RE YOU SUPPOSED TO BE? YOU'RE TOO DARK TO PLAY DUTCH.
TWO TONKOTSU RAMEN WITH PORK BELLY, PLEASE.
GOOD NOODLES?
BEST AROUND.
SO, YOU REALLY THINK IT'S SEPARATISTS? THESE "SONS OF COLUMBUS"?
THE SONS DON'T LIKE EVERYONE COEXISTING. THEY WANT TO DESTABILIZE THE STATUS QUO ANY WAY THEY CAN.
THEY ALWAYS SAY THEY WANT TO SEE "HARD LINES" ON THE MAP.
OF COURSE. IT'S THE FIVE-CENTURY GRUDGE OVER NOT GETTING THEIR SHARE OF THE NEW WORLD.
AND WHO BETTER TO BLAME THAN THE ROMANS?

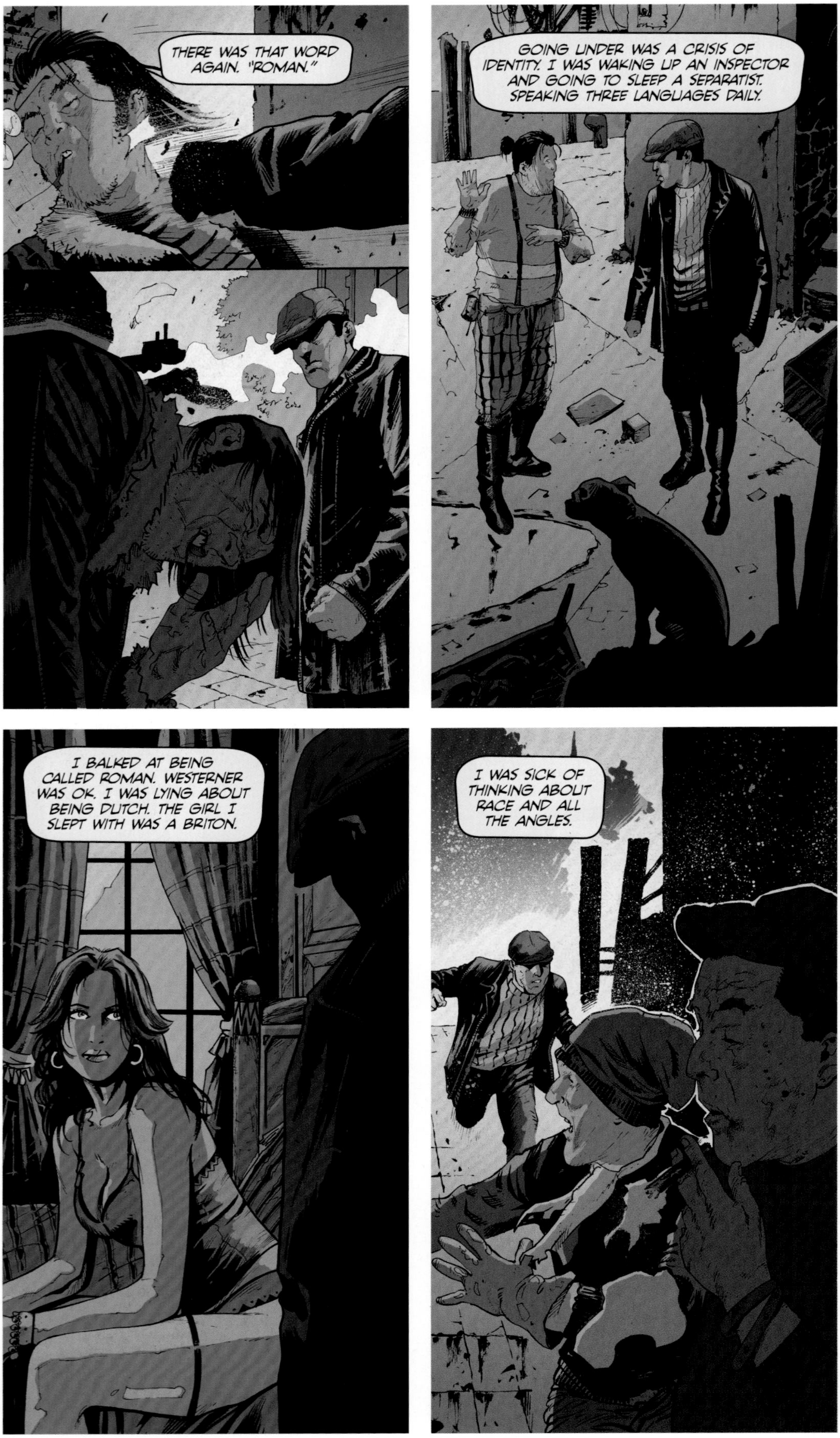
THERE WAS THAT WORD AGAIN. "ROMAN."
GOING UNDER WAS A CRISIS OF IDENTITY. I WAS WAKING UP AN INSPECTOR AND GOING TO SLEEP A SEPARATIST. SPEAKING THREE LANGUAGES DAILY.
I BALKED AT BEING CALLED ROMAN. WESTERNER WAS OK. I WAS LYING ABOUT BEING DUTCH. THE GIRL I SLEPT WITH WAS A BRITON.
I WAS SICK OF THINKING ABOUT RACE AND ALL THE ANGLES.

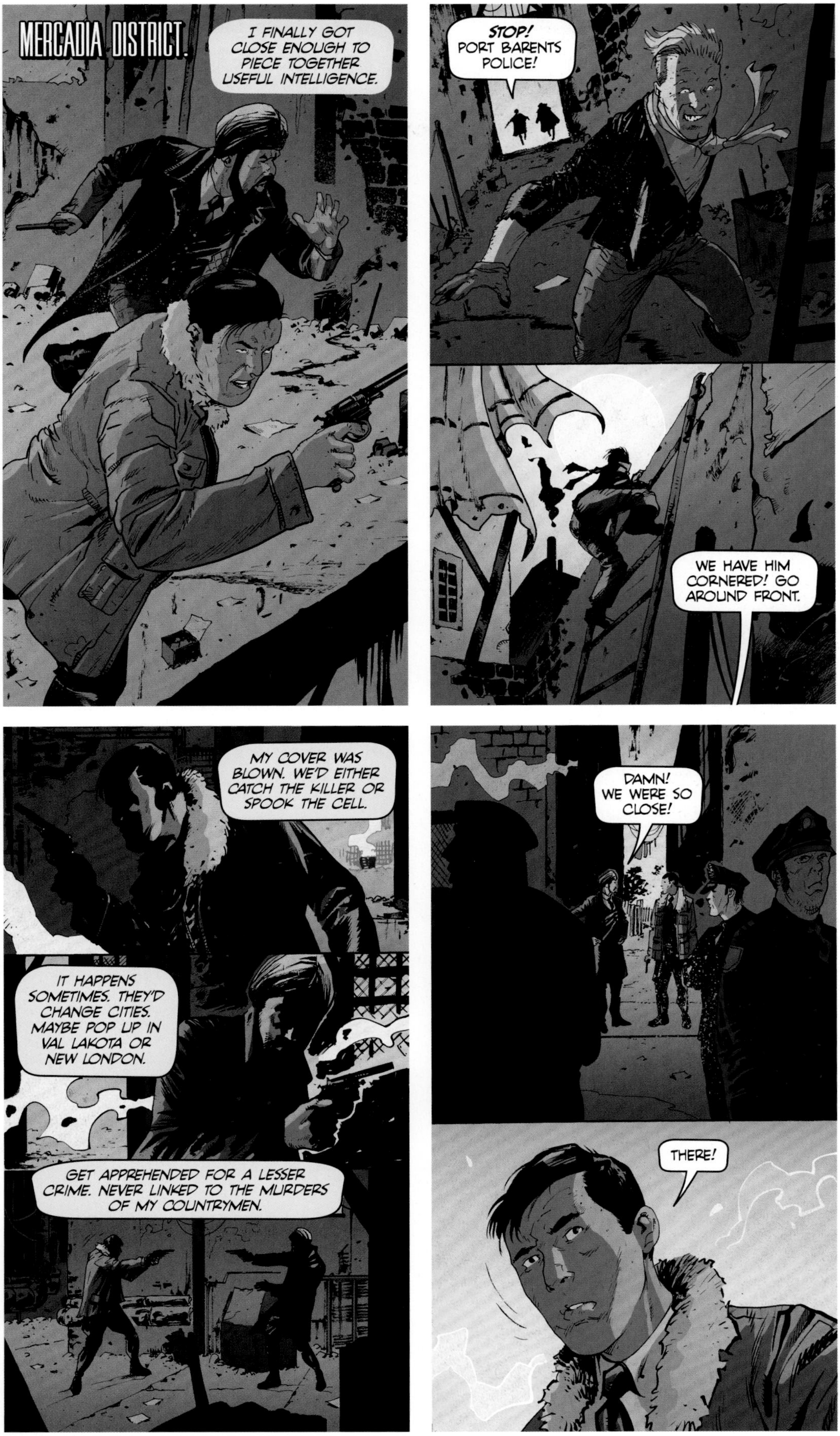
MERCADIA DISTRICT.
I FINALLY GOT CLOSE ENOUGH TO PIECE TOGETHER USEFUL INTELLIGENCE.
STOP! PORT BARENTS POLICE!
WE HAVE HIM CORNERED! GO AROUND FRONT.
MY COVER WAS BLOWN. WE'D EITHER CATCH THE KILLER OR SPOOK THE CELL.
IT HAPPENS SOMETIMES. THEY'D CHANGE CITIES. MAYBE POP UP IN VAL LAKOTA OR NEW LONDON.
GET APPREHENDED FOR A LESSER CRIME. NEVER LINKED TO THE MURDERS OF MY COUNTRYMEN.
DAMN! WE WERE SO CLOSE!
THERE!

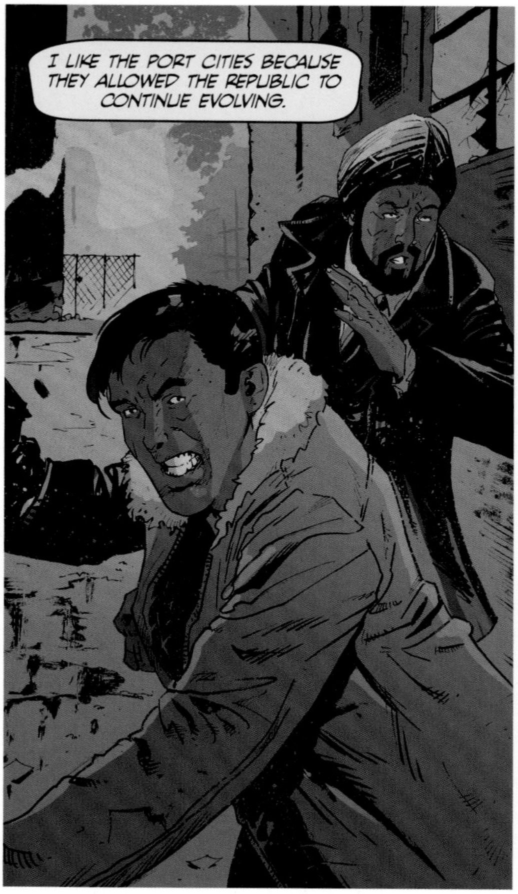
I LIKE THE PORT CITIES BECAUSE THEY ALLOWED THE REPUBLIC TO CONTINUE EVOLVING.

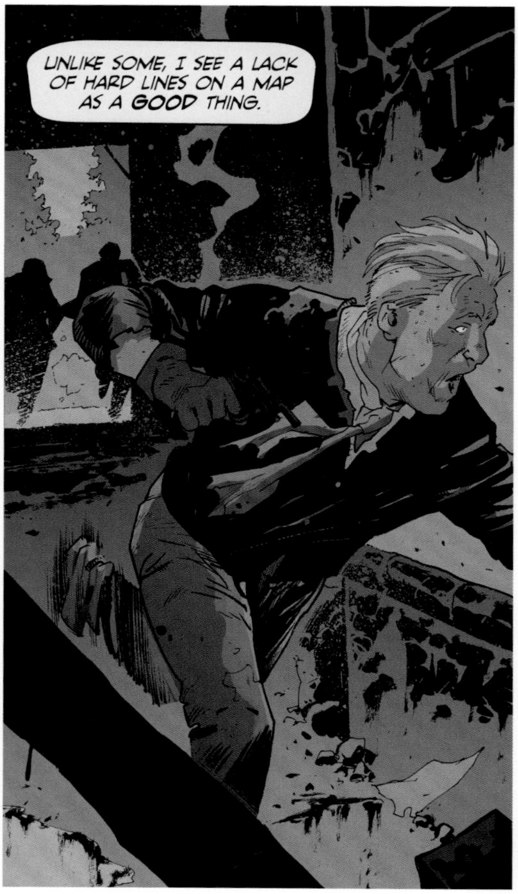
UNLIKE SOME, I SEE A LACK OF HARD LINES ON A MAP AS A GOOD THING.

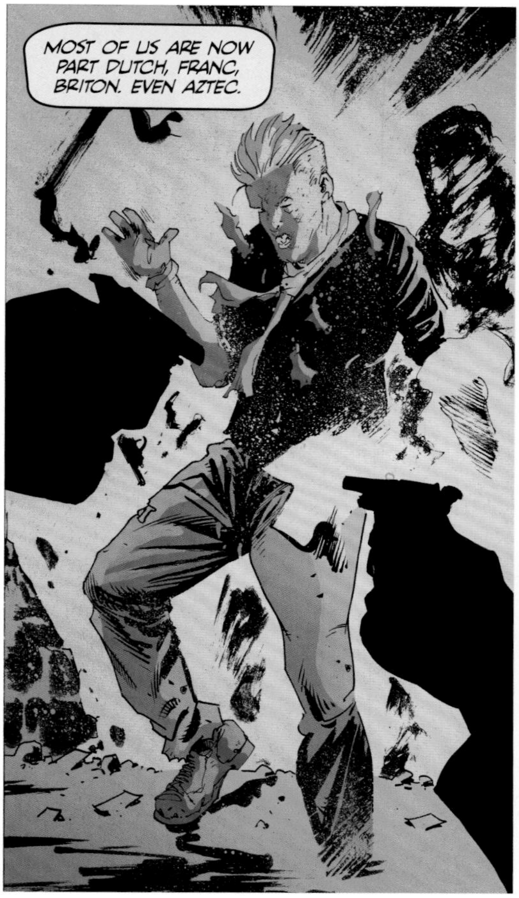
MOST OF US ARE NOW PART DUTCH, FRANC, BRITON. EVEN AZTEC.

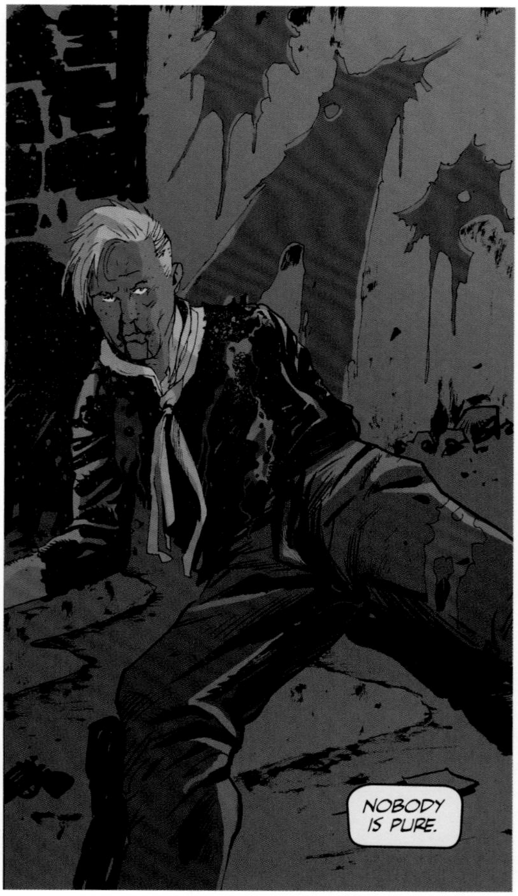
NOBODY IS PURE.

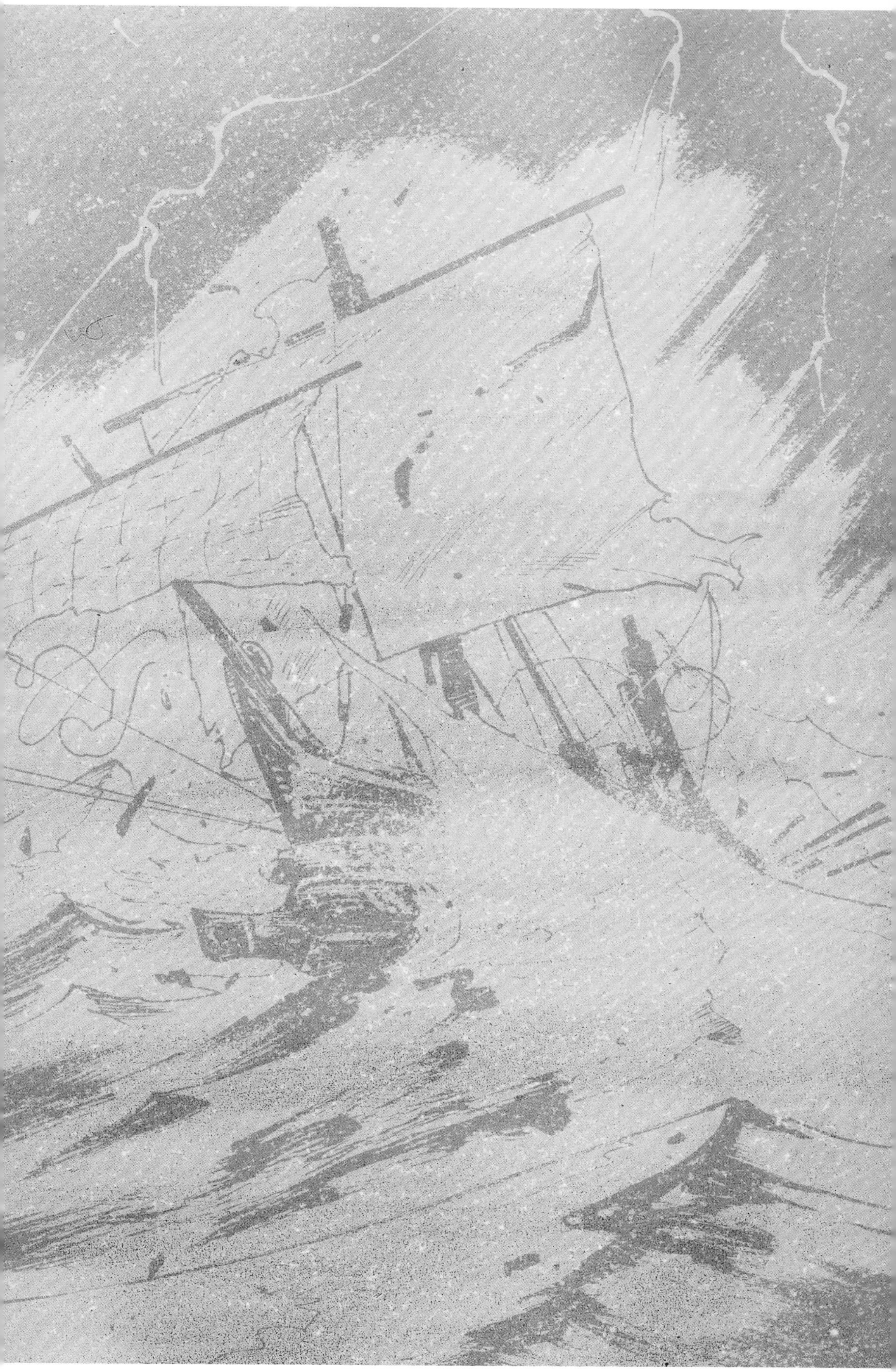

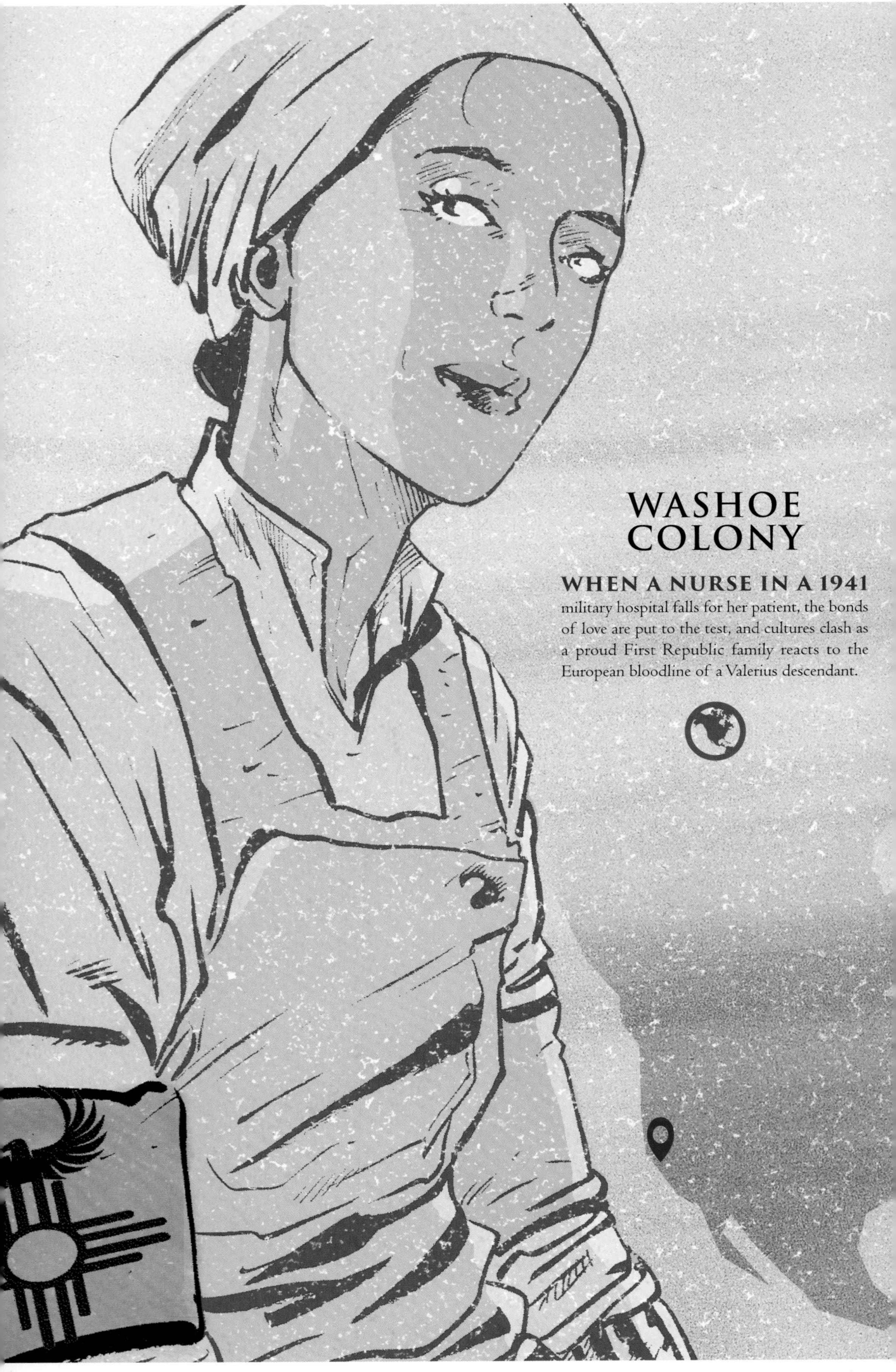

WASHOE COLONY

WHEN A NURSE IN A 1941 military hospital falls for her patient, the bonds of love are put to the test, and cultures clash as a proud First Republic family reacts to the European bloodline of a Valerius descendant.

1941.
WASHOE COLONY (LAKE TAHOE, CALIFORNIA).
THE JOURNAL OF DENA BESHKO.

The moment I laid eyes on Lonan, I knew I couldn't live without him. He pulled at something inside me, and I'd do anything to be with him.

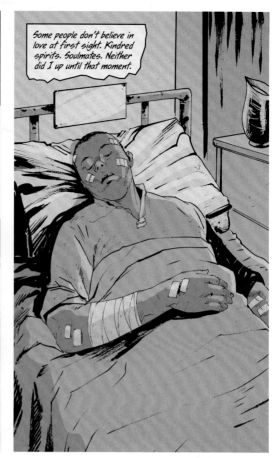

Some people don't believe in love at first sight. Kindred spirits. Soulmates. Neither did I up until that moment.

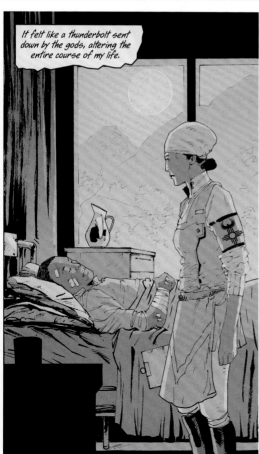

It felt like a thunderbolt sent down by the gods, altering the entire course of my life.

I knew things would never be the same.

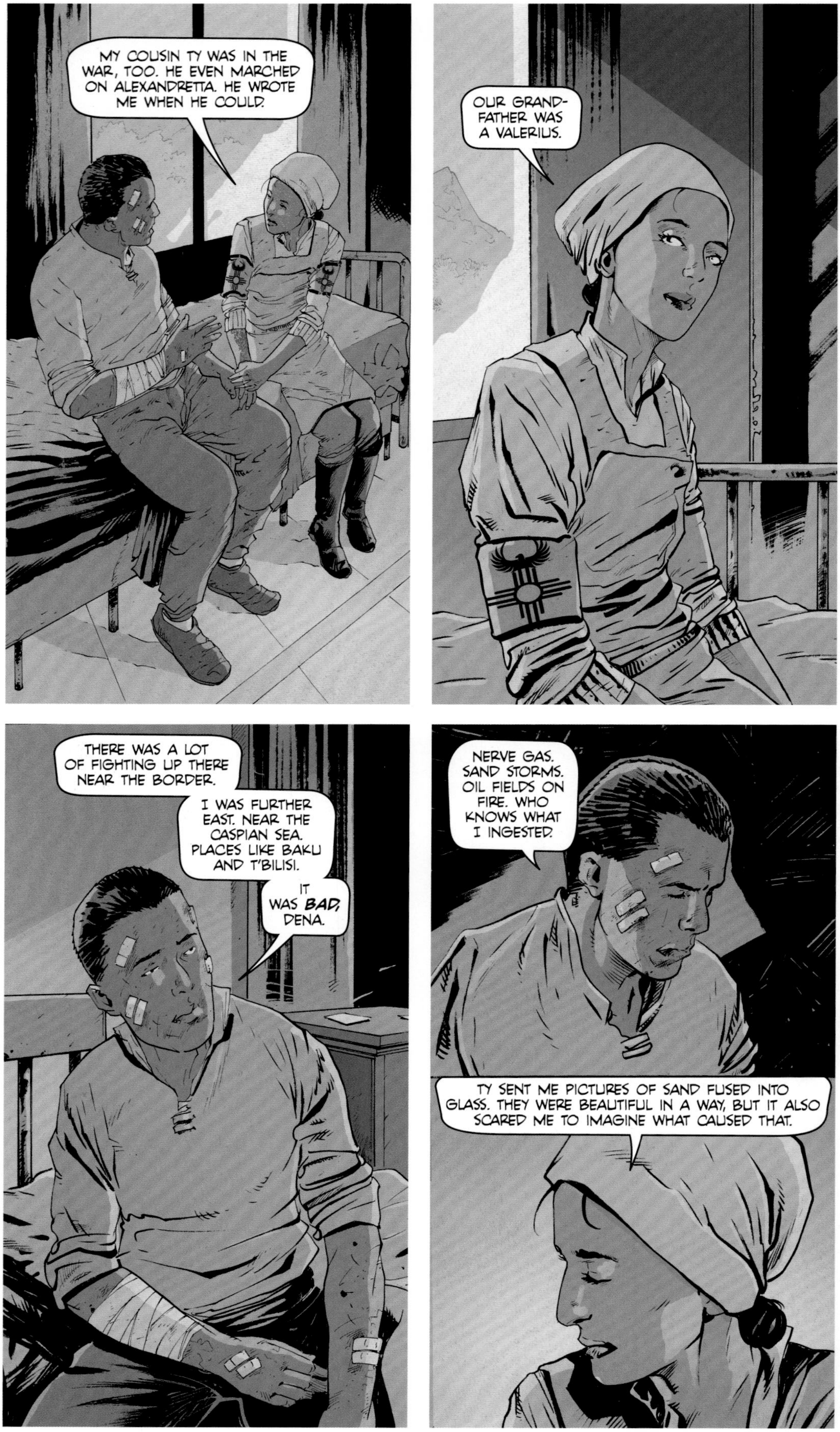
MY COUSIN TY WAS IN THE WAR, TOO. HE EVEN MARCHED ON ALEXANDRETTA. HE WROTE ME WHEN HE COULD.
OUR GRAND-FATHER WAS A VALERIUS.
THERE WAS A LOT OF FIGHTING UP THERE NEAR THE BORDER.
I WAS FURTHER EAST. NEAR THE CASPIAN SEA. PLACES LIKE BAKU AND T'BILISI.
IT WAS BAD, DENA.
NERVE GAS. SAND STORMS. OIL FIELDS ON FIRE. WHO KNOWS WHAT I INGESTED.
TY SENT ME PICTURES OF SAND FUSED INTO GLASS. THEY WERE BEAUTIFUL IN A WAY, BUT IT ALSO SCARED ME TO IMAGINE WHAT CAUSED THAT.

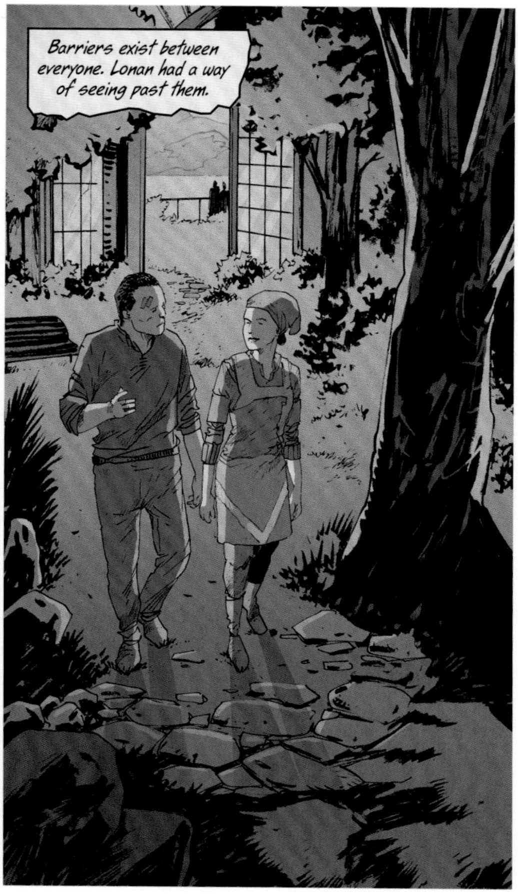
Barriers exist between everyone. Lonan had a way of seeing past them.

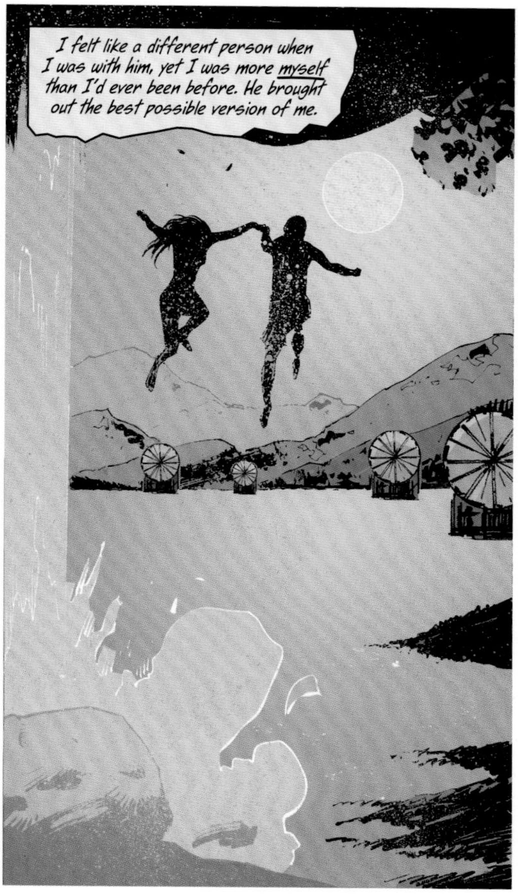
I felt like a different person when I was with him, yet I was more myself than I'd ever been before. He brought out the best possible version of me.

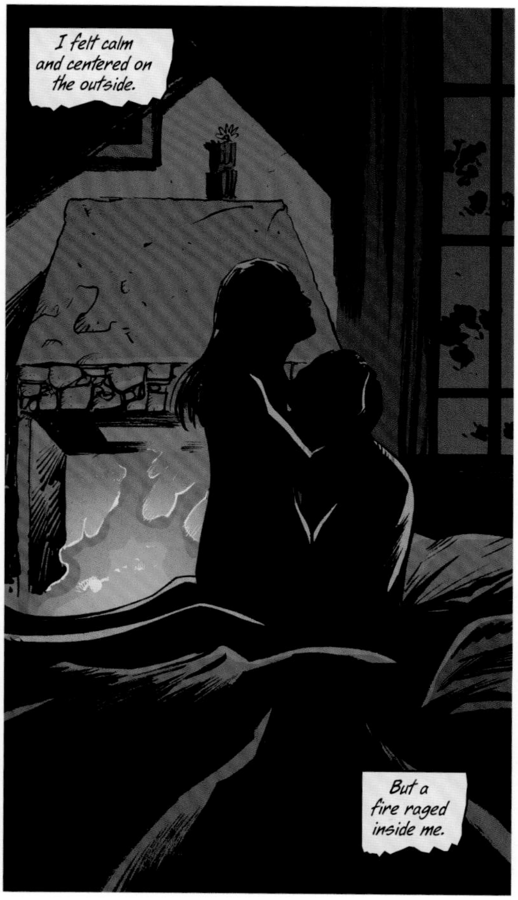
I felt calm and centered on the outside.
But a fire raged inside me.

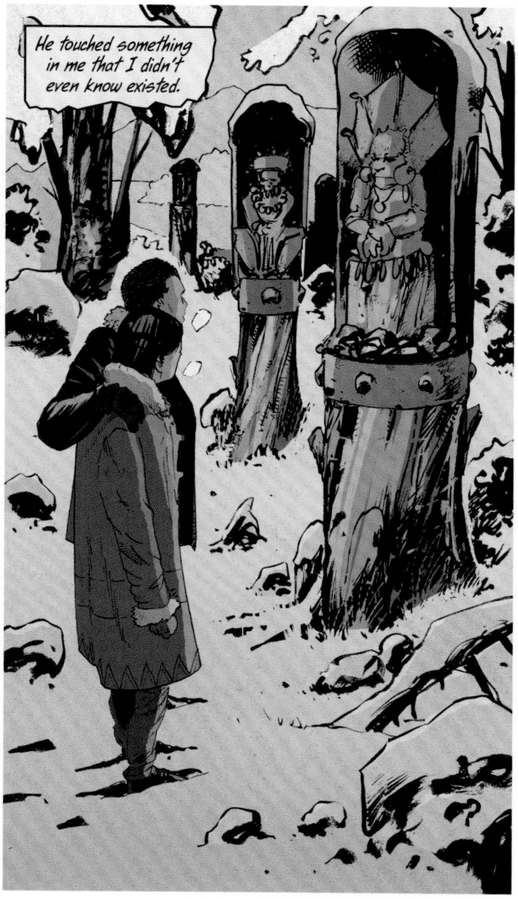
He touched something in me that I didn't even know existed.

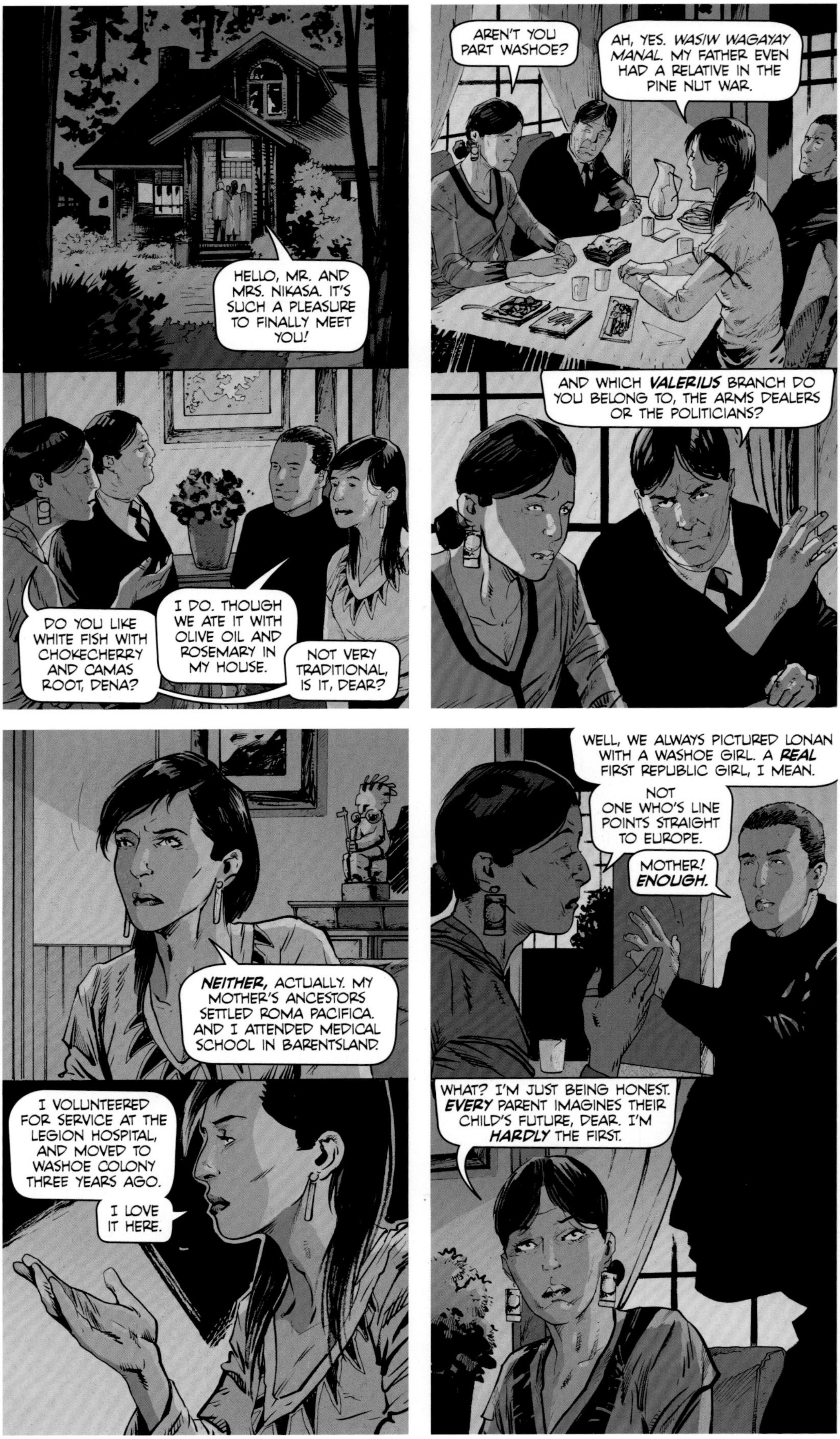
HELLO, MR. AND MRS. NIKASA. IT'S SUCH A PLEASURE TO FINALLY MEET YOU!
AREN'T YOU PART WASHOE?
AH, YES. WASIW WAGAYAY MANAL. MY FATHER EVEN HAD A RELATIVE IN THE PINE NUT WAR.
DO YOU LIKE WHITE FISH WITH CHOKECHERRY AND CAMAS ROOT, DENA?
I DO. THOUGH WE ATE IT WITH OLIVE OIL AND ROSEMARY IN MY HOUSE.
NOT VERY TRADITIONAL, IS IT, DEAR?
AND WHICH VALERIUS BRANCH DO YOU BELONG TO, THE ARMS DEALERS OR THE POLITICIANS?
NEITHER, ACTUALLY. MY MOTHER'S ANCESTORS SETTLED ROMA PACIFICA. AND I ATTENDED MEDICAL SCHOOL IN BARENTSLAND.
I VOLUNTEERED FOR SERVICE AT THE LEGION HOSPITAL, AND MOVED TO WASHOE COLONY THREE YEARS AGO.
I LOVE IT HERE.
WELL, WE ALWAYS PICTURED LONAN WITH A WASHOE GIRL. A REAL FIRST REPUBLIC GIRL, I MEAN.
NOT ONE WHO'S LINE POINTS STRAIGHT TO EUROPE.
MOTHER! ENOUGH.
WHAT? I'M JUST BEING HONEST. EVERY PARENT IMAGINES THEIR CHILD'S FUTURE, DEAR. I'M HARDLY THE FIRST.

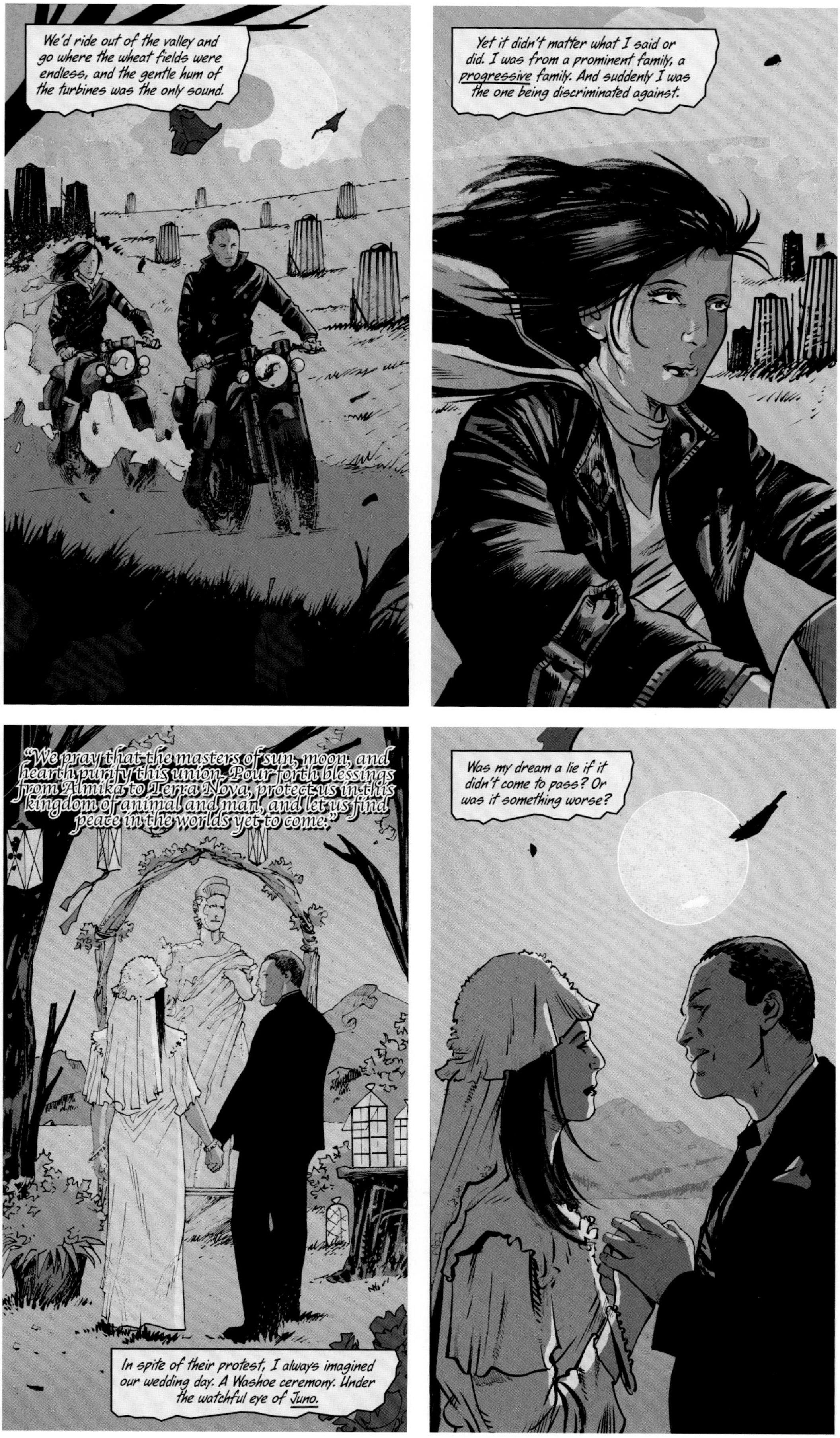
We'd ride out of the valley and go where the wheat fields were endless, and the gentle hum of the turbines was the only sound.
Yet it didn't matter what I said or did. I was from a prominent family, a progressive family. And suddenly I was the one being discriminated against.
"We pray that the masters of sun, moon, and hearth purify this union. Pour forth blessings from Almika to Terra Nova, protect us in this kingdom of animal and man, and let us find peace in the worlds yet to come."
In spite of their protest, I always imagined our wedding day. A Washoe ceremony. Under the watchful eye of Juno.
Was my dream a lie if it didn't come to pass? Or was it something worse?

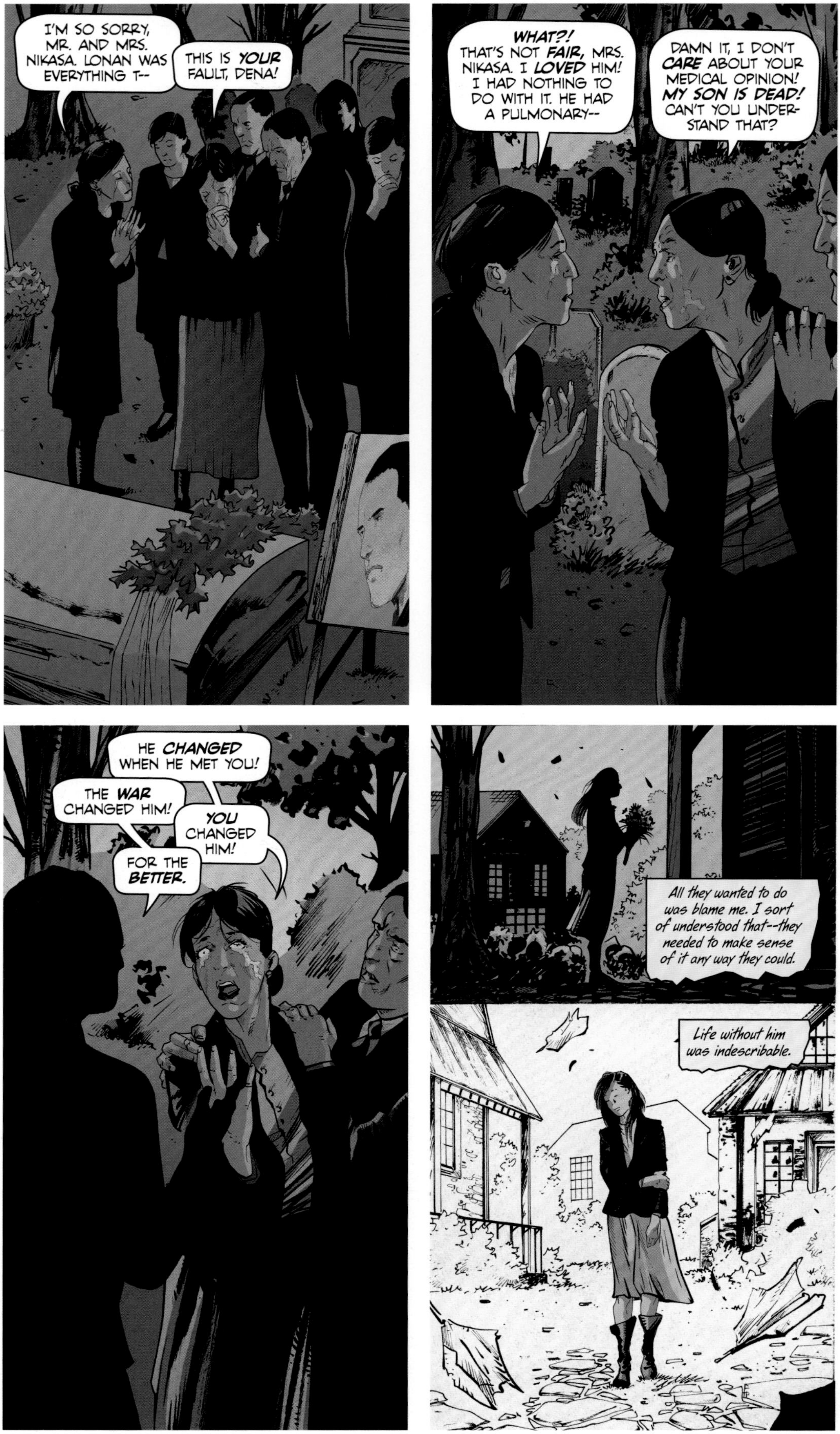
I'M SO SORRY, MR. AND MRS. NIKASA. LONAN WAS EVERYTHING T--
THIS IS YOUR FAULT, DENA!
WHAT?! THAT'S NOT FAIR, MRS. NIKASA. I LOVED HIM! I HAD NOTHING TO DO WITH IT. HE HAD A PULMONARY--
DAMN IT, I DON'T CARE ABOUT YOUR MEDICAL OPINION! MY SON IS DEAD! CAN'T YOU UNDERSTAND THAT?
HE CHANGED WHEN HE MET YOU!
THE WAR CHANGED HIM!
YOU CHANGED HIM!
FOR THE BETTER.
All they wanted to do was blame me. I sort of understood that--they needed to make sense of it any way they could.
Life without him was indescribable.

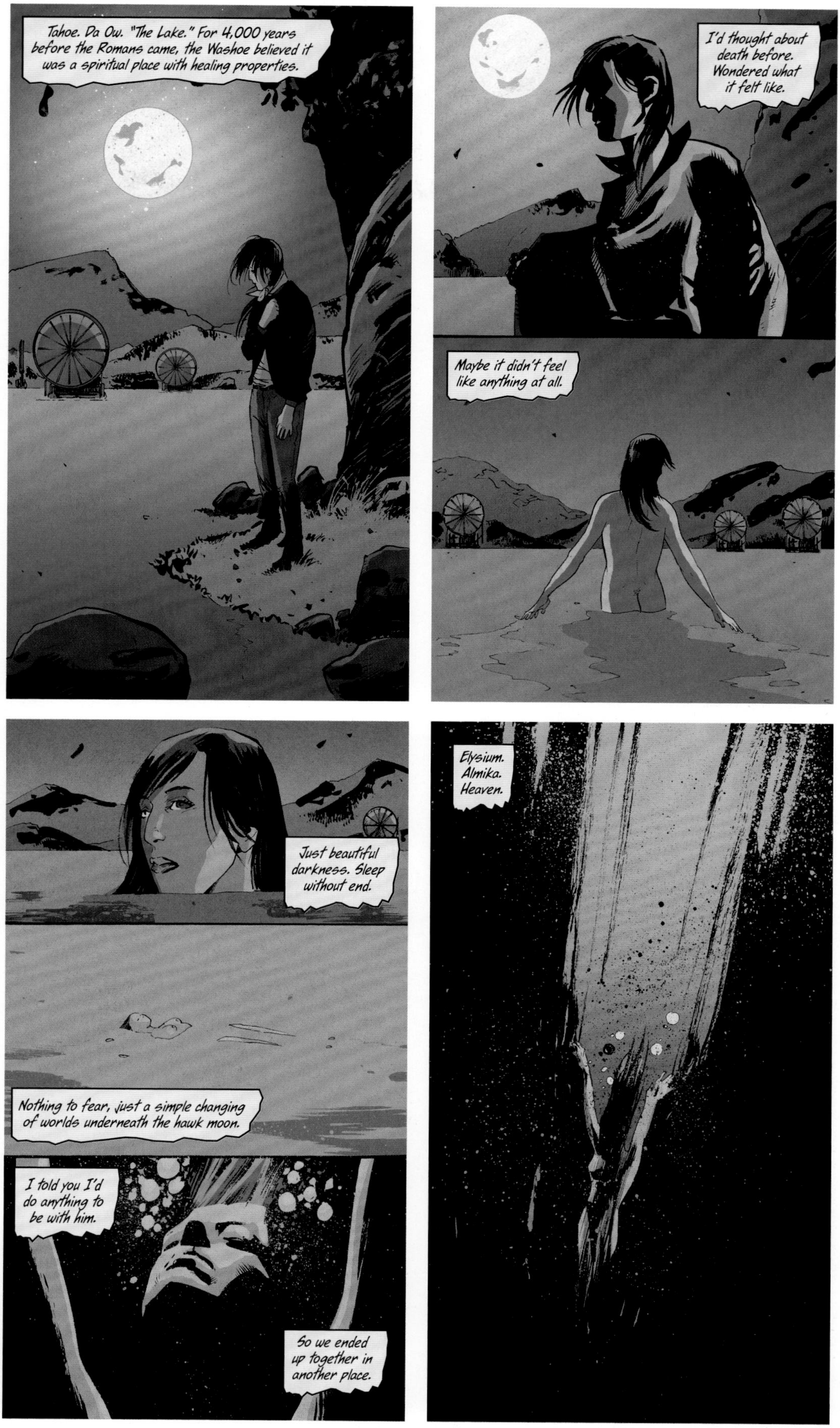
Tahoe. Da Ow. "The Lake." For 4,000 years before the Romans came, the Washoe believed it was a spiritual place with healing properties.
I'd thought about death before. Wondered what it felt like.
Maybe it didn't feel like anything at all.
Just beautiful darkness. Sleep without end.
Nothing to fear, just a simple changing of worlds underneath the hawk moon.
I told you I'd do anything to be with him.
So we ended up together in another place.
Elysium. Almika. Heaven.

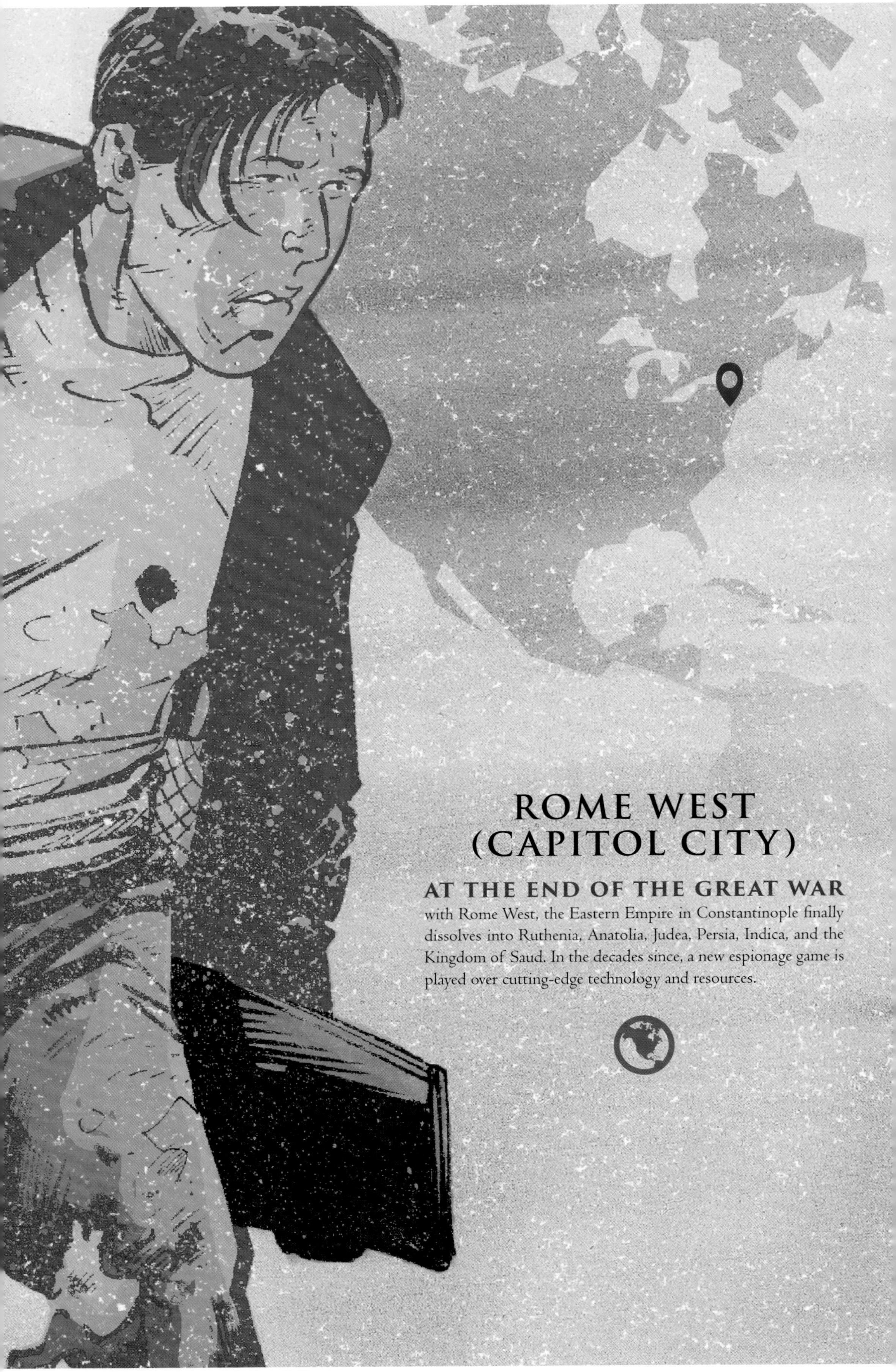

ROME WEST (CAPITOL CITY)

AT THE END OF THE GREAT WAR

with Rome West, the Eastern Empire in Constantinople finally dissolves into Ruthenia, Anatolia, Judea, Persia, Indica, and the Kingdom of Saud. In the decades since, a new espionage game is played over cutting-edge technology and resources.

1979.
ROME WEST, CAPITOL CITY
(NEW YORK, NEW YORK).
ROMAN SECURITY BUREAU (RSB)
OPERATIONS CENTER.

THE SAUD INFORMANT GAVE UP AGENT VALERIUS, MA'AM.

MOST PEOPLE START WITH "GOOD MORNING," MANDY.

THE MISSION CLOCK IS ALSO CODED RED. HE'S BEEN HIT. SMALL ARMS. *GOOD MORNING.*

HE DID MANAGE TO PULSE THE MAGSAT WITH HIS LAST LOCATION ON THE RUTHENIAN SIDE OF THE BORDER.

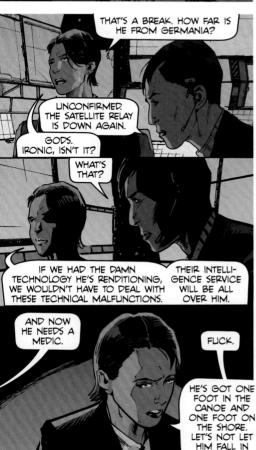

THAT'S A BREAK. HOW FAR IS HE FROM GERMANIA?

UNCONFIRMED. THE SATELLITE RELAY IS DOWN AGAIN.

GODS. IRONIC, ISN'T IT?

WHAT'S THAT?

IF WE HAD THE DAMN TECHNOLOGY HE'S RENDITIONING, WE WOULDN'T HAVE TO DEAL WITH THESE TECHNICAL MALFUNCTIONS.

THEIR INTELLIGENCE SERVICE WILL BE ALL OVER HIM.

AND NOW HE NEEDS A MEDIC.

FUCK.

HE'S GOT ONE FOOT IN THE CANOE AND ONE FOOT ON THE SHORE. LET'S NOT LET HIM FALL IN THE RIVER.

OK, I WANT DIRECT COMMUNICATION. GET ME IAN WHITAKER ON A SECURE LINE. AND FIND SENATOR AVENTINE.

IN THAT ORDER.

RUTHENIA.
OPERATION LAZY TERRORIST.
MISSION STATUS: RUNNING.

MY MOTHER WILL BE SAD WHEN SHE HEARS THAT I WAS KILLED IN PRAGUE OVER THE WIRELESS.

BUT SHE'LL HAVE A *PANIC ATTACK* WHEN SHE REALIZES I NEVER REALLY WORKED FOR THE AGRICULTURE BUREAU.

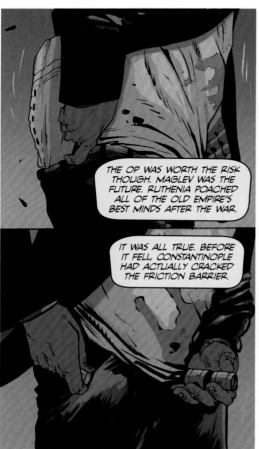

THE OP WAS WORTH THE RISK THOUGH. MAGLEV WAS THE FUTURE. RUTHENIA POACHED ALL OF THE OLD EMPIRE'S BEST MINDS AFTER THE WAR.

IT WAS ALL TRUE. BEFORE IT FELL, CONSTANTINOPLE HAD ACTUALLY CRACKED THE FRICTION BARRIER.

UNLIKE THE EAST, ROME WEST DIDN'T RELY HEAVILY ON CRUDE.

WE STARTED WITH HYDRO AND WIND FARMS. THEY WERE MUCH CLEANER.

NOW WE WERE MOSTLY SOLAR AND ELECTRO-MAGNETIC.

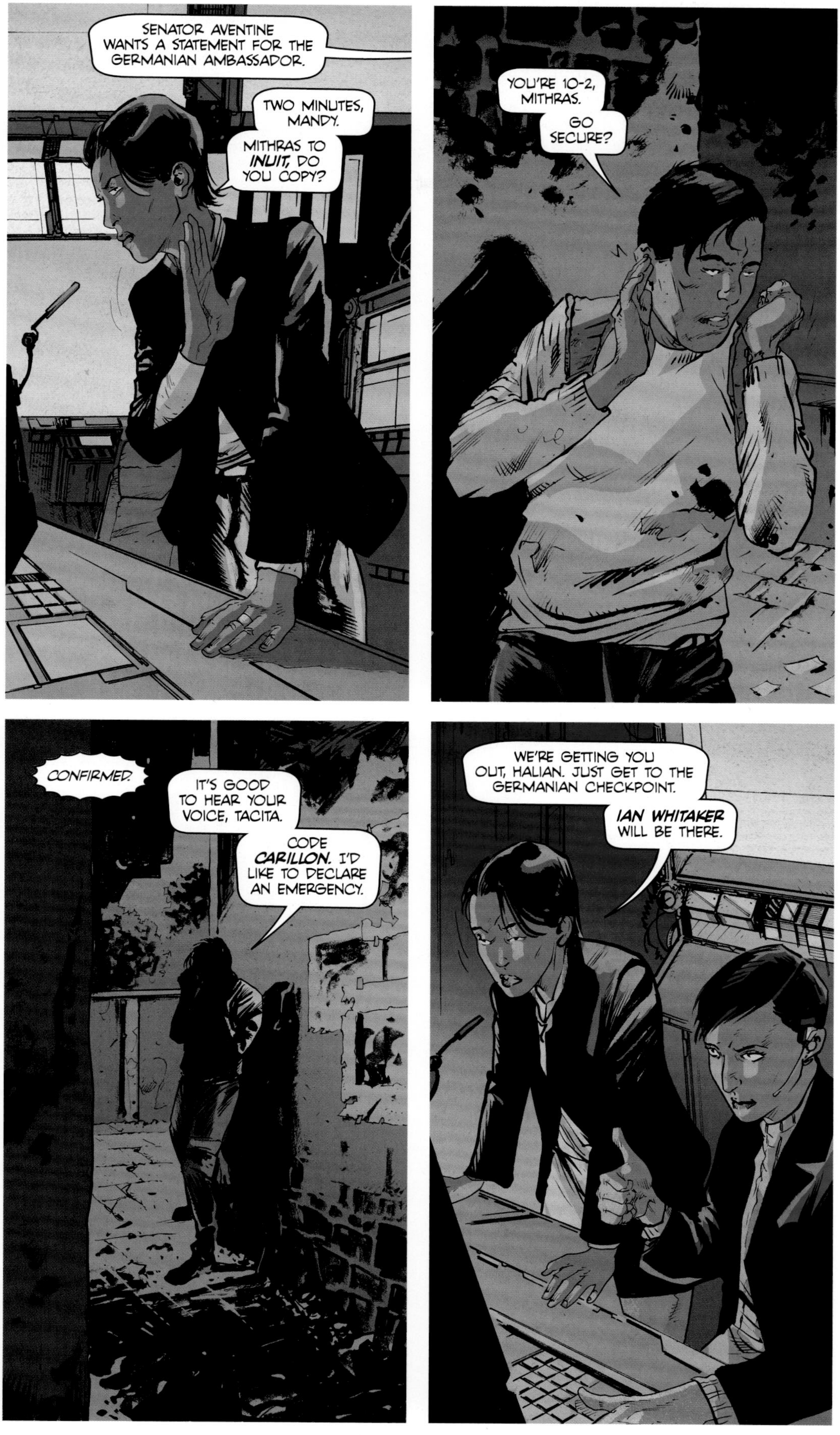
SENATOR AVENTINE WANTS A STATEMENT FOR THE GERMANIAN AMBASSADOR.
TWO MINUTES, MANDY.
MITHRAS TO *INUIT,* DO YOU COPY?
YOU'RE 10-2, MITHRAS.
GO SECURE?
CONFIRMED.
IT'S GOOD TO HEAR YOUR VOICE, TACITA.
CODE *CARILLON.* I'D LIKE TO DECLARE AN EMERGENCY.
WE'RE GETTING YOU OUT, HALIAN. JUST GET TO THE GERMANIAN CHECKPOINT.
IAN WHITAKER WILL BE THERE.

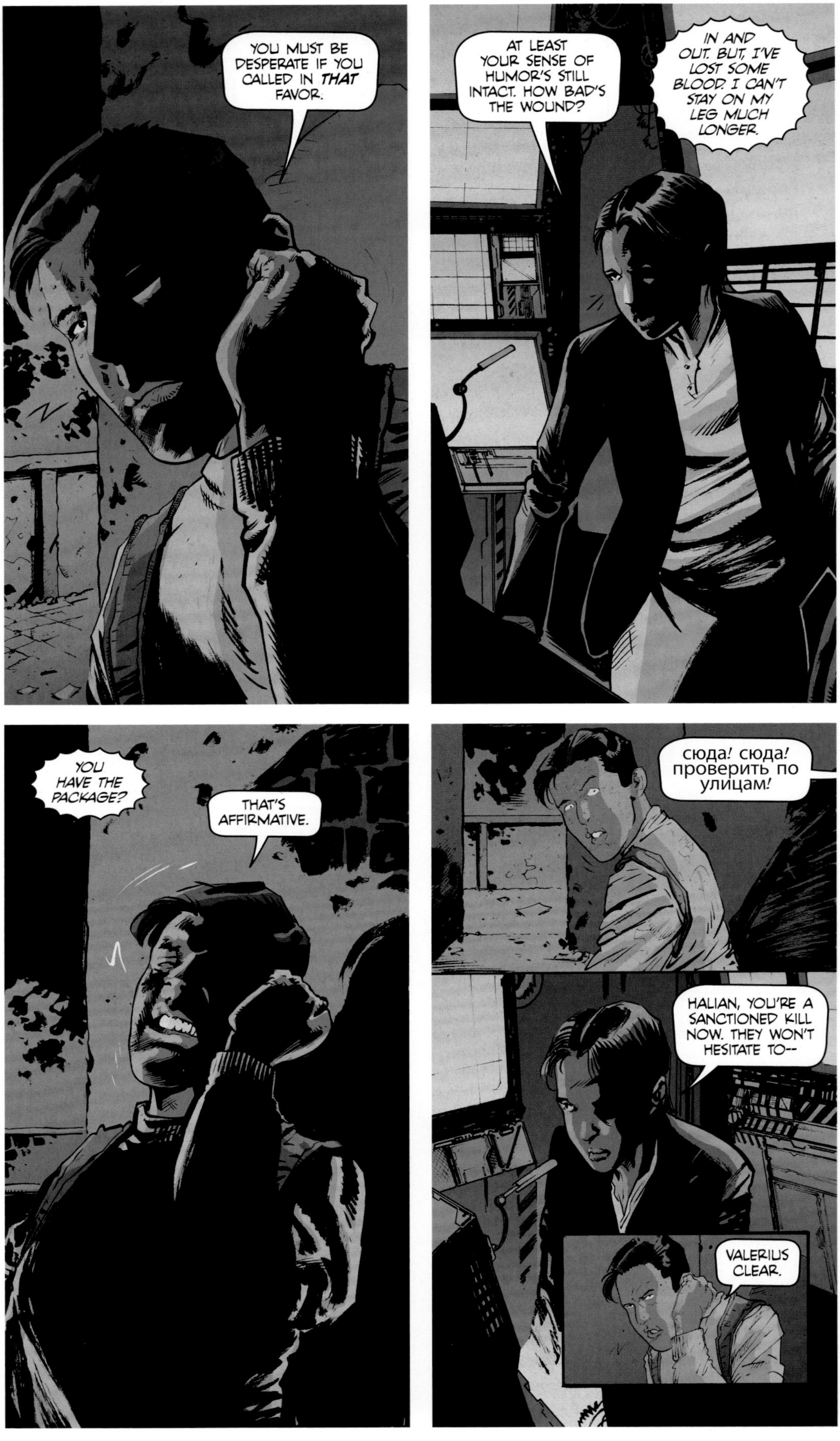
YOU MUST BE DESPERATE IF YOU CALLED IN *THAT* FAVOR.
AT LEAST YOUR SENSE OF HUMOR'S STILL INTACT. HOW BAD'S THE WOUND?
IN AND OUT. BUT, I'VE LOST SOME BLOOD. I CAN'T STAY ON MY LEG MUCH LONGER.
YOU HAVE THE PACKAGE?
THAT'S AFFIRMATIVE.
сюда! сюда! проверить по улицам!
HALIAN, YOU'RE A SANCTIONED KILL NOW. THEY WON'T HESITATE TO--
VALERIUS CLEAR.

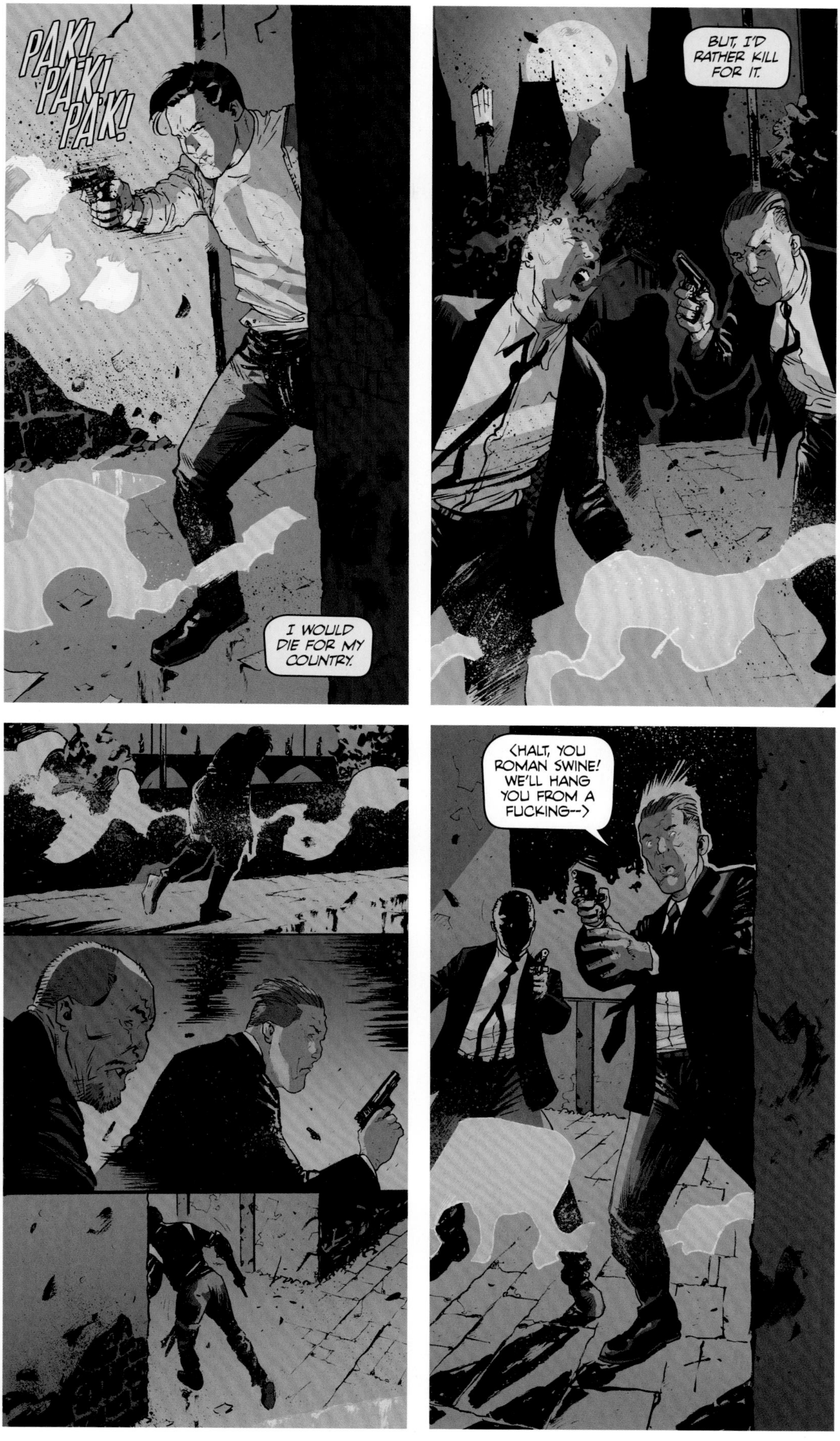
PAK! PAK! PAK!
I WOULD DIE FOR MY COUNTRY.
BUT, I'D RATHER KILL FOR IT.
<HALT, YOU ROMAN SWINE! WE'LL HANG YOU FROM A FUCKING-->

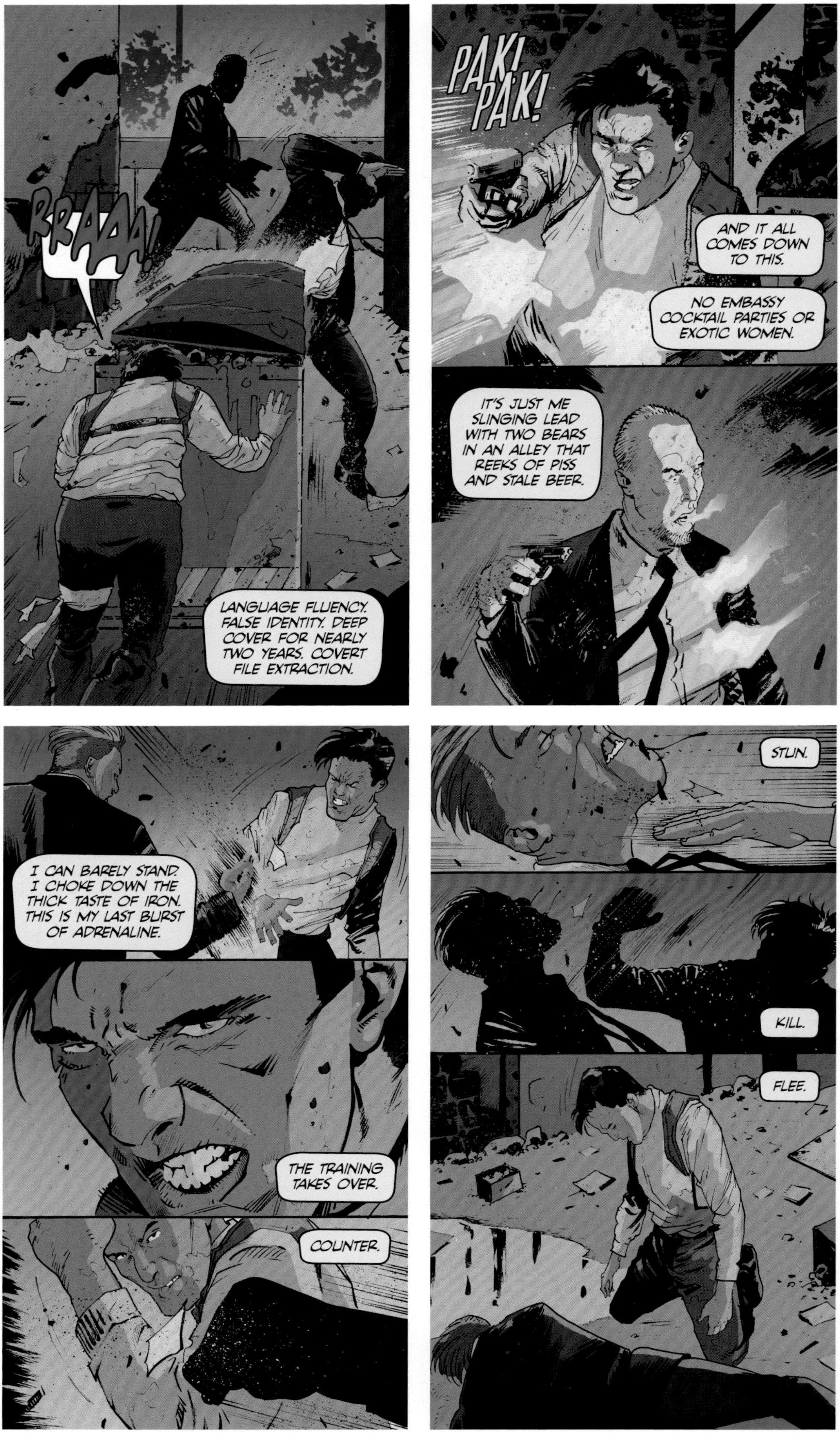
RRAAA!
LANGUAGE FLUENCY. FALSE IDENTITY. DEEP COVER FOR NEARLY TWO YEARS. COVERT FILE EXTRACTION.
PAK! PAK!
AND IT ALL COMES DOWN TO THIS.
NO EMBASSY COCKTAIL PARTIES OR EXOTIC WOMEN.
IT'S JUST ME SLINGING LEAD WITH TWO BEARS IN AN ALLEY THAT REEKS OF PISS AND STALE BEER.
I CAN BARELY STAND. I CHOKE DOWN THE THICK TASTE OF IRON. THIS IS MY LAST BURST OF ADRENALINE.
THE TRAINING TAKES OVER.
COUNTER.
STUN.
KILL.
FLEE.

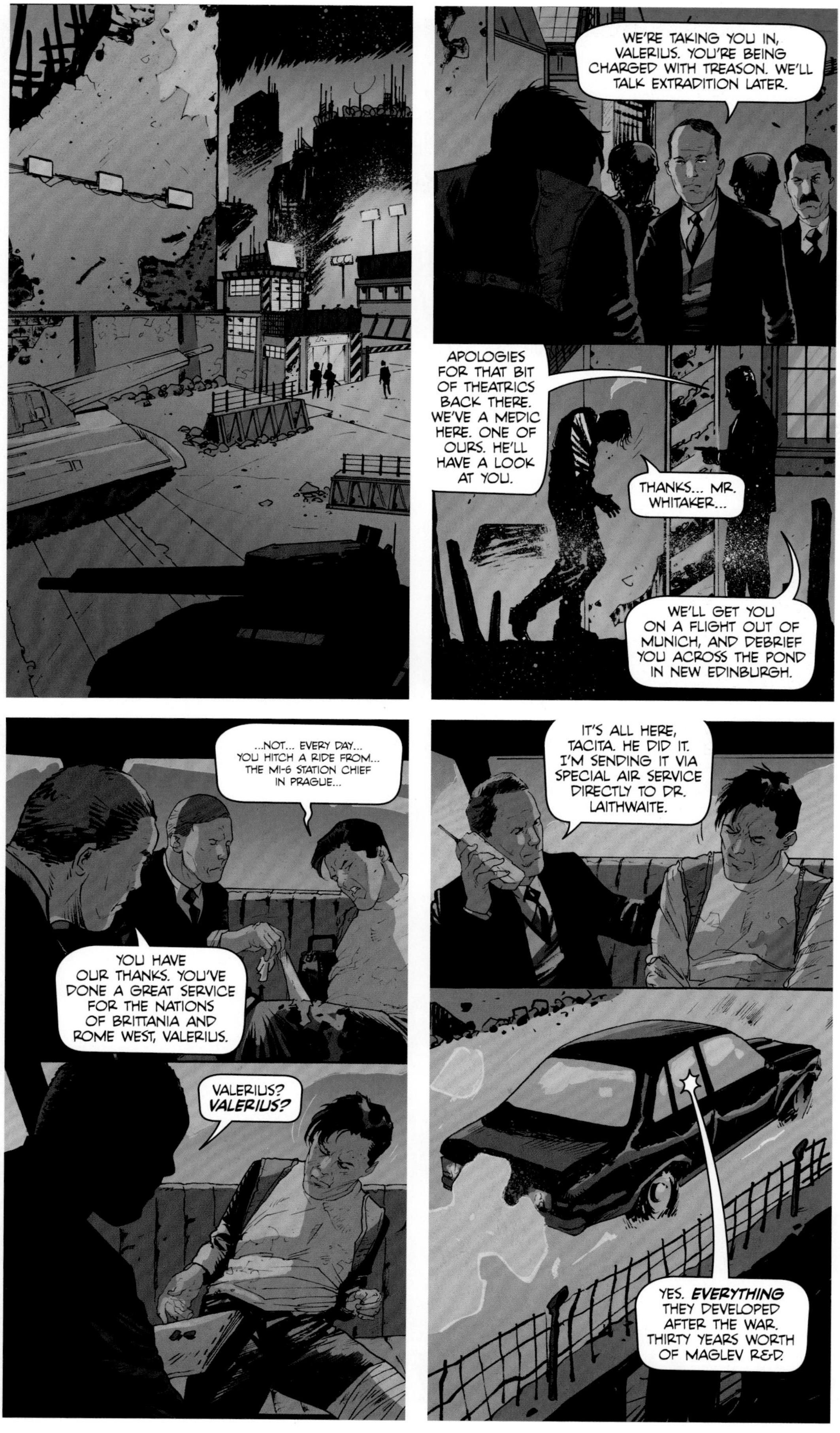
WE'RE TAKING YOU IN, VALERIUS. YOU'RE BEING CHARGED WITH TREASON. WE'LL TALK EXTRADITION LATER.
APOLOGIES FOR THAT BIT OF THEATRICS BACK THERE. WE'VE A MEDIC HERE. ONE OF OURS. HE'LL HAVE A LOOK AT YOU.
THANKS... MR. WHITAKER...
WE'LL GET YOU ON A FLIGHT OUT OF MUNICH, AND DEBRIEF YOU ACROSS THE POND IN NEW EDINBURGH.
...NOT... EVERY DAY... YOU HITCH A RIDE FROM... THE MI-6 STATION CHIEF IN PRAGUE...
YOU HAVE OUR THANKS. YOU'VE DONE A GREAT SERVICE FOR THE NATIONS OF BRITTANIA AND ROME WEST, VALERIUS.
VALERIUS? ***VALERIUS?***
IT'S ALL HERE, TACITA. HE DID IT. I'M SENDING IT VIA SPECIAL AIR SERVICE DIRECTLY TO DR. LAITHWAITE.
YES. ***EVERYTHING*** THEY DEVELOPED AFTER THE WAR. THIRTY YEARS WORTH OF MAGLEV R&D.

ROMA BOREAS REPUBLIC UNIVERSITY

WITH MUCH OF THE REPUBLIC SUFFERING under authoritarianism and social decay, it doesn't matter if it's past, present, or future; it's always dangerous to hold the name Valerius.

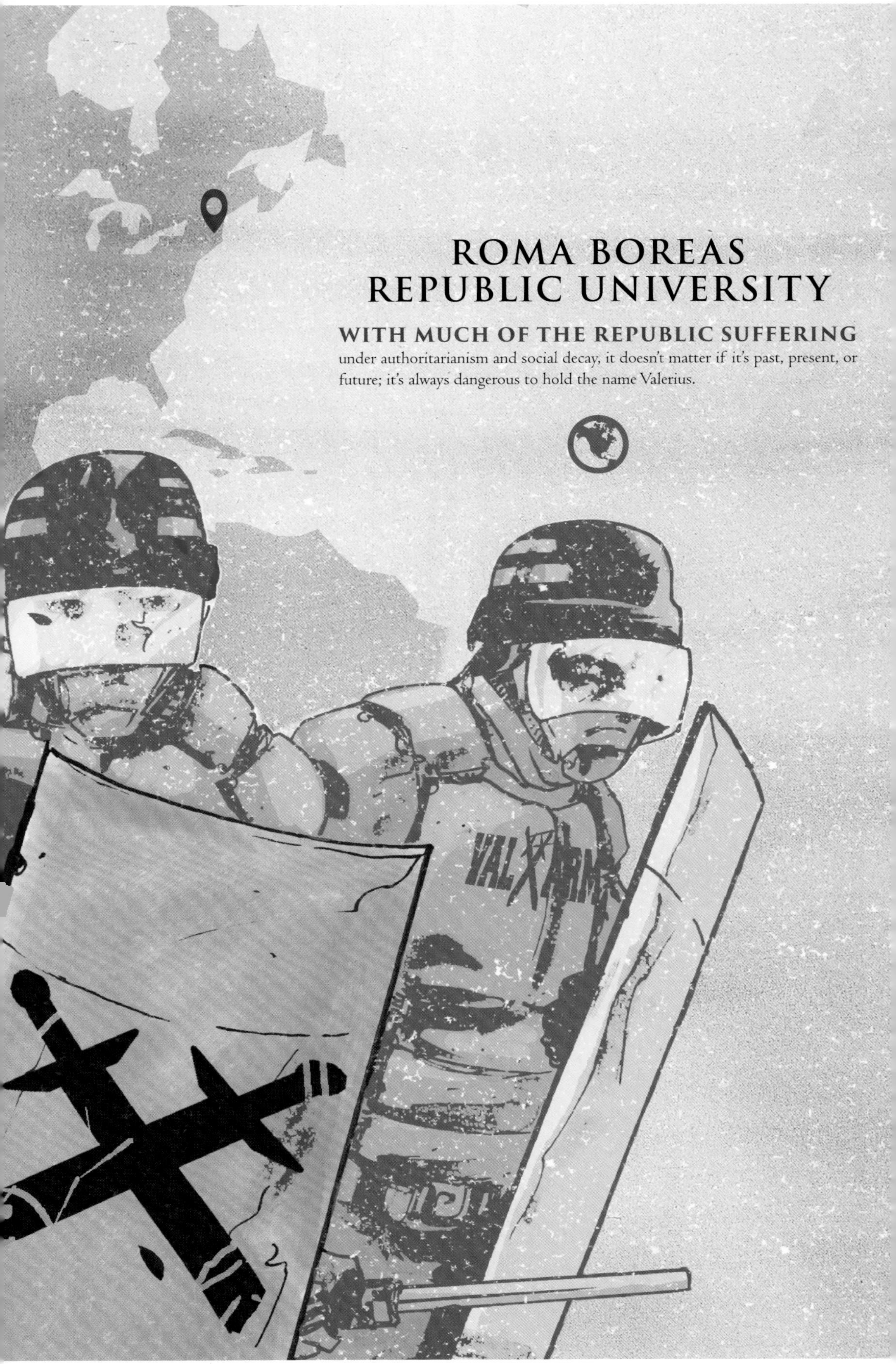

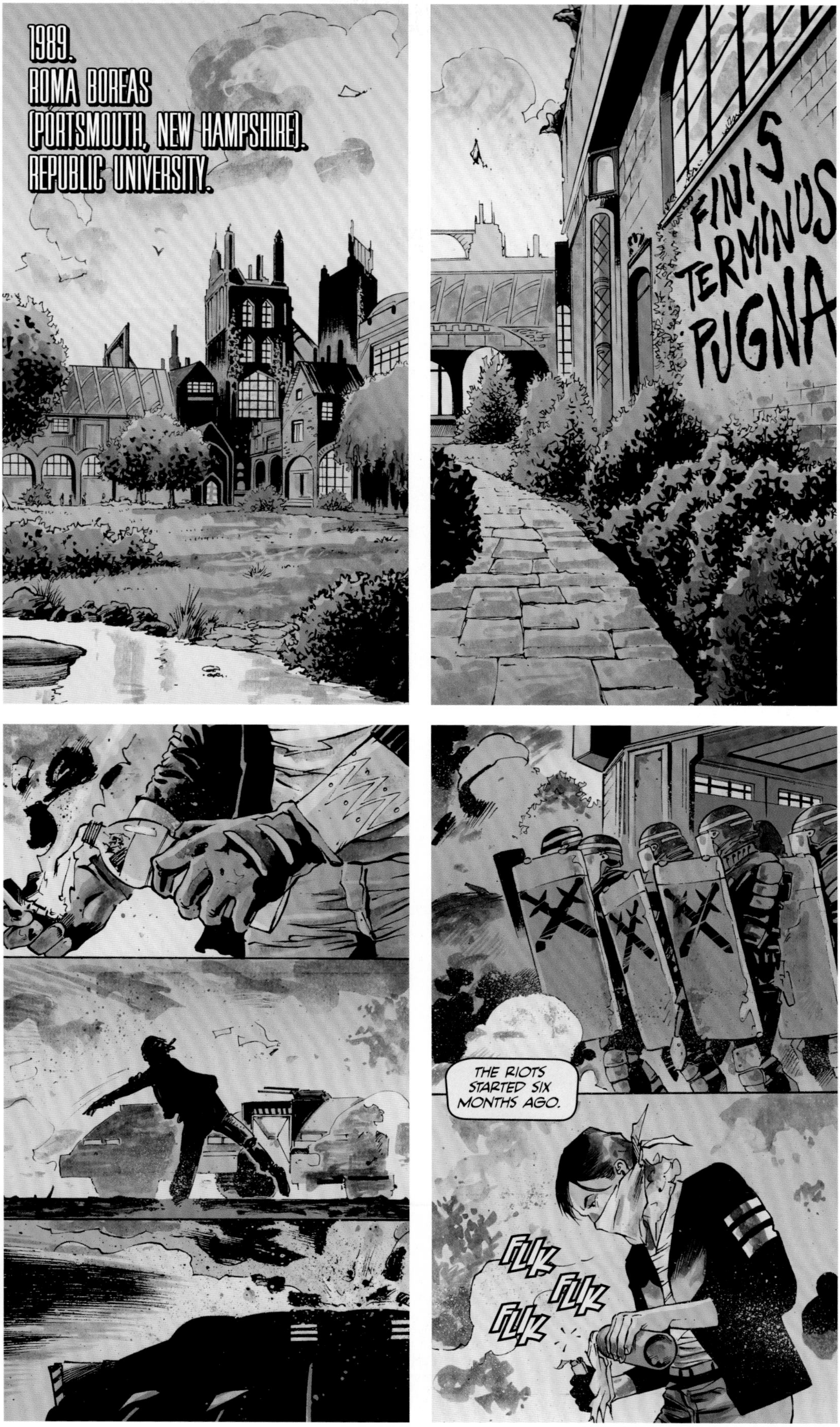
1989.
ROMA BOREAS
(PORTSMOUTH, NEW HAMPSHIRE).
REPUBLIC UNIVERSITY.
FINIS
TERMINUS
PUGNA
THE RIOTS STARTED SIX MONTHS AGO.
FLIK
FLIK
FLIK

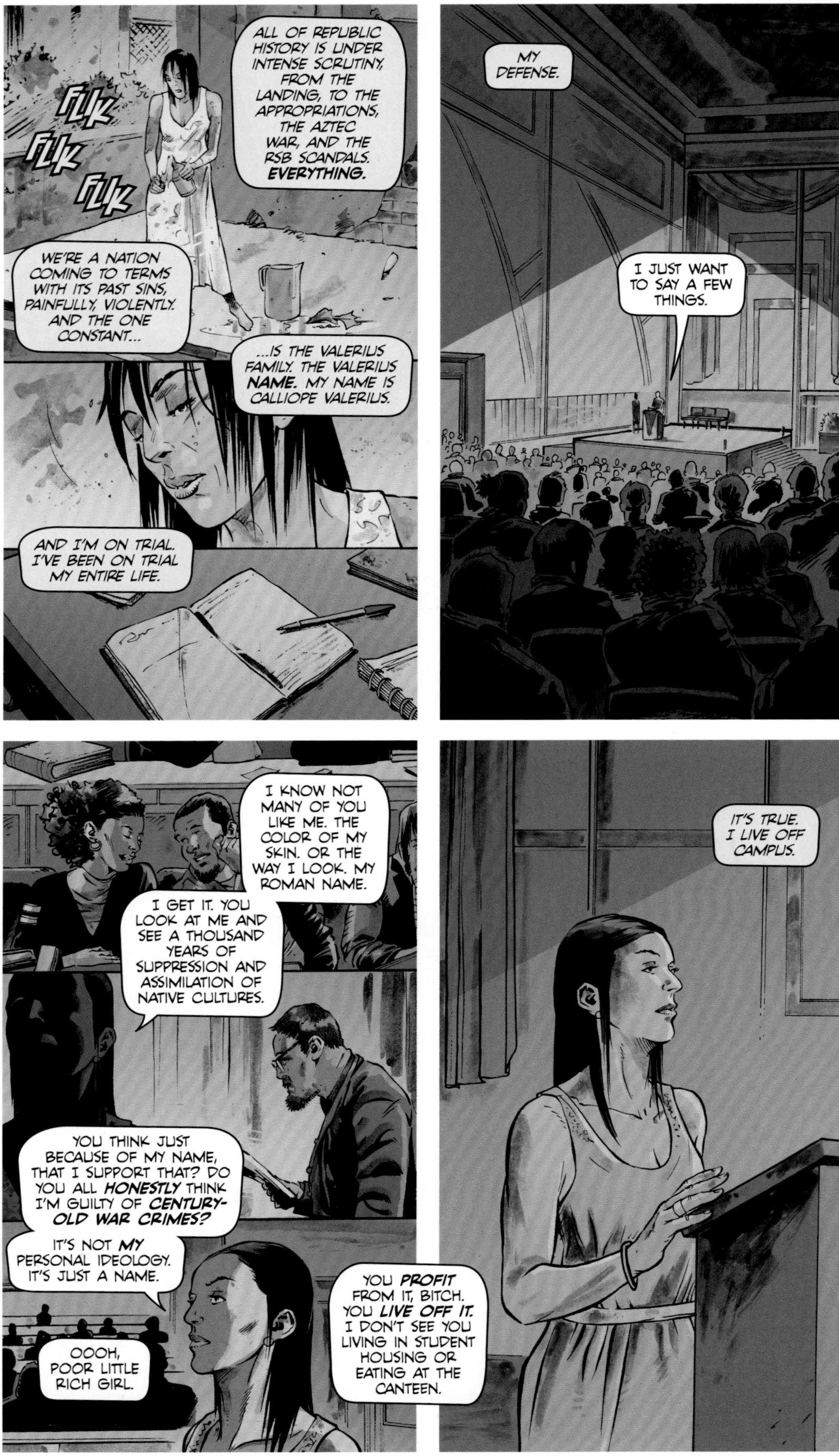
ALL OF REPUBLIC HISTORY IS UNDER INTENSE SCRUTINY, FROM THE LANDING, TO THE APPROPRIATIONS, THE AZTEC WAR, AND THE RSB SCANDALS. EVERYTHING.
FLIK
FLIK
FLIK
WE'RE A NATION COMING TO TERMS WITH ITS PAST SINS, PAINFULLY, VIOLENTLY. AND THE ONE CONSTANT...
...IS THE VALERIUS FAMILY. THE VALERIUS NAME. MY NAME IS CALLIOPE VALERIUS.
AND I'M ON TRIAL. I'VE BEEN ON TRIAL MY ENTIRE LIFE.
MY DEFENSE.
I JUST WANT TO SAY A FEW THINGS.
I KNOW NOT MANY OF YOU LIKE ME. THE COLOR OF MY SKIN. OR THE WAY I LOOK. MY ROMAN NAME.
I GET IT. YOU LOOK AT ME AND SEE A THOUSAND YEARS OF SUPPRESSION AND ASSIMILATION OF NATIVE CULTURES.
YOU THINK JUST BECAUSE OF MY NAME, THAT I SUPPORT THAT? DO YOU ALL HONESTLY THINK I'M GUILTY OF CENTURY-OLD WAR CRIMES?
IT'S NOT MY PERSONAL IDEOLOGY. IT'S JUST A NAME.
OOOH, POOR LITTLE RICH GIRL.
YOU PROFIT FROM IT, BITCH. YOU LIVE OFF IT. I DON'T SEE YOU LIVING IN STUDENT HOUSING OR EATING AT THE CANTEEN.
IT'S TRUE. I LIVE OFF CAMPUS.

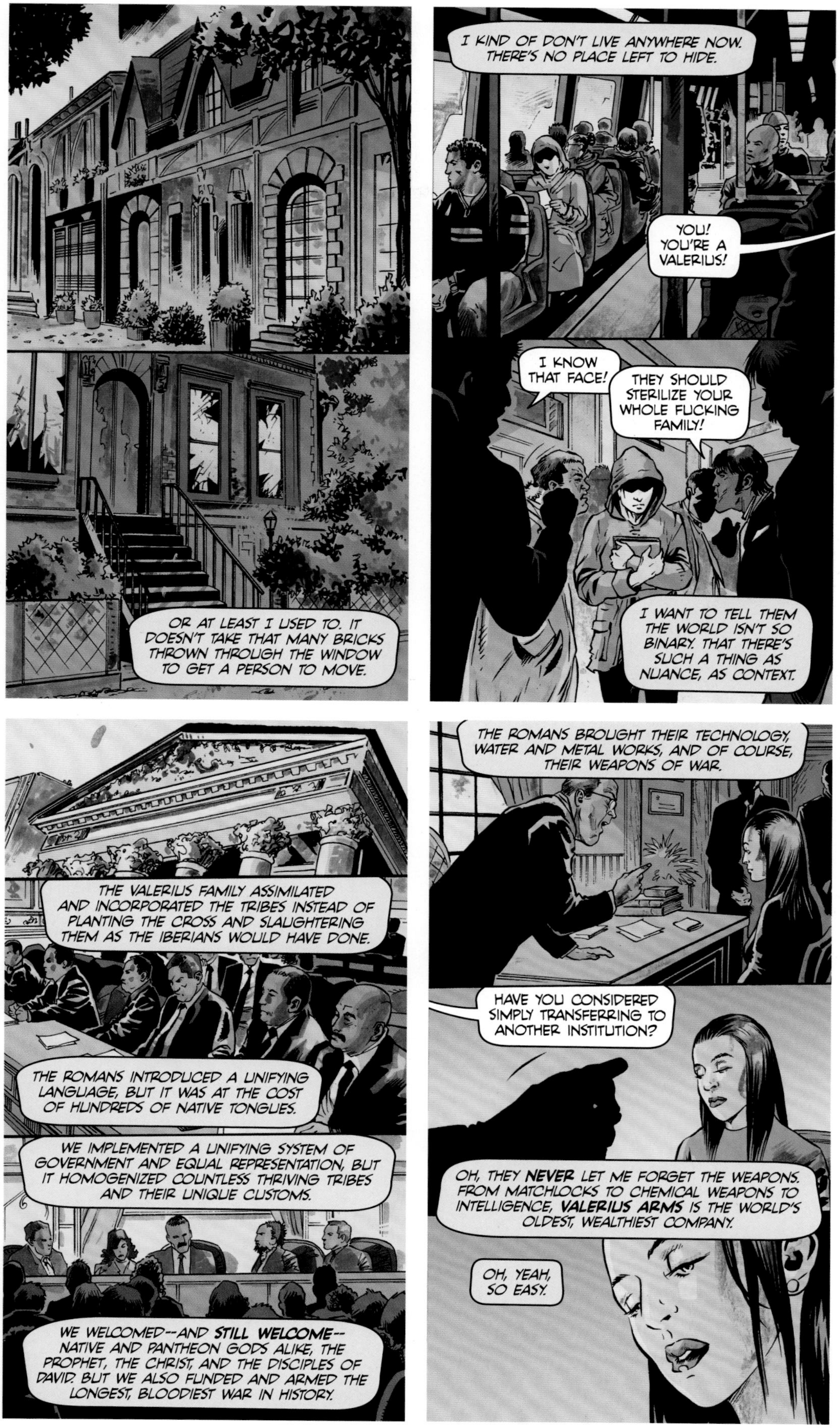
OR AT LEAST I USED TO. IT DOESN'T TAKE THAT MANY BRICKS THROWN THROUGH THE WINDOW TO GET A PERSON TO MOVE.
I KIND OF DON'T LIVE ANYWHERE NOW. THERE'S NO PLACE LEFT TO HIDE.
YOU! YOU'RE A VALERIUS!
I KNOW THAT FACE!
THEY SHOULD STERILIZE YOUR WHOLE FUCKING FAMILY!
I WANT TO TELL THEM THE WORLD ISN'T SO BINARY. THAT THERE'S SUCH A THING AS NUANCE, AS CONTEXT.
THE VALERIUS FAMILY ASSIMILATED AND INCORPORATED THE TRIBES INSTEAD OF PLANTING THE CROSS AND SLAUGHTERING THEM AS THE IBERIANS WOULD HAVE DONE.
THE ROMANS INTRODUCED A UNIFYING LANGUAGE, BUT IT WAS AT THE COST OF HUNDREDS OF NATIVE TONGUES.
WE IMPLEMENTED A UNIFYING SYSTEM OF GOVERNMENT AND EQUAL REPRESENTATION, BUT IT HOMOGENIZED COUNTLESS THRIVING TRIBES AND THEIR UNIQUE CUSTOMS.
WE WELCOMED--AND **STILL WELCOME**--NATIVE AND PANTHEON GODS ALIKE, THE PROPHET, THE CHRIST, AND THE DISCIPLES OF DAVID. BUT WE ALSO FUNDED AND ARMED THE LONGEST, BLOODIEST WAR IN HISTORY.
THE ROMANS BROUGHT THEIR TECHNOLOGY, WATER AND METAL WORKS, AND OF COURSE, THEIR WEAPONS OF WAR.
HAVE YOU CONSIDERED SIMPLY TRANSFERRING TO ANOTHER INSTITUTION?
OH, THEY **NEVER** LET ME FORGET THE WEAPONS. FROM MATCHLOCKS TO CHEMICAL WEAPONS TO INTELLIGENCE, **VALERIUS ARMS** IS THE WORLD'S OLDEST, WEALTHIEST COMPANY.
OH, YEAH, SO EASY.

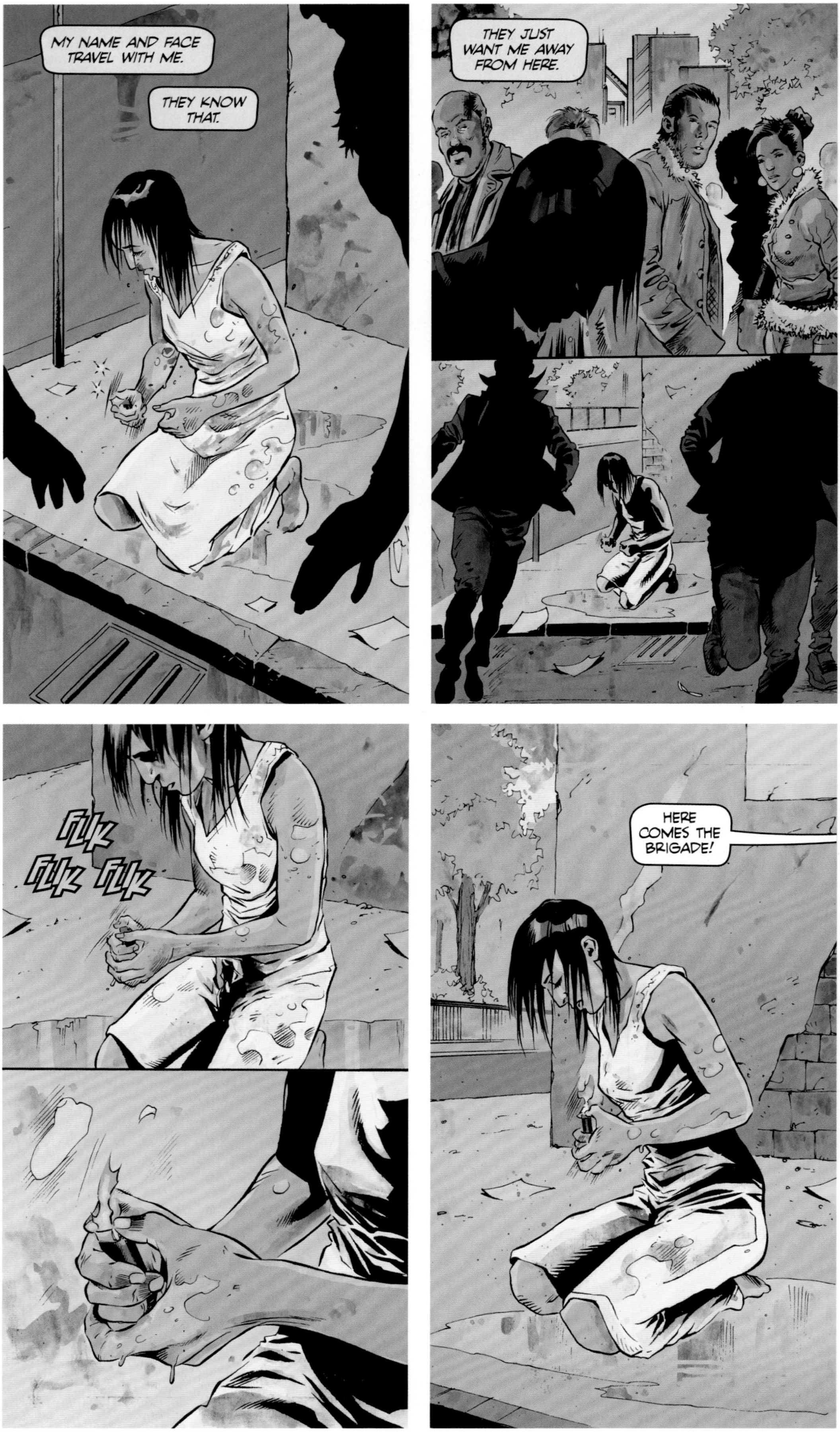
MY NAME AND FACE TRAVEL WITH ME.
THEY KNOW THAT.
THEY JUST WANT ME AWAY FROM HERE.
FLIK
FLIK FLIK
HERE COMES THE BRIGADE!

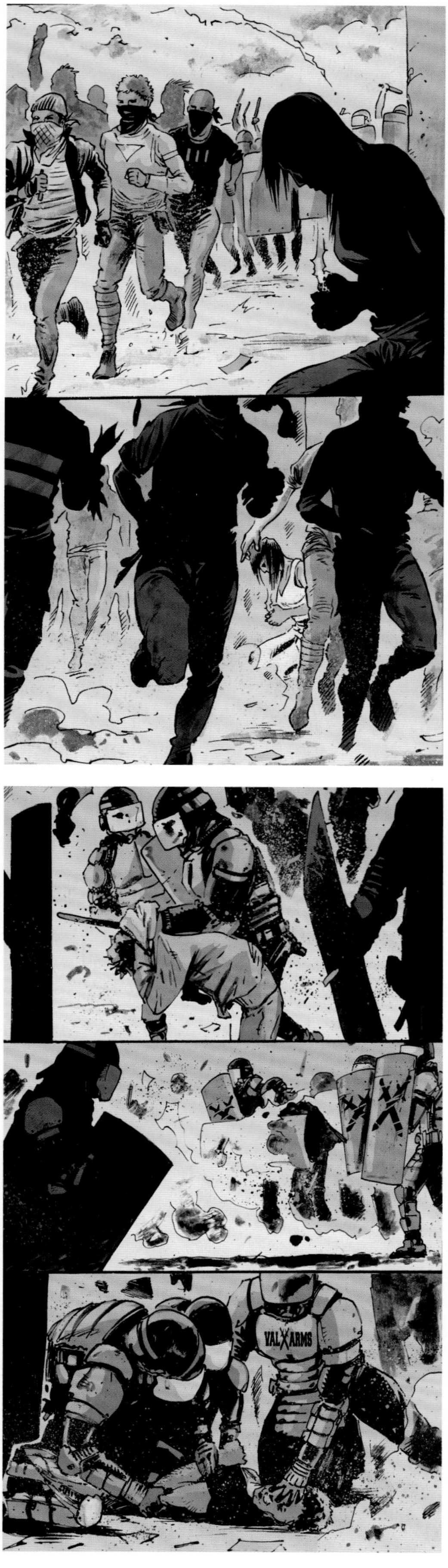
VAL ARMS

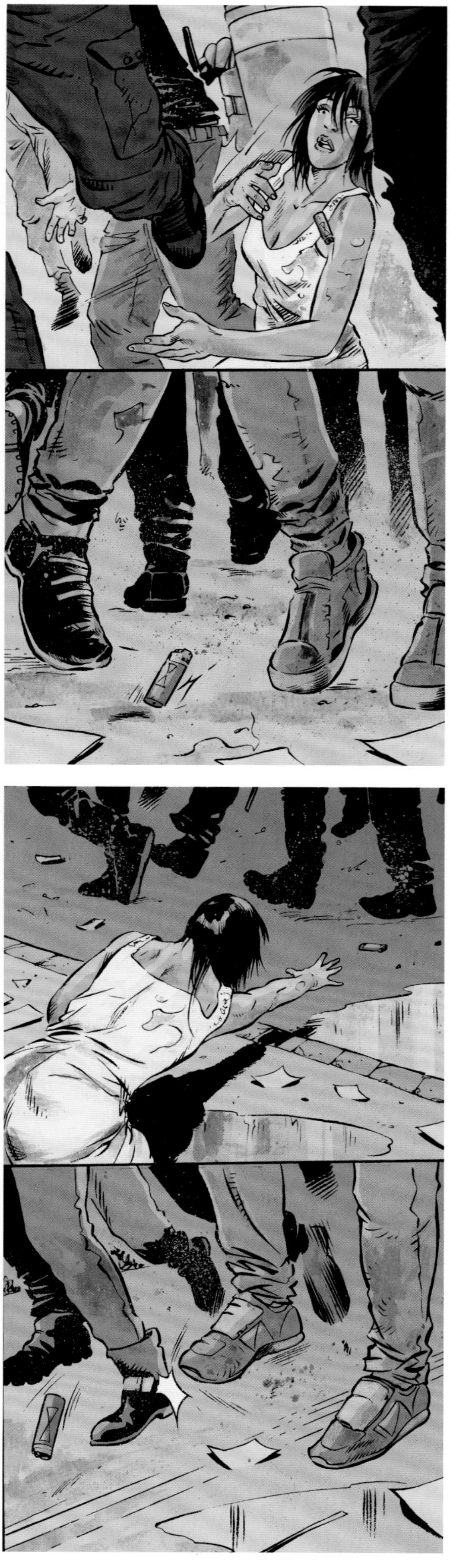

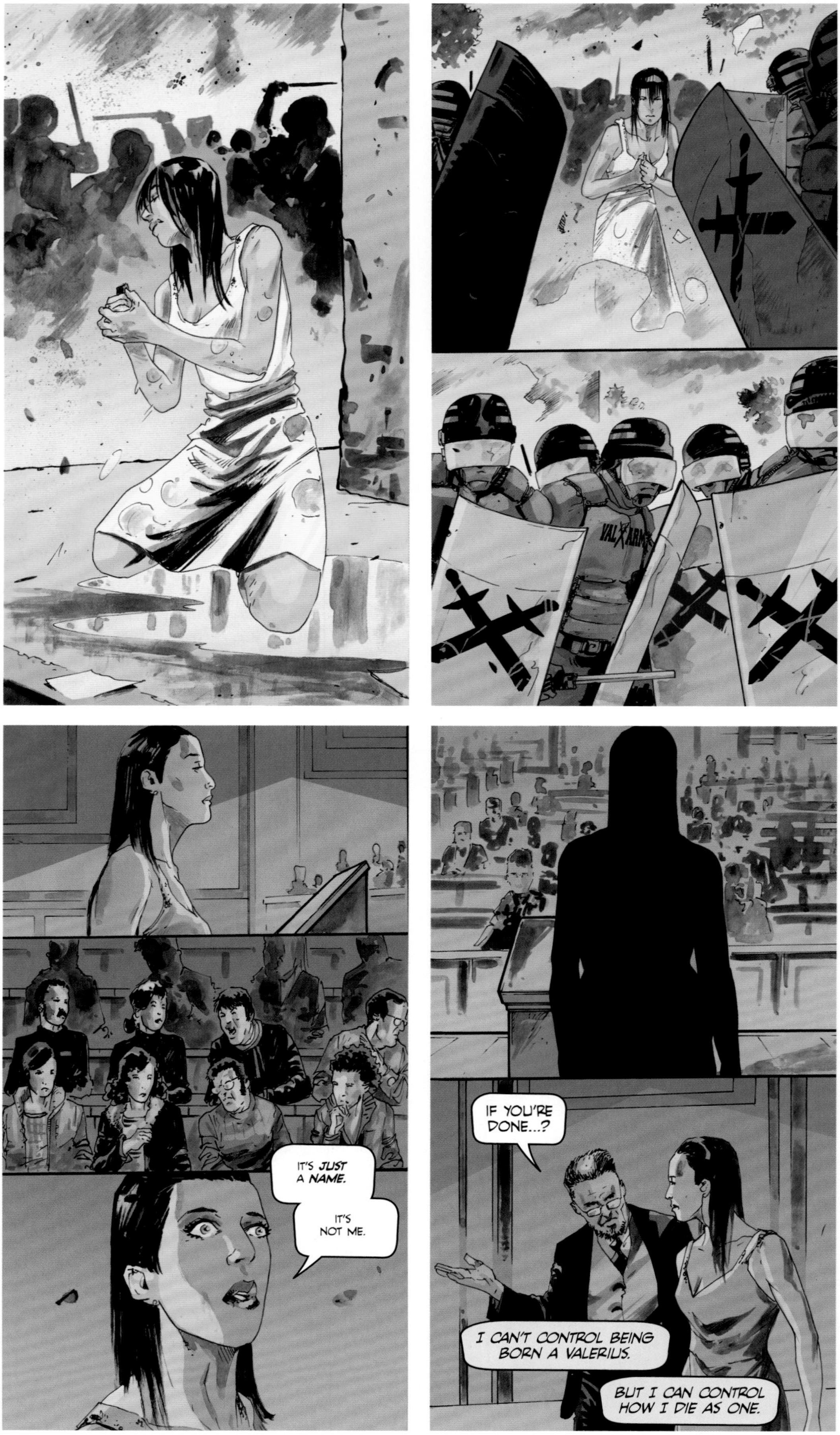
IT'S JUST A NAME.
IT'S NOT ME.
IF YOU'RE DONE...?
I CAN'T CONTROL BEING BORN A VALERIUS.
BUT I CAN CONTROL HOW I DIE AS ONE.

I CAN BURN IT AWAY.

VAL

SHIELDS UP! SHIELDS UP! SHE'S DOUSED IN PETROLINE!

VAL

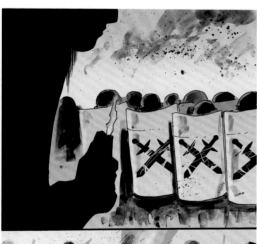

THIS REPUBLIC WAS NEVER PLANNED.

NEVER SOME GRAND SCHEME AS THE REVISIONIST HISTORY BOOKS WOULD HAVE YOU BELIEVE.

ROME WEST WAS BORN IN A DESPERATE BID TO STAY ALIVE.

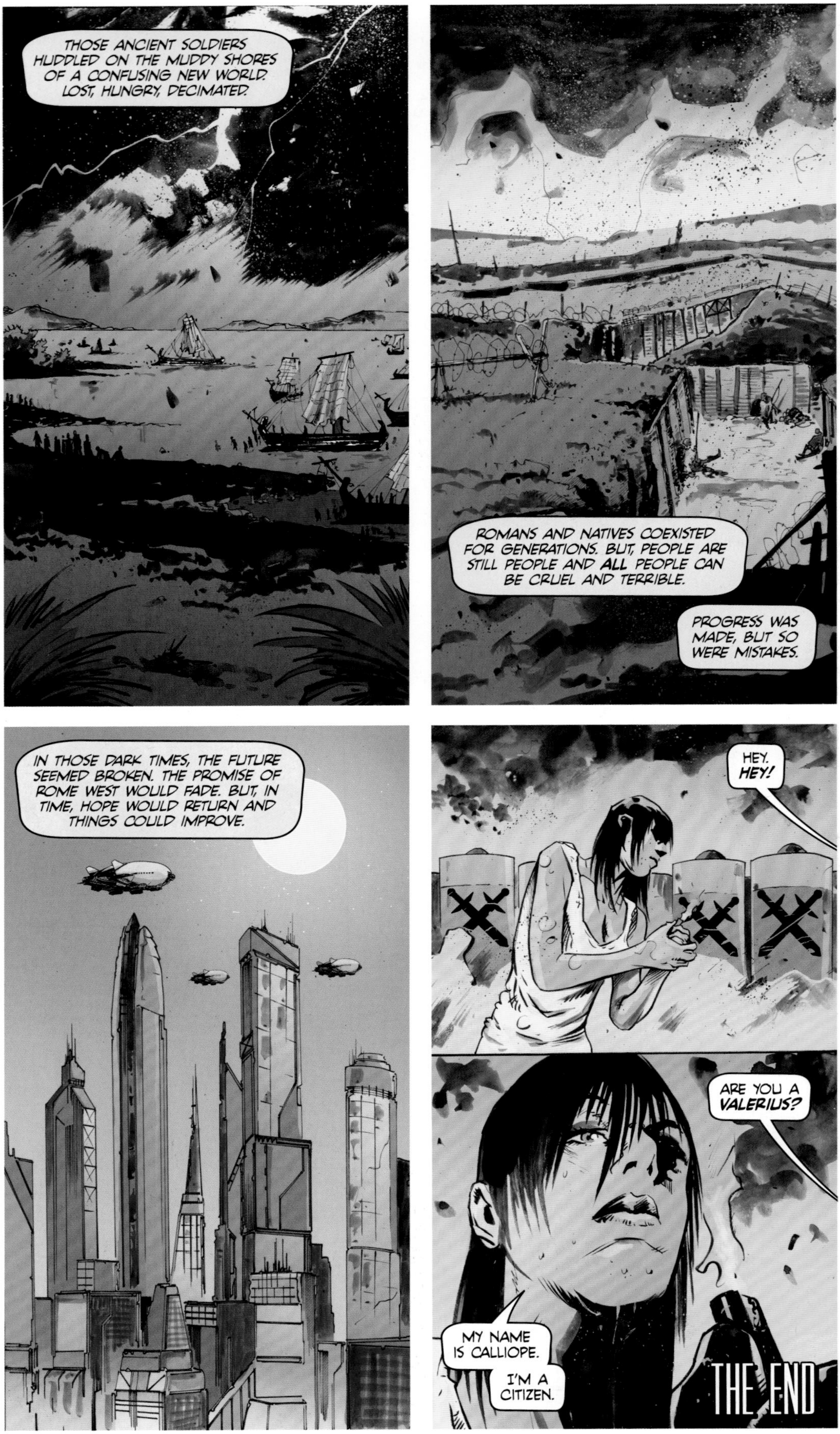
THOSE ANCIENT SOLDIERS HUDDLED ON THE MUDDY SHORES OF A CONFUSING NEW WORLD. LOST, HUNGRY, DECIMATED.
ROMANS AND NATIVES COEXISTED FOR GENERATIONS. BUT, PEOPLE ARE STILL PEOPLE AND ALL PEOPLE CAN BE CRUEL AND TERRIBLE.
PROGRESS WAS MADE, BUT SO WERE MISTAKES.
IN THOSE DARK TIMES, THE FUTURE SEEMED BROKEN. THE PROMISE OF ROME WEST WOULD FADE. BUT, IN TIME, HOPE WOULD RETURN AND THINGS COULD IMPROVE.
HEY. HEY!
ARE YOU A VALERIUS?
MY NAME IS CALLIOPE.
I'M A CITIZEN.
THE END

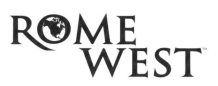

ROME WEST™

The following pages include special behind-the-scenes material used to create the character concepts and the world of *Rome West*.

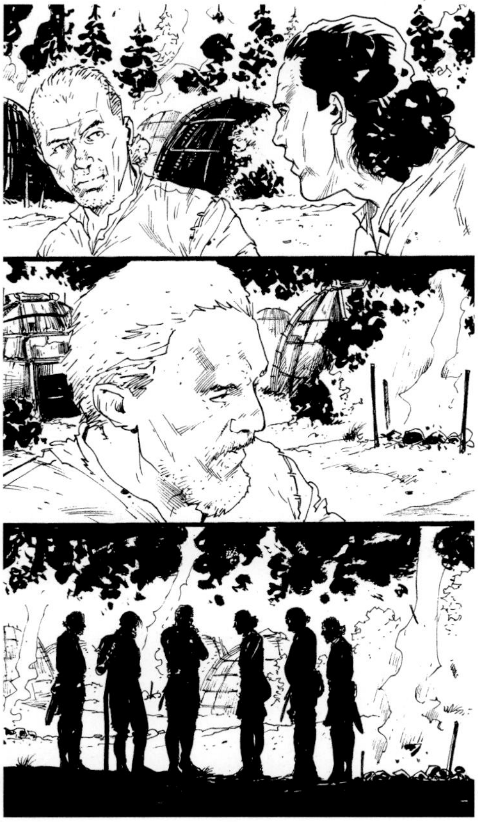

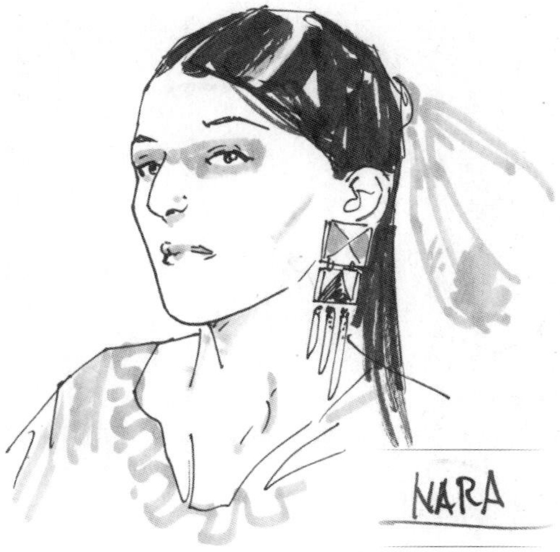
NARA

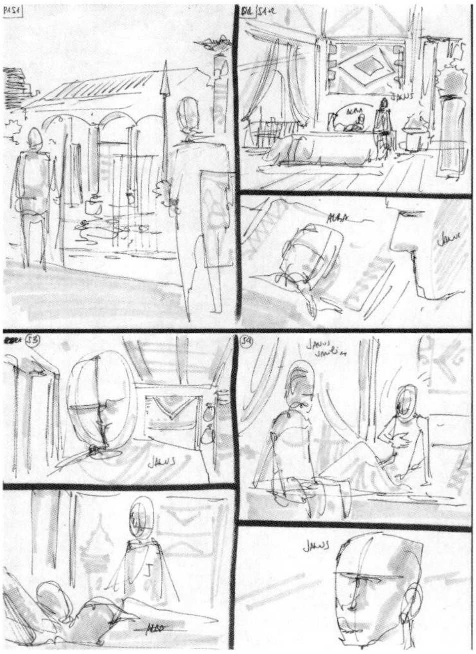

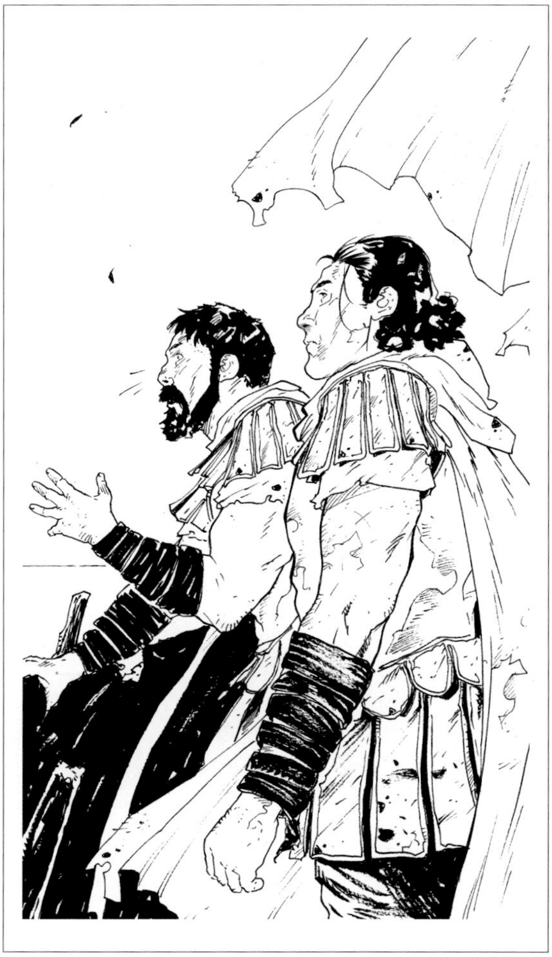

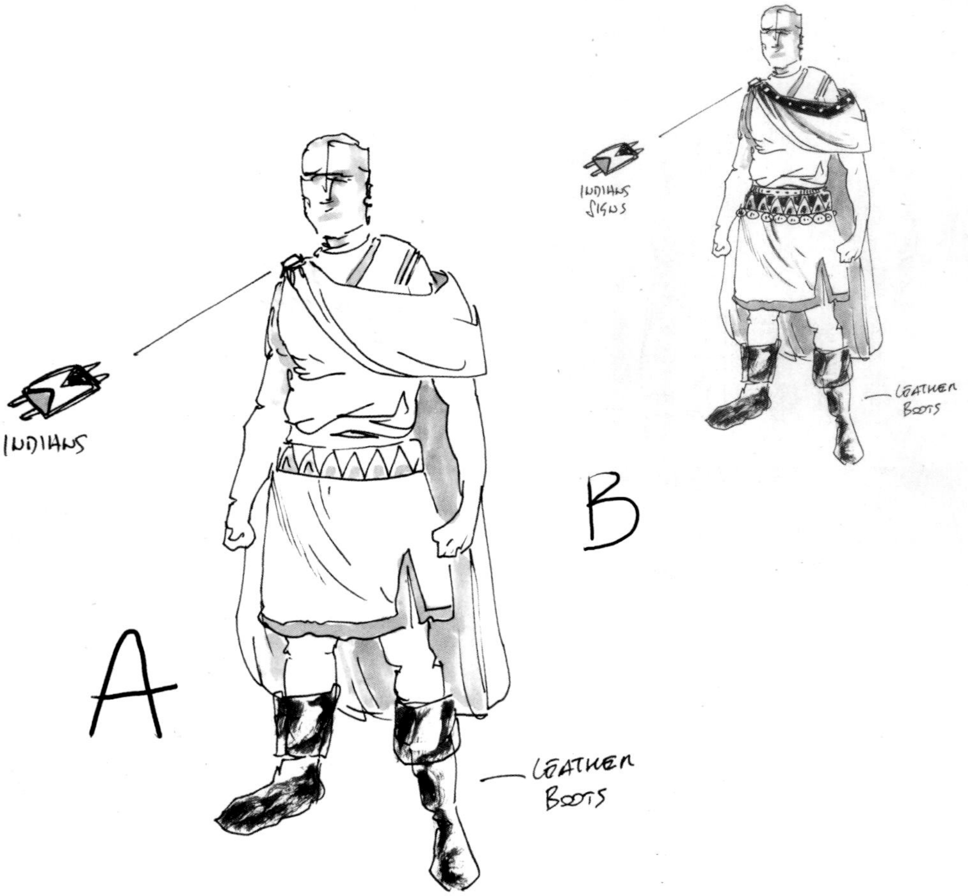
INDIANS SIGNS
LEATHER BOOTS
INDIANS
B
A
LEATHER BOOTS

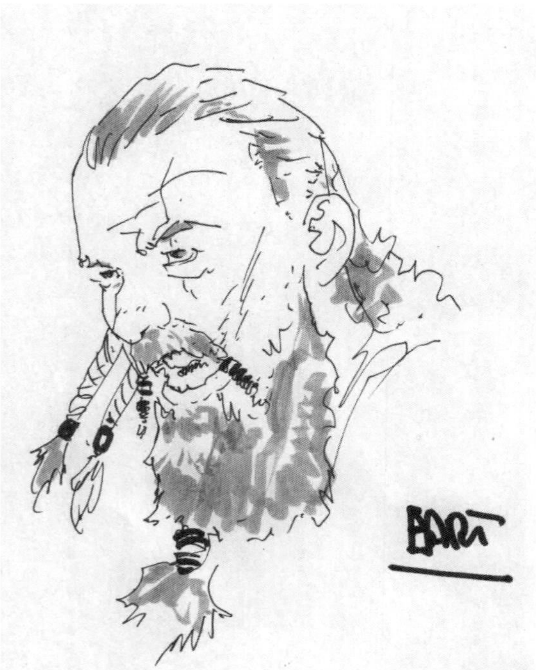
BART

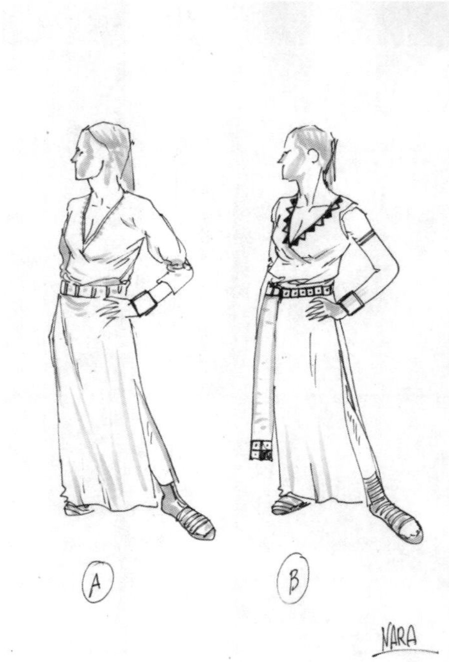
A
B
NARA

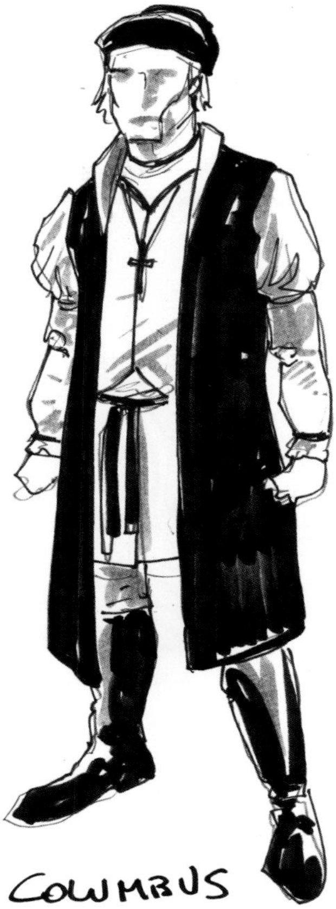
COLUMBUS

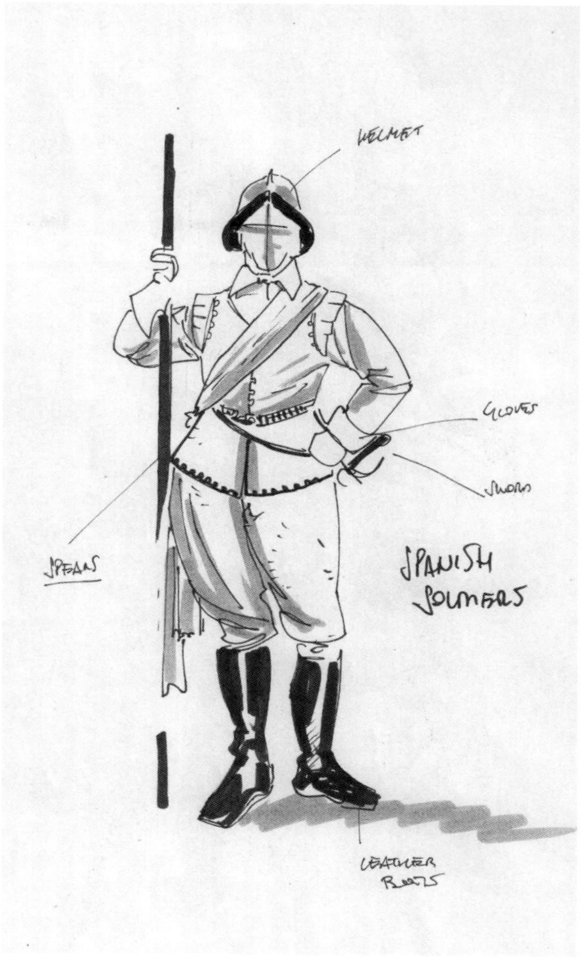
HELMET
GLOVES
SWORD
SPEARS
SPANISH SOLDIERS
LEATHER BOOTS

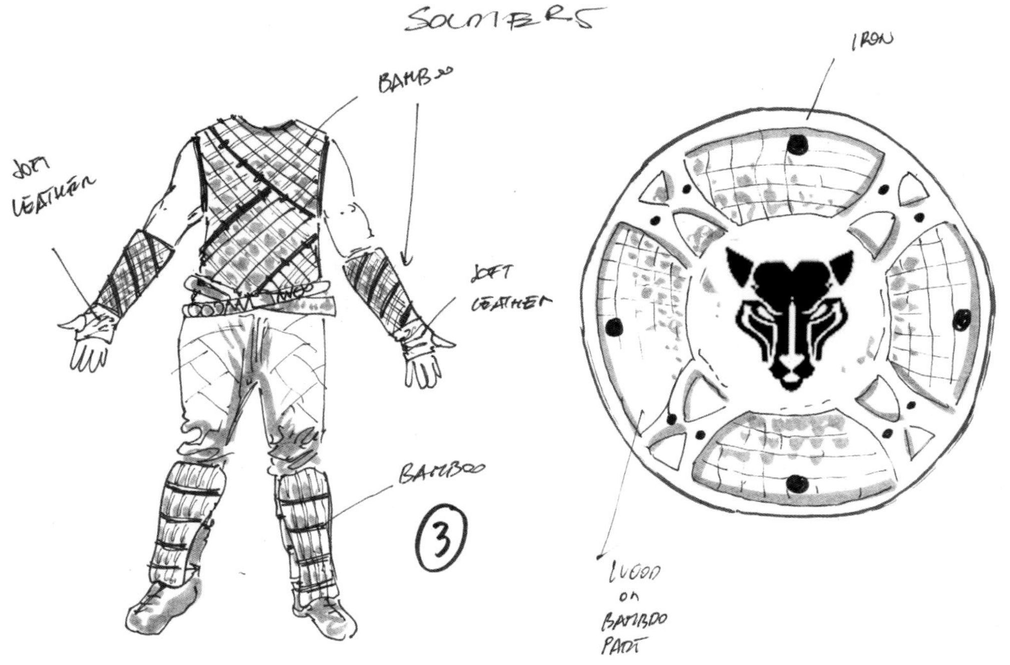
SOLDIERS
BAMBOO
SOFT LEATHER
SOFT LEATHER
BAMBOO
3
IRON
WOOD ON BAMBOO PART

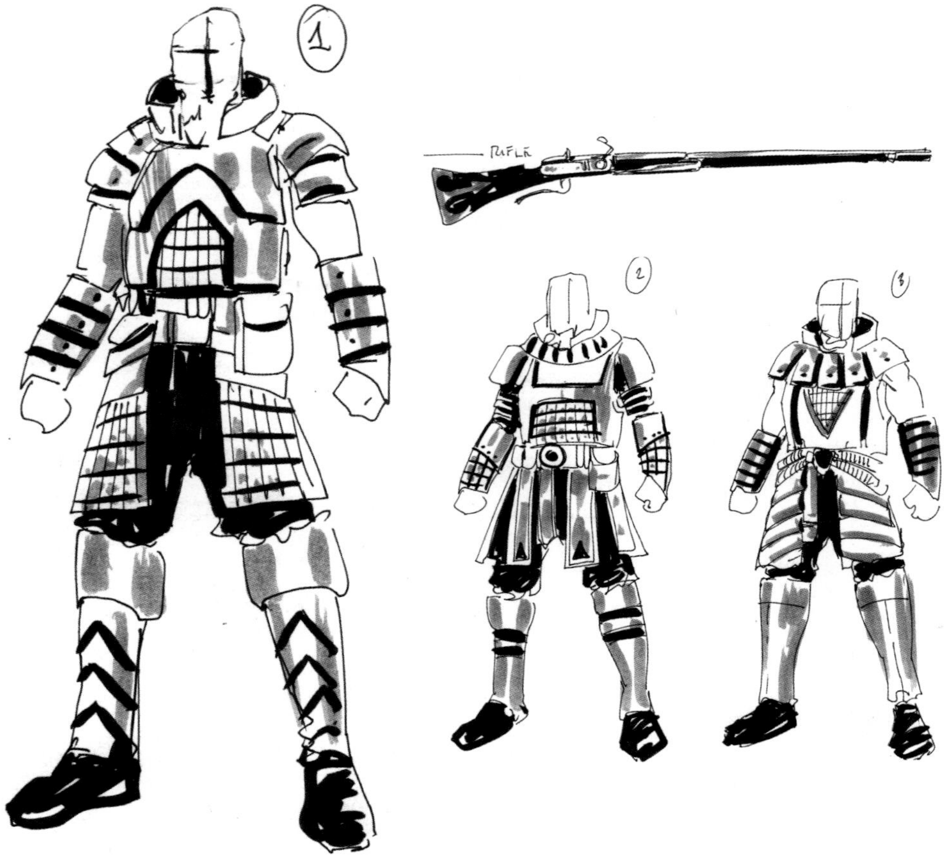
1
RIFLE
2
3

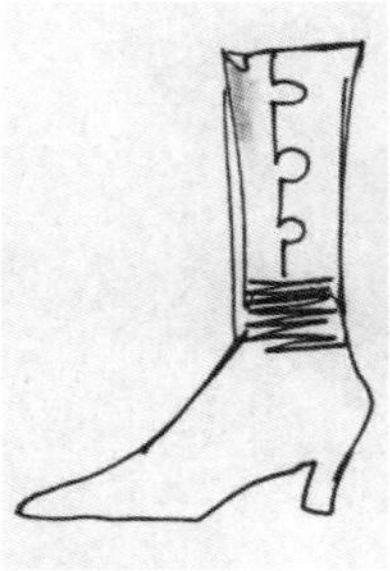

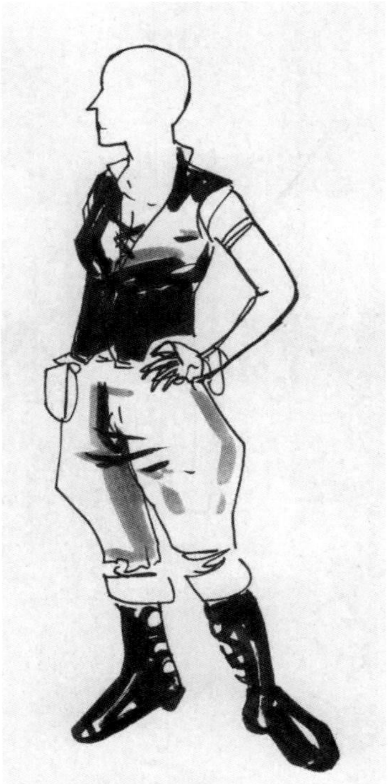

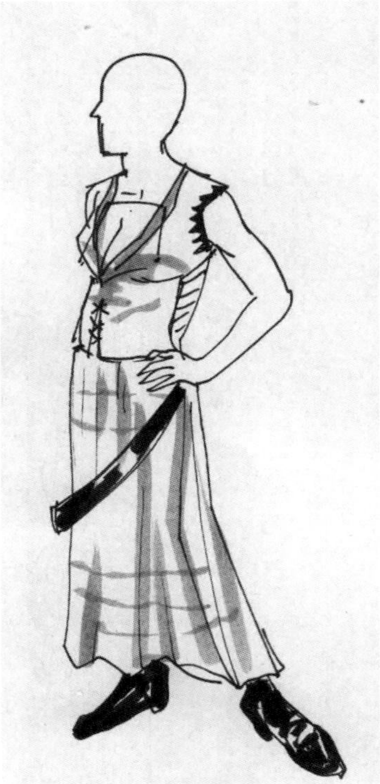

VAL ARMS

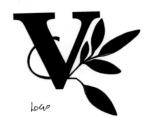

LOGO

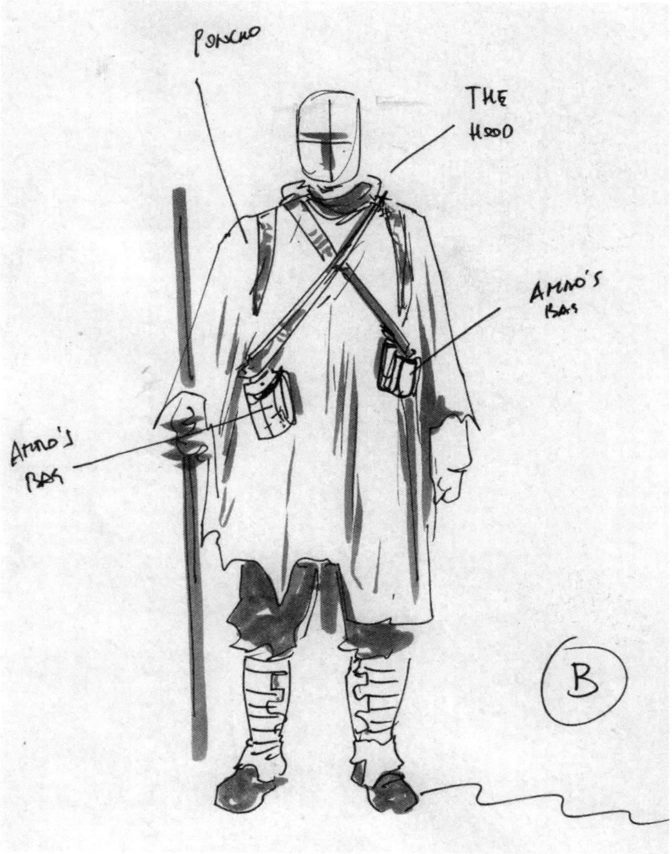
PONCHO
THE HOOD
AMMO'S BAG
AMMO'S BAG
B

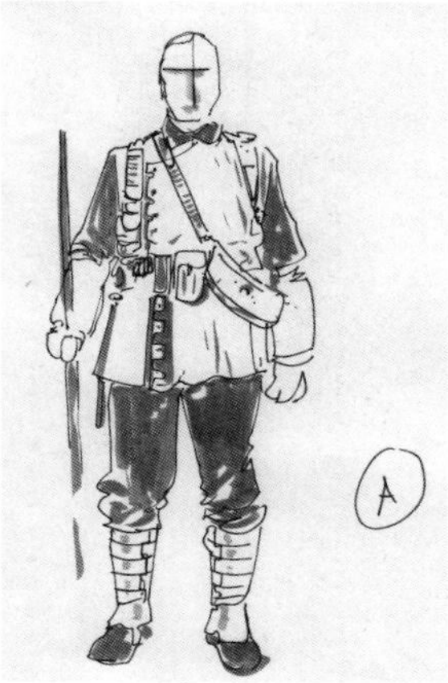
A

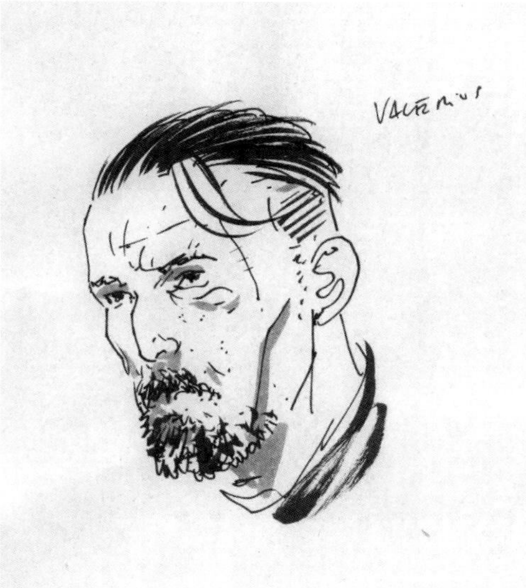
VALERIUS

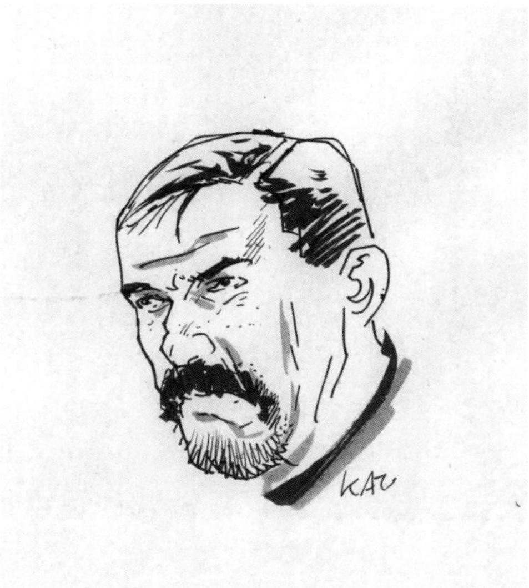
KAL

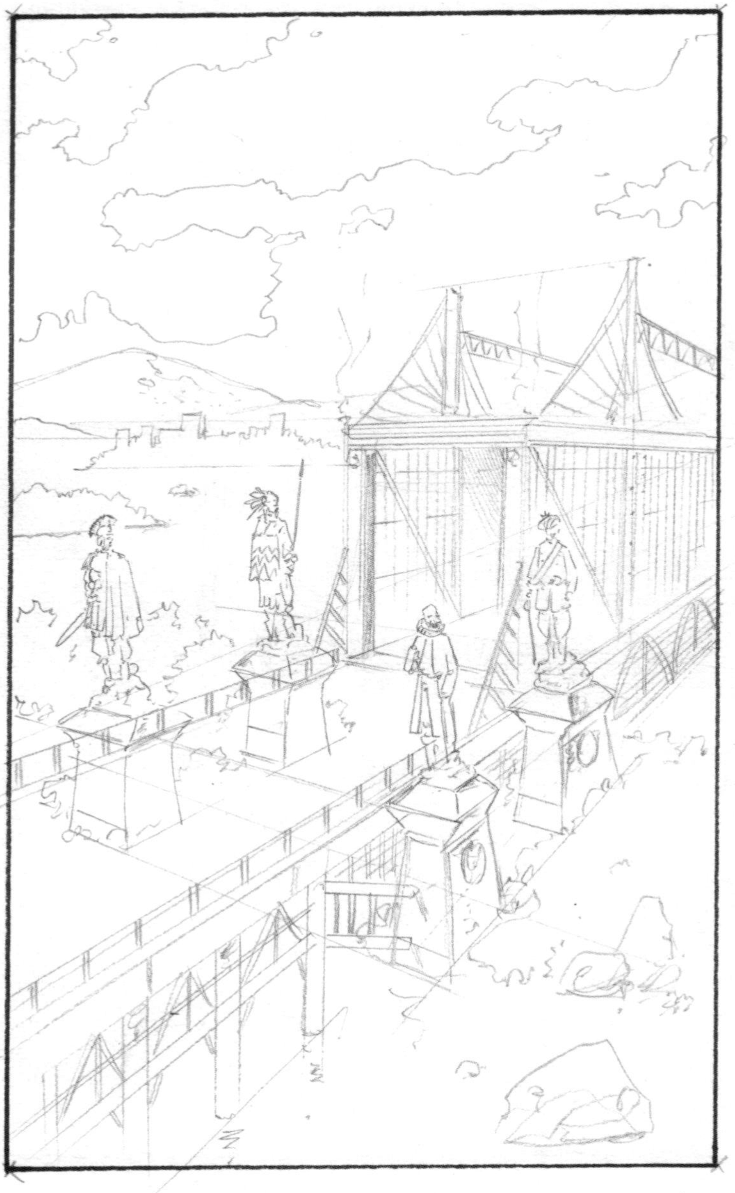

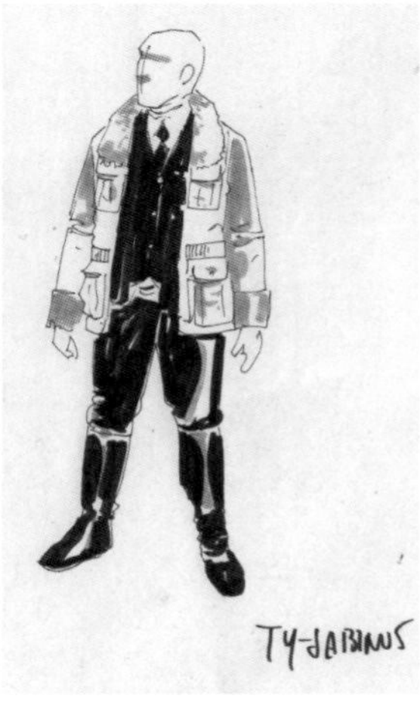
TY-JABINUS

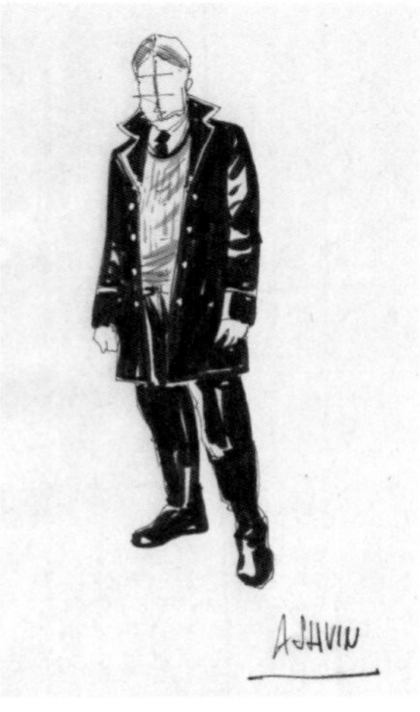
AJHVIN

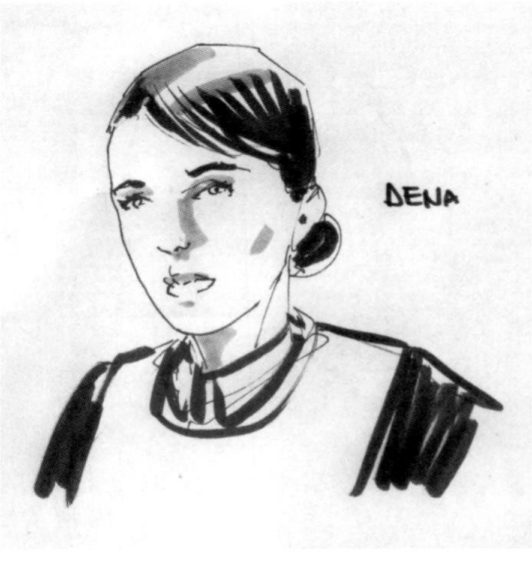
DENA